The Map of Life

by

William Edward Hartpole Lecky

The Echo Library 2009

Published by

The Echo Library

Echo Library
131 High St.
Teddington
Middlesex TW11 8HH

www.echo-library.com

Please report serious faults in the text to complaints@echo-library.com

ISBN 978-1-40685-193-9

THE MAP OF LIFE

Conduct and Character

by

WILLIAM EDWARD HARTPOLE LECKY

'La vie n'est pas un plaisir ni une douleur, mais une affaire
grave
dont nous sommes chargés, et qu'il faut conduire et terminer à
notre honneur'   TOCQUEVILLE

New Impression

Longmans, Green, and Co.
39 Paternoster Row, London
New York and Bombay
1904

4

CONTENTS

THE MAP OF LIFE

CHAPTER I

One of the first questions that must naturally occur to every writer who deals with the subject of this book is, what influence mere discussion and reasoning can have in promoting the happiness of men. The circumstances of our lives and the dispositions of our characters mainly determine the measure of happiness we enjoy, and mere argument about the causes of happiness and unhappiness can do little to affect them. It is impossible to read the many books that have been written on these subjects without feeling how largely they consist of mere sounding generalities which the smallest experience shows to be perfectly impotent in the face of some real and acute sorrow, and it is equally impossible to obtain any serious knowledge of the world without perceiving that a large proportion of the happiest lives and characters are to be found where introspection, self-analysis and reasonings about the good and evil of life hold the smallest place. Happiness, indeed, like health, is one of the things of which men rarely think except when it is impaired, and much that has been written on the subject has been written under the stress of some great depression. Such writers are like the man in Hogarth's picture occupying himself in the debtors' prison with plans for the payment of the National Debt. There are moments when all of us feel the force of the words of Voltaire: 'Travaillons sans raisonner, c'est le seul moyen de rendre la vie supportable.'

That there is much truth in such considerations is incontestable, and it is only within a restricted sphere that the province of reasoning extends. Man comes into the world with mental and moral characteristics which he can only very imperfectly influence, and a large proportion of the external circumstances of his life lie wholly or mainly beyond his control. At the same time, every one recognises the power of skill, industry and perseverance to modify surrounding circumstances; the power of temperance and prudence to strengthen a naturally weak constitution, prolong life, and diminish the chances of disease; the power of education and private study to develop, sharpen and employ to the best advantage our intellectual faculties. Every one also recognises how large a part of the unhappiness of most men may be directly traced to their own voluntary and deliberate acts. The power each man possesses in the education and management of his character, and especially in the cultivation of the dispositions and tendencies which most largely contribute to happiness, is less recognised and is perhaps less extensive, but it is not less real.

The eternal question of free will and determinism here naturally meets us, but on such a subject it is idle to suppose that a modern writer can do more than define the question and state his own side. The Determinist says that the real question is not whether a man can do what he desires, but whether he can do what he does not desire; whether the will can act without a motive; whether that motive can in the last analysis be other than the strongest pleasure. The illusion of free will, he maintains, is only due to the conflict of our motives. Under many forms and disguises pleasure and pain have an absolute empire over conduct. The will is nothing more than the last and strongest desire; or it is like a piece of iron surrounded by magnets and necessarily drawn by the most powerful; or (as has been ingeniously imagined) like a weathercock, conscious of its own motion, but not conscious of the winds that are moving it. The law of compulsory causation applies to the world of mind as truly as to the world of matter. Heredity and Circumstance make us what we are. Our actions are the inevitable result of the mental and moral constitutions with which we came into the world, operated on by external influences.

The supporters of free will, on the other hand, maintain that it is a fact of consciousness that there is a clear distinction between the Will and the Desires, and that although they are closely connected no sound analysis will confuse them. Coleridge ingeniously compared their relations to 'the co-instantaneous yet reciprocal action of the air and the vital energy of the lungs in breathing.'[1] If the will is powerfully acted on by the desires, it has also in its turn a power of acting upon them, and it is not a mere slave to pleasure and pain. The supporters of this view maintain that it is a fact of the plainest consciousness that we can do things which we do not like; that we can suspend the force of imperious desires, resist the bias of our nature, pursue for the sake of duty the course which gives least pleasure without deriving or expecting from it any pleasure, and select at a given moment between alternate courses. They maintain that when various motives pass before the mind, the mind retains a power of choosing and judging, of accepting and rejecting; that it can by force of reason or by force of imagination bring one motive into prominence, concentrating its attention on it and thus intensifying its power; that it has a corresponding power of resisting other motives, driving them into the background and thus gradually diminishing their force; that the will itself becomes stronger by exercise, as the desires do by indulgence. The conflict between the will and the desires, the reality of self-restraint and the power of Will to modify character, are among the most familiar facts of moral life. In the words of Burke, 'It is the prerogative of man to be in a great degree a creature of his own making.' There are men whose whole lives are spent in willing one thing and desiring the opposite, and all morality depends upon the supposition that we have at least some freedom of choice between good and evil. 'I ought,' as Kant says, necessarily implies 'I can.' The feeling of moral responsibility is an essential part of healthy and developed human nature, and it inevitably presupposes free will. The best argument in its favour is that it is impossible really to disbelieve it. No human being can prevent himself from viewing certain acts with an indignation, shame, remorse, resentment, gratitude, enthusiasm, praise or blame, which would be perfectly unmeaning and irrational if these acts could not have been avoided. We can have no higher evidence on the subject than is derived from this fact. It is impossible

---

[1] *Aids to Reflection*, p. 68.

to explain the mystery of free will, but until a man ceases to feel these emotions he has not succeeded in disbelieving in it. The feelings of all men and the vocabularies of all languages attest the universality of the belief.

Newman, in a well-known passage in his 'Apologia,' describes the immense effect which the sentence of Augustine, 'Securus judicat orbis terrarum,' had upon his opinions in determining him to embrace the Church of Rome. The force of this consideration in relation to the subject to which Dr. Newman refers does not appear to have great weight. It means only that at a time when the Christian Church included but a small fraction of the human race; when all questions of orthodoxy or the reverse were practically in the hands of the priesthood; when ignorance, credulity and superstition were at their height and the habits of independence and impartiality of judgment running very low; and when every kind of violent persecution was directed against those who dissented from the prevailing dogmas,—certain councils of priests found it possible to attain unanimity on such questions as the two natures in Christ or the relations of the Persons in the Trinity, and to expel from the Church those who differed from their views, and that the once formidable sects which held slightly different opinions about these inscrutable relations gradually faded away. Such an unanimity on such subjects and attained by such methods does not appear to me to carry with it any overwhelming force. There are, however, a certain number of beliefs that are not susceptible of demonstrative proof, and which must always rest essentially on the universal assent of mankind. Such is the existence of the external world. Such, in my opinion, is the existence of a distinction between right and wrong, different from and higher than the distinction between pleasure and pain, and subsisting in all human nature in spite of great diversities of opinion about the acts and qualities that are comprised in either category; and such also is the kindred belief in a self-determining will. If men contend that these things are mere illusions and that their faculties are not to be trusted, it will no doubt be difficult or impossible to refute them; but a scepticism of this kind has no real influence on either conduct or feeling.

CHAPTER II

Men continually forget that Happiness is a condition of Mind and not a disposition of circumstances, and one of the most common of errors is that of confusing happiness with the means of happiness, sacrificing the first for the attainment of the second. It is the error of the miser, who begins by seeking money for the enjoyment it procures and ends by making the mere acquisition of money his sole object, pursuing it to the sacrifice of all rational ends and pleasures. Circumstances and Character both contribute to Happiness, but the proportionate attention paid to one or other of these great departments not only varies largely with different individuals, but also with different nations and in different ages. Thus Religion acts mainly in the formation of dispositions, and it is especially in this field that its bearing on human happiness should be judged. It influences, it is true, vastly and variously the external circumstances of life, but its chief power of comforting and supporting lies in its direct and immediate action upon the human soul. The same thing is true of some systems of philosophy of which Stoicism is the most conspicuous. The paradox of the Stoic that good and evil are so entirely from within that to a wise man all external circumstances are indifferent, represents this view of life in its extreme form. Its more moderate form can hardly be better expressed than in the saying of Dugald Stewart that 'the great secret of happiness is to study to accommodate our own minds to things external rather than to accommodate things external to ourselves.'[2] It is eminently the characteristic of Eastern nations to place their ideals mainly in states of mind or feeling rather than in changes of circumstances, and in such nations men are much less desirous than in European countries of altering the permanent conditions of their lives.

On the other hand, the tendency of those philosophies which treat man—his opinions and his character—essentially as the result of circumstances, and which aggrandise the influence of the external world upon mankind, is in the opposite direction. All the sensational philosophies from Bacon and Locke to our own day tend to concentrate attention on the external circumstances and conditions of happiness. And the same tendency will be naturally found in the most active, industrial and progressive nations; where life is very full and busy; where its competitions are most keen; where scientific discoveries are rapidly multiplying pleasures or diminishing pains; where town life with its constant hurry and change is the most prominent. In such spheres men naturally incline to seek happiness from without rather than from within, or, in other words, to seek it much less by acting directly on the mind and character than through the indirect method of improved circumstances.

English character on both sides of the Atlantic is an eminently objective one—a character in which thoughts, interests and emotions are most habitually thrown on that which is without. Introspection and self-analysis are not congenial to it. No one

---

[2] *Active and Moral Powers*, ii. 312.

can compare English life with life even in the Continental nations which occupy the same rank in civilisation without perceiving how much less Englishmen are accustomed either to dwell upon their emotions or to give free latitude to their expression. Reticence and self-restraint are the lessons most constantly inculcated. The whole tone of society favours it. In times of great sorrow a degree of shame is attached to demonstrations of grief which in other countries would be deemed perfectly natural. The disposition to dilate upon and perpetuate an old grief by protracted mournings, by carefully observed anniversaries, by long periods of retirement from the world, is much less common than on the Continent and it is certainly diminishing. The English tendency is to turn away speedily from the past, and to seek consolation in new fields of activity. Emotions translate themselves speedily into action, and they lose something of their intensity by the transformation. Philanthropy is nowhere more active and more practical, and religion has in few countries a greater hold on the national life, but English Protestantism reflects very clearly the national characteristics. It, no doubt, like all religions, lays down rules for the government of thought and feeling, but these are of a very general character. Preeminently a regulator of conduct, it lays comparatively little stress upon the inner life. It discourages, or at least neglects that minutely introspective habit of thought which the confessional is so much calculated to promote, which appears so prominently in the writings of the Catholic Saints, and which finds its special representation in the mystics and the religious contemplative orders. Improved conduct and improved circumstances are to an English mind the chief and almost the only measures of progress.

That this tendency is on the whole a healthy one, I, at least, firmly believe, but it brings with it certain manifest limitations and somewhat incapacitates men from judging other types of character and happiness. The part that circumstances play in the formation of our characters is indeed very manifest, and it is a humiliating truth that among these circumstances mere bodily conditions which we share with the animals hold a foremost place. In the long run and to the great majority of men health is probably the most important of all the elements of happiness. Acute physical suffering or shattered health will more than counterbalance the best gifts of fortune, and the bias of our nature and even the processes of our reasoning are largely influenced by physical conditions. Hume has spoken of that 'disposition to see the favourable rather than the unfavourable side of things which it is more happiness to possess than to be heir to an estate of 10,000*l.* a year;' but this gift of a happy temperament is very evidently greatly due to bodily conditions. On the other hand, it is well known how speedily and how powerfully bodily ailments react upon our moral natures. Every one is aware of the morbid irritability that is produced by certain maladies of the nerves or of the brain; of the deep constitutional depression which often follows diseases of the liver, or prolonged sleeplessness and other hypochondriacal maladies, and which not only deprives men of most of their capacity of enjoyment, but also infallibly gives a colour and a bias to their reasonings on life; of the manner in which animal passions as well as animal spirits are affected by certain well-known conditions of age and health. In spite of the 'coelum non animum mutant' of Horace, few men fail to experience how different is the range of spirits in the limbo-like atmosphere of a London winter and beneath the glories of an Italian sky or in the keen bracing atmosphere of the mountain side, and it is equally apparent how differently we judge the world when we are jaded by a long spell of excessive work or refreshed after a night of tranquil sleep. Poetry and Painting are probably not wrong in associating a certain bilious temperament with a predisposition to envy, or an anæmic or lymphatic temperament with a saintly life, and there are well-attested cases in which an acute illness has fundamentally altered characters, sometimes replacing an habitual gloom by buoyancy and light.[3] That invaluable gift which enables some men to cast aside trouble and turn their thoughts and energies swiftly and decisively into new channels can be largely strengthened by the action of the will, but according to some physiologists it has a well-ascertained physical antecedent in the greater or less contractile power of the blood-vessels which feed the brain causing the flow of blood into it to be stronger or less rapid. If it be true that 'a healthy mind in a healthy body' is the supreme condition of happiness, it is also true that the healthy mind depends more closely than we like to own on the healthy body.

These are but a few obvious instances of the manner in which the body acts upon happiness. They do not mean that the will is powerless in the face of bodily conditions, but that in the management of character it has certain very definite predispositions to encounter. In reasonings on life, even more than on other things, a good reasoner will consider not only the force of the opposing arguments, but also the bias to which his own mind is subject. To raise the level of national health is one of the surest ways of raising the level of national happiness, and in estimating the value of different pleasures many which, considered in themselves, might appear to rank low upon the scale, will rank high, if in addition to the immediate and transient enjoyment they procure, they contribute to form a strong and healthy body. No branch of legislation is more really valuable than that which is occupied with the health of the people, whether it takes the form of encouraging the means by which remedies may be discovered and diffused, or of extirpating by combined efforts particular diseases, or of securing that the mass of labour in the community should as far as possible be carried on under sound sanitary conditions. Fashion also can do much, both for good and ill. It exercises over great multitudes an almost absolute empire, regulating their dress, their education, their hours, their amusements, their food, their scale of expenditure; determining the qualities to which they principally aspire, the work in which they may engage, and even the form of beauty which they most cultivate. It is happy for a nation when this mighty influence is employed in encouraging habits of life which are beneficial or at least not gravely prejudicial to health. Nor is any form of individual education more really valuable than that which teaches the main conditions of a healthy life and forms those habits of temperance and self-restraint that are most likely to attain it.

---

[3] Much curious information on this subject will be found in Cabanis' *Rapports du physique et du moral de l'homme.*

With its great recuperative powers Youth can do with apparent impunity many things which in later life bring a speedy Nemesis; but on the other hand Youth is pre-eminently the period when habits and tastes are formed, and the yoke which is then lightly, willingly, wantonly assumed will in after years acquire a crushing weight. Few things are more striking than the levity of the motives, the feebleness of the impulses under which in youth fatal steps are taken which bring with them a weakened life and often an early grave. Smoking in manhood, when practised in moderation, is a very innocent and probably beneficent practice, but it is well known how deleterious it is to young boys, and how many of them have taken to it through no other motive than a desire to appear older than they are—that surest of all signs that we are very young. How often have the far more pernicious habits of drinking, or gambling, or frequenting corrupt society been acquired through a similar motive, or through the mere desire to enjoy the charm of a forbidden pleasure or to stand well with some dissipated companions! How large a proportion of lifelong female debility is due to an early habit of tight lacing, springing only from the silliest vanity! How many lives have been sacrificed through the careless recklessness which refused to take the trouble of changing wet clothes! How many have been shattered and shortened by excess in things which in moderation are harmless, useful, or praiseworthy,—by the broken blood-vessel, due to excess in some healthy athletic exercise or game; by the ruined brain overstrained in order to win some paltry prize! It is melancholy to observe how many lives have been broken down, ruined or corrupted in attempts to realise some supreme and unattainable desire; through the impulse of overmastering passion, of powerful and perhaps irresistible temptation. It is still sadder to observe how large a proportion of the failures of life may be ultimately traced to the most insignificant causes and might have been avoided without any serious effort either of intellect or will.

The success with which medicine and sanitary science have laboured to prolong life, to extirpate or diminish different forms of disease and to alleviate their consequences is abundantly proved. In all civilised countries the average of life has been raised, and there is good reason to believe that not only old age but also active, useful, enjoyable old age has become much more frequent. It is true that the gain to human happiness is not quite as great as might at first sight be imagined. Death is least sad when it comes in infancy or in extreme old age, and the increased average of life is largely due to the great diminution in infant mortality, which is in truth a very doubtful blessing. If extreme old age is a thing to be desired, it is perhaps chiefly because it usually implies a constitution which gives many earlier years of robust and healthy life. But with all deductions the triumphs of sanitary reform as well as of medical science are perhaps the brightest page in the history of our century. Some of the measures which have proved most useful can only be effected at some sacrifice of individual freedom and by widespread coercive sanitary regulations, and are thus more akin to despotism than to free government. How different would have been the condition of the world, and how far greater would have been the popularity of strong monarchy if at the time when such a form of government generally prevailed rulers had had the intelligence to put before them the improvement of the health and the prolongation of the lives of their subjects as the main object of their policy rather than military glory or the acquisition of territory or mere ostentatious and selfish display!

There is, however, some reason to believe that the diminution of disease and the prolongation of average human life are not necessarily or even generally accompanied by a corresponding improvement in general health. 'Acute diseases,' says an excellent judge, 'which are eminently fatal, prevail, on the contrary, in a population where the standard of health is high.... Thus a high rate of mortality may often be observed in a community where the number of persons affected with disease is small, and on the other hand general physical depression may concur with the prevalence of chronic maladies and yet be unattended with a great proportion of deaths.'[4] An anæmic population, free from severe illness, but living habitually at a low level of health and with the depressed spirits and feeble capacity of enjoyment which such a condition produces, is far from an ideal state, and there is much reason to fear that this type is an increasing one. Many things in modern life, among which ill-judged philanthropy and ill-judged legislation have no small part, contribute to produce it, but two causes probably dominate over all others. The one is to be found in sanitary science itself, which enables great numbers of constitutionally weak children who in other days would have died in infancy to grow up and marry and propagate a feeble offspring. The other is the steady movement of population from the country to the towns, which is one of the most conspicuous features of modern civilisation. These two influences inevitably and powerfully tend to depress the vitality of a nation, and by doing so to lower the level of animal spirits which is one of the most essential elements of happiness. Whether our improved standards of living and our much greater knowledge of sanitary conditions altogether counteract them is very doubtful.

In this as in most questions affecting life there are opposite dangers to be avoided, and wisdom lies mainly in a just sense of proportion and degree. That sanitary reform, promoted by governments, has on the whole been a great blessing seems to me scarcely open to reasonable question, but many of the best judges are of opinion that it may easily be pushed to dangerous extremes. Pew things are more curious than to observe how rapidly during the past generation the love of individual liberty has declined; how contentedly the English race are submitting great departments of their lives to a web of regulations restricting and encircling them. Each individual case must be considered on its merits, and few persons will now deny that the right of adult men and women to regulate the conditions of their own work and to determine the risks that they will assume may be wisely infringed in more cases than the Manchester School would have admitted. At the same time the marked tendency of this generation to extend the stringency and area of coercive legislation in the fields of industry and sanitary reform is one that should be carefully watched. Its exaggerations may in more ways than one greatly injure the very classes it is intended to benefit.

---

[4] Kay's *Moral and Physical Condition of the Working Classes*, p. 75

A somewhat corresponding statement may be made about individual sanitary education. It is, as I have said, a matter of the most vital importance that we should acquire in youth the knowledge and the habits that lead to a healthy life. The main articles of the sanitary creed are few and simple. Moderation and self-restraint in all things—an abundance of exercise, of fresh air, and of cold water—a sufficiency of steady work not carried to excess—occasional change of habits and abstinence from a few things which are manifestly injurious to health, are the cardinal rules to be observed. In the great lottery of life, men who have observed them all may be doomed to illness, weak vitality, and early death, but they at least add enormously to the chances of a strong and full life. The parent will need further knowledge for the care of his children, but for self-guidance little more is required, and with early habits an observance of the rules of health becomes almost instinctive and unconscious. But while no kind of education is more transcendently important than this, it is not unfrequently carried to an extreme which defeats its own purpose. The habit that so often grows upon men with slight chronic maladies, or feeble temperament, or idle lives, of making their own health and their own ailments the constant subject of their thoughts soon becomes a disease very fatal to happiness and positively injurious to health. It is well known how in an epidemic the panic-stricken are most liable to the contagion, and the life of the habitual valetudinarian tends promptly to depress the nerve energy which provides the true stamina of health. In the words of an eminent physician, 'It is not by being anxious in an inordinate or unduly fussy fashion that men can hope to live long and well. The best way to live well is to work well. Good work is the daily test and safeguard of personal health.... The practical aim should be to live an orderly and natural life. We were not intended to pick our way through the world trembling at every step.... It is worse than vain, for it encourages and increases the evil it attempts to relieve.... I firmly believe one half of the confirmed invalids of the day could be cured of their maladies if they were compelled to live busy and active lives and had no time to fret over their miseries.... One of the most seductive and mischievous of errors in self-management is the practice of giving way to inertia, weakness and depression.... Those who desire to live should settle this well in their minds, that nerve power is the force of life and that the will has a wondrously strong and direct influence over the body through the brain and the nervous system.'[5]

[5] Mortimer Granville's *How to Make the Best of Life*

CHAPTER III

Before entering into a more particular account of the chief elements of a happy life it may be useful to devote a few pages to some general considerations on the subject.

One of the first and most clearly recognised rules to be observed is that happiness is most likely to be attained when it is not the direct object of pursuit. In early youth we are accustomed to divide life broadly into work and play, regarding the first as duty or necessity and the second as pleasure. One of the great differences between childhood and manhood is that we come to like our work more than our play. It becomes to us, if not the chief pleasure, at least the chief interest of our lives, and even when it is not this, an essential condition of our happiness. Few lives produce so little happiness as those that are aimless and unoccupied. Apart from all considerations of right and wrong, one of the first conditions of a happy life is that it should be a full and busy one, directed to the attainment of aims outside ourselves. Anxiety and Ennui are the Scylla and Charybdis on which the bark of human happiness is most commonly wrecked. If a life of luxurious idleness and selfish ease in some measure saves men from the first danger, it seldom fails to bring with it the second. No change of scene, no multiplicity of selfish pleasures will in the long run enable them to escape it. As Carlyle says, 'The restless, gnawing ennui which, like a dark, dim, ocean flood, communicating with the Phlegethons and Stygian deeps, begirdles every human life so guided—is it not the painful cry even of that imprisoned heroism?... You ask for happiness. "Oh give me happiness," and they hand you ever new varieties of covering for the skin, ever new kinds of supply for the digestive apparatus.... Well, rejoice in your upholsteries and cookeries if so be they will make you "happy." Let the varieties of them be continual and innumerable. In all things let perpetual change, if that is a perpetual blessing to you, be your portion instead of mine. Incur the prophet's curse and in all things in this sublunary world "make yourselves like unto a wheel." Mount into your railways; whirl from place to place at the rate of fifty or, if you like, of five hundred miles an hour; you cannot escape from that inexorable, all-encircling ocean moan of ennui. No; if you could mount to the stars and do yacht voyages under the belts of Jupiter or stalk deer on the ring of Saturn it would still begirdle you. You cannot escape from it; you can but change your place in it without solacement except one moment's. That prophetic Sermon from the Deeps will continue with you till you wisely interpret it and do it or else till the Crack of Doom swallow it and you.'[6]

It needs but a few years of life experience to realise the profound truth of this passage. An ideal life would be furnished with abundant work of a kind that is congenial both to our intellects and our characters and that brings with it much interest and little anxiety. Few of us can command this. Most men's work is largely determined for them by circumstances, though in the guidance of life there are many

---

[6] *Latter-day Pamphlets:* 'Jesuitism.'

alternatives and much room for skilful pilotage. But the first great rule is that we must do something—that life must have a purpose and an aim—that work should be not merely occasional and spasmodic, but steady and continuous. Pleasure is a jewel which will only retain its lustre when it is in a setting of work, and a vacant life is one of the worst of pains, though the islands of leisure that stud a crowded, well-occupied life may be among the things to which we look back with the greatest delight.

Another great truth is conveyed in the saying of Aristotle that a wise man will make it his aim rather to avoid suffering than to attain pleasure. Men can in reality do very little to mitigate the force of the great bereavements and the other graver calamities of life. All our systems of philosophy and reasoning are vain when confronted with them. Innate temperament which we cannot greatly change determines whether we sink crushed beneath the blow or possess the buoyancy that can restore health to our natures. The conscious and deliberate pursuit of pleasure is attended by many deceptions and illusions, and rarely leads to lasting happiness. But we can do very much by prudence, self-restraint and intelligent regulation so to manage life as to avoid a large proportion of its calamities and at the same time, by preserving the affections pure and undimmed, by diversifying interests and forming active habits, to combat its tedium and despondency.

Another truth is that both the greatest pleasures and the keenest pains of life lie much more in those humbler spheres which are accessible to all than on the rare pinnacles to which only the most gifted or the most fortunate can attain. It would probably be found upon examination that most men who have devoted their lives successfully to great labours and ambitions, and who have received the most splendid gifts from Fortune, have nevertheless found their chief pleasure in things unconnected with their main pursuits and generally within the reach of common men. Domestic pleasures, pleasures of scenery, pleasures of reading, pleasures of travel or of sport have been the highest enjoyment of men of great ambition, intellect, wealth and position. There is a curious passage in Lord Althorp's Life in which that most popular and successful statesman, towards the close of his long parliamentary life, expressed his emphatic conviction that 'the thing that gave him the greatest pleasure in the world' was 'to see sporting dogs hunt.'[7] I can myself recollect going over a country place with an old member of Parliament who had sat in the House of Commons for nearly fifty years of the most momentous period of modern English history. If questioned he could tell about the stirring scenes of the great Reform Bill of 1832, but it was curious to observe how speedily and inevitably he passed from such matters to the history of the trees on his estate which he had planted and watched at every stage of their growth, and how evidently in the retrospect of life it was to these things and not to the incidents of a long parliamentary career that his affections naturally turned. I once asked an illustrious public man who had served his country with brilliant success in many lands, and who was spending the evening of his life as an active

---

[7] Le Marchant's *Life of Althorp*, p. 143

country gentleman in a place which he dearly loved, whether he did not find this sphere too contracted for his happiness. 'Never for a day,' he answered; 'and in every country where I have been, in every post which I have filled, the thought of this place has always been at the back of my mind.' A great writer who had devoted almost his whole life to one gigantic work, and to his own surprise brought it at last to a successful end, sadly observed that amid the congratulations that poured in to him from every side he could not help feeling, when he analysed his own emotions, how tepid was the satisfaction which such a triumph could give him, and what much more vivid gratification he had come to take in hearing the approaching steps of some little children whom he had taught to love him.

It is one of the paradoxes of human nature that the things that are most struggled for and the things that are most envied are not those which give either the most intense or the most unmixed joy. Ambition is the luxury of the happy. It is sometimes, but more rarely, the consolation and distraction of the wretched; but most of those who have trodden its paths, if they deal honestly with themselves, will acknowledge that the gravest disappointments of public life dwindle into insignificance compared with the poignancy of suffering endured at the deathbed of a wife or of a child, and that within the small circle of a family life they have found more real happiness than the applause of nations could ever give.

> Look down, look down from your glittering heights,
>   And tell us, ye sons of glory,
> The joys and the pangs of your eagle flights,
>   The triumph that crowned the story,
>
> The rapture that thrilled when the goal was won,
>   The goal of a life's desire;
> And a voice replied from the setting sun,
>   Nay, the dearest and best lies nigher.
>
> How oft in such hours our fond thoughts stray
>   To the dream of two idle lovers;
> To the young wife's kiss; to the child at play;
>   Or the grave which the long grass covers!
>
> And little we'd reck of power or gold,
>   And of all life's vain endeavour,
> If the heart could glow as it glowed of old,
>   And if youth could abide for ever.

Another consideration in the cultivation of happiness is the importance of acquiring the habit of realising our blessings while they last. It is one of the saddest facts of human nature that we commonly only learn their value by their loss. This, as I have already noticed, is very evidently the case with health. By the laws of our being we are almost unconscious of the action of our bodily organs as long as they are working well. It is only when they are deranged, obstructed or impaired that our attention becomes concentrated upon them. In consequence of this a state of perfect health is rarely fully appreciated until it is lost and during a short period after it has been regained. Gray has described the new sensation of pleasure which convalescence gives in well-known lines:

> See the wretch who long has tost
>   On the thorny bed of pain,
> At length repair his vigour lost
>   And breathe and walk again;
> The meanest floweret of the vale,
> The simplest note that swells the gale,
>   The common sun, the air, the skies,
>   To him are opening Paradise.

And what is true of health is true of other things. It is only when some calamity breaks the calm tenor of our ways and deprives us of some gift of fortune we have long enjoyed that we feel how great was the value of what we have lost. There are times in the lives of most of us when we would have given all the world to be as we were but yesterday, though that yesterday had passed over us unappreciated and unenjoyed. Sometimes, indeed, our perception of this contrast brings with it a lasting and salutary result. In the medicine of Nature a chronic and abiding disquietude or morbidness of temperament is often cured by some keen though more transient sorrow which violently changes the current of our thoughts and imaginations.

The difference between knowledge and realisation is one of the facts of our nature that are most worthy of our attention. Every human mind contains great masses of inert, passive, undisputed knowledge which exercise no real influence on thought or character till something occurs which touches our imagination and quickens this knowledge into activity. Very few things contribute so much to the happiness of life as a constant realisation of the blessings we enjoy. The difference between a naturally contented and a naturally discontented nature is one of the marked differences of innate temperament, but we can do much to cultivate that habit of dwelling on the benefits of our lot which converts acquiescence into a more positive enjoyment. Religion in this field does much, for it inculcates thanksgiving as well as prayer, gratitude for the present and the past as well as hope for the future. Among secular influences, contrast and comparison have the greatest value. Some minds are always looking on the fortunes that are above them and comparing their own penury with the opulence of others. A wise nature will take an opposite course and will cultivate the habit of looking rather at the round of the ladder of fortune which is below our own and realising the countless points in which our lot is better than that of others. As Dr. Johnson says, 'Few are placed in a situation so gloomy and distressful as not to see every day beings yet more forlorn and miserable from whom they may learn to rejoice in their own lot.'

The consolation men derive amid their misfortunes from reflecting upon the still greater misfortunes of others and thus lightening their own by contrast is a topic which must be delicately used, but when so used it is not wrong and it often proves very efficacious. Perhaps the pleasure La Rochefoucauld pretends that men take in the misfortunes of their best friends, if it is a real thing, is partly due to this consideration, as the feeling of pity which is inspired by some sudden death or great trouble falling on others is certainly not wholly unconnected with the realisation that such calamities might fall upon ourselves. It is worthy of notice, however, that while all moralists recognise content as one of the chief ingredients of happiness, some of the strongest influences of modern industrial civilisation are antagonistic to it. The whole theory of progress as taught by Political Economy rests upon the importance of creating wants and desires as a stimulus to exertion. There are countries, especially in southern climates, where the wants of men are very few, and where, as long as those wants are satisfied, men will live a careless and contented life, enjoying the present, thinking very little of the future. Whether the sum of enjoyment in such a population is really less than in our more advanced civilisation is at least open to question. It is a remark of Schopenhauer that the Idyll, which is the only form of poetry specially devoted to the description of human felicity, always paints life in its simplest and least elaborated form, and he sees in this an illustration of his doctrine that the greatest happiness will be found in the simplest and even most uniform life provided it escapes the evil of ennui. The political economist, however, will pronounce the condition of such a people as I have described a deplorable one, and in order to raise them his first task will be to infuse into them some discontent with their lot, to persuade them to multiply their wants and to aspire to a higher standard of comfort, to a fuller and a larger existence. A discontent with existing circumstances is the chief source of a desire to improve them, and this desire is the mainspring of progress. In this theory of life, happiness is sought, not in content, but in improved circumstances, in the development of new capacities of enjoyment, in the pleasure which active existence naturally gives. To maintain in their due proportion in our nature the spirit of content and the desire to improve, to combine a realised appreciation of the blessings we enjoy with a healthy and well-regulated ambition, is no easy thing, but it is the problem which all who aspire to a perfect life should set before themselves. In medio tutissimus ibis is eminently true of the cultivation of character, and some of its best elements become pernicious in their extremes. Thus prudent forethought, which is one of the first conditions of a successful life, may easily degenerate into that most miserable state of mind in which men are perpetually anticipating and dwelling upon the uncertain dangers and evils of an uncertain future. How much indeed of the happiness and misery of men may be included under those two words, realisation and anticipation!

There is no such thing as a Eudæmometer measuring with accuracy the degrees of happiness realised by men in different ages, under different circumstances, and with different characters. Perhaps if such a thing existed it might tend to discourage us by showing that diversities and improvements of circumstances affect real happiness in a smaller degree than we are accustomed to imagine. Our nature accommodates itself speedily to improved circumstances, and they cease to give positive pleasure while their loss is acutely painful. Advanced civilisation brings with it countless and inestimable benefits, but it also brings with it many forms of suffering from which a ruder existence is exempt. There is some reason to believe that it is usually accompanied with a lower range of animal spirits, and it is certainly accompanied with an increased sensitiveness to pain. Some philosophers have contended that this is the best of all possible worlds. It is difficult to believe so, as the whole object of human effort is to make it a better one. But the success of that effort is more apparent in the many terrible forms of human suffering which it has abolished or diminished than in the higher level of positive happiness that has been attained.

CHAPTER IV

Though the close relationship that subsists between morals and happiness is universally acknowledged, I do not belong to the school which believes that pleasure and pain, either actual or anticipated, are the only motives by which the human will can be governed; that virtue resolves itself ultimately into well-considered interest and finds its ultimate reason in the happiness of those who practise it; that 'all our virtues,' as La Rochefoucauld has said, 'end in self-love as the rivers in the sea.' Such a proverb as 'Honesty is the best policy' represents no doubt a great truth, though it has been well said that no man is really honest who is only honest through this motive, and though it is very evident that it is by no means an universal truth but depends largely upon changing and precarious conditions of laws, police, public opinion, and individual circumstances. But in the higher realms of morals the coincidence of happiness and virtue is far more doubtful. It is certainly not true that the highest nature is necessarily or even naturally the happiest. Paganism has produced no more perfect type than the profoundly pathetic figure of Marcus Aurelius, while Christianity finds its ideal in one who was known as the 'Man of Sorrows.' The conscience of Mankind has ever recognised self-sacrifice as the supreme element of virtue, and self-sacrifice is never real when it is only the exchange of a less happiness for a greater one. No moral chemistry can transmute the worship of Sorrow, which Goethe described as the essence of Christianity, into the worship of happiness, and probably with most men health and temperament play a far larger part in the real happiness of their lives than any of the higher virtues. The satisfaction of accomplished duty which some moralists place among the chief pleasures of life is a real thing in so far as it saves men from internal reproaches, but it is probable that it is among the worst men that pangs of conscience are least dreaded, and it is certainly not among the best men that they are least felt. Conscience, indeed, when it is very sensitive and very lofty, is far more an element of suffering than the reverse. It aims at an ideal higher than we can attain. It takes the lowest view of our own achievements. It suffers keenly from the many shortcomings of which it is acutely sensible. Far from indulging in the pleasurable retrospect of a well-spent life, it urges men to constant, painful, and often unsuccessful effort. A nature that is strung to the saintly or the heroic level will find itself placed in a jarring world, will provoke much friction and opposition, and will be pained by many things in which a lower nature would placidly acquiesce. The highest form of intellectual virtue is that love of truth for its own sake which breaks up prejudices, tempers enthusiasm by the full admission of opposing arguments and qualifying circumstances, and places in the sphere of possibility or probability many things which we would gladly accept as certainties. Candour and impartiality are in a large degree virtues of temperament; but no one who has any real knowledge of human nature can doubt how much more pleasurable it is to most men to live under the empire of invincible prejudice, deliberately shutting out every consideration that could shake or qualify cherished beliefs. 'God,' says Emerson, 'offers to every mind its choice between truth and repose. Take which you please. You can never have both.' One of the strongest arguments of natural religion rests upon the fact that virtue so often fails to bring its reward; upon the belief that is so deeply implanted in human nature that this is essentially unjust and must in some future state be remedied.

For such reasons as these I believe it to be impossible to identify virtue with happiness, and the views of the opposite school seem to me chiefly to rest upon an unnatural and deceptive use of words. Even when the connection between virtue and pleasure is most close, it is true, as the old Stoics said, that though virtue gives pleasure, this is not the reason why a good man will practise it; that pleasure is the companion and not the guide of his life; that he does not love virtue because it gives pleasure, but it gives pleasure because he loves it.[8] A true account of human nature will recognise that it has the power of aiming at something which is different from happiness and something which may be intelligibly described as higher, and that on the predominance of this loftier aim the nobility of life essentially depends. It is not even true that the end of man should be to find peace at the last. It should be to do his duty and tell the truth.

But while this great truth of the existence of a higher aim than happiness should be always maintained, the relations between morals and happiness are close and intimate and well worthy of investigation. As far as the lower or more commonplace virtues are concerned there can be no mistake. It is very evident that a healthy, long and prosperous life is more likely to be attained by industry, moderation and purity than by the opposite courses. It is very evident that drunkenness and sensuality ruin health and shorten life; that idleness, gambling and disorderly habits ruin prosperity; that ill-temper, selfishness and envy kill friendship and provoke animosities and dislike; that in every well-regulated society there is at least a general coincidence between the path of duty and the path of prosperity; dishonesty, violence and disregard for the rights of others naturally and usually bringing their punishment either from law or from public opinion or from both. Bishop Butler has argued that the general tendency of virtue to lead to happiness and the general tendency of vice to lead to unhappiness prove that even in its present state there is a moral government of the world, and whatever controversy may be raised about the inference there can at least be no doubt about the substantial truth of the facts. Happiness, as I have already said, is best attained when it is not the direct or at least the main object that is aimed at. A wasted and inactive life not only palls in itself but deprives men of the very real and definite pleasure that naturally arises from the healthful activity of all our powers, while a life of egotism excludes the pleasures of sympathy which play so large a part in human happiness. One of the lessons which experience most clearly teaches is that work, duty and the discipline of character are essential elements of lasting happiness. The pleasures of vice are often real, but they are commonly transient and they leave legacies of suffering, weakness, or care behind them. The nobler pleasures for the most part grow and strengthen with advancing years. The passions of youth, when duly

---

[8] Seneca, *De Vita Beata*

regulated, gradually transform themselves into habits, interests and steady affections, and it is in the long forecasts of life that the superiority of virtue as an element of happiness becomes most apparent.

It has been truly said that such words as 'pastime' and 'diversion' applied to our pleasures are among the most melancholy in the language, for they are the confession of human nature that it cannot find happiness in itself, but must seek for something that will fill up time, will cover the void which it feels, and divert men's thoughts from the conditions and prospects of their own lives. How much of the pleasure of Society, and indeed of all amusements, depends on their power of making us forget ourselves! The substratum of life is sad, and few men who reflect on the dangers and uncertainties that surround it can find it even tolerable without much extraneous aid. The first and most vital of these aids is to be found in the creation of strong interests. It is one of the laws of our being that by seeking interests rather than by seeking pleasures we can best encounter the gloom of life. But those only have the highest efficiency which are of an unselfish nature. By throwing their whole nature into the interests of others men most effectually escape the melancholy of introspection; the horizon of life is enlarged; the development of the moral and sympathetic feelings chases egotistic cares, and by the same paradox that we have seen in other parts of human nature men best attain their own happiness by absorbing themselves in the pursuit of the happiness of others.

The aims and perspective of a well-regulated life have never, I think, been better described than in one of the letters of Burke to the Duke of Richmond. 'It is wise indeed, considering the many positive vexations and the innumerable bitter disappointments of pleasure in the world, to have as many resources of satisfaction as possible within one's power. Whenever we concentre the mind on one sole object, that object and life itself must go together. But though it is right to have reserves of employment, still some one object must be kept principal; greatly and eminently so; and the other masses and figures must preserve their due subordination, to make out the grand composition of an important life.'[9] It is equally true that among these objects the disinterested and the unselfish should hold a predominant place. With some this side of their activity is restricted to the narrow circle of home or to the isolated duties and charities of their own neighbourhood. With others it takes the form of large public interests, of a keen participation in social, philanthropic, political or religious enterprises. Character plays a larger part than intellect in the happiness of life, and the cultivation of the unselfish part of our nature is not only one of the first lessons of morals but also of wisdom.

Like most other things its difficulties lie at the beginning, and it is by steady practice that it passes into a second and instinctive nature. The power of man to change organically his character is a very limited one, but on the whole the improvement of character is probably more within his reach than intellectual

---

[9]Burke's *Correspondence*, i. 376, 377.

development. Time and Opportunity are wanting to most men for any considerable intellectual study, and even were it otherwise every man will find large tracts of knowledge and thought wholly external to his tastes, aptitudes and comprehension. But every one can in some measure learn the lesson of self-sacrifice, practise what is right, correct or at least mitigate his dominant faults. What fine examples of self-sacrifice, quiet courage, resignation in misfortune, patient performance of painful duty, magnanimity and forgiveness under injury may be often found among those who are intellectually the most commonplace!

The insidious growth of selfishness is a disease against which men should be most on their guard; but it is a grave though a common error to suppose that the unselfish instincts may be gratified without restraint. There is here, however, one important distinction to be noted. The many and great evils that have sprung from lavish and ill-considered charities do not always or perhaps generally spring from any excess or extravagance of the charitable feeling. They are much more commonly due to its defect. The rich man who never cares to inquire into the details of the cases that are brought before him or to give any serious thought to the ulterior consequences of his acts, but who is ready to give money at any solicitation and who considers that by so doing he has discharged his duty, is far more likely to do harm in this way than the man who devotes himself to patient, plodding, house to house work among the poor. The many men and the probably still larger number of women who give up great portions of their lives to such work soon learn to trace with considerable accuracy the consequences of their charities and to discriminate between the worthy and the unworthy. That such persons often become exclusive and one-sided, and acquire a kind of professional bent which induces them to subordinate all national considerations to their own subject and lose sight of the true proportion of things, is undoubtedly true, but it will probably not be found with the best workers that such a life tends to unduly intensify emotion. As Bishop Butler has said with profound truth, active habits are strengthened and passive impressions weakened by repetition, and a life spent in active charitable work is quite compatible with much sobriety and even coldness of judgment in estimating each case as it arises. It is not the surgeon who is continually employed in operations for the cure of his patients who is most moved at the sight of suffering.

This is, I believe, on the whole true, but it is also true that there are grave diseases which attach themselves peculiarly to the unselfish side of our nature, and they are peculiarly dangerous because men, feeling that the unselfish is the virtuous and nobler side of their being, are apt to suffer these tendencies to operate without supervision or control. Yet it is hardly possible to exaggerate the calamities that have sprung from misjudged unselfish actions. The whole history of religious persecution abundantly illustrates it, for there can be little question that a large proportion of the persecutors were sincerely seeking what they believed to be the highest good of mankind. And if this dark page of human history is now almost closed, there are still many other ways in which a similar evil is displayed. Crotchets, sentimentalities and fanaticisms cluster especially around the unselfish side of our nature, and they work evil in many curious and subtle ways. Few things have done more harm in the world than disproportioned compassion. It is a law of our being that we are only deeply moved by sufferings we distinctly realise, and the degrees in which different kinds of suffering appeal to the imagination bear no proportion to their real magnitude. The most benevolent man will read of an earthquake in Japan or a plague in South America with a callousness he would never display towards some untimely death or some painful accident in his immediate neighbourhood, and in general the suffering of a prominent and isolated individual strikes us much more forcibly than that of an undistinguished multitude. Few deaths are so prominent, and therefore few produce such widespread compassion, as those of conspicuous criminals. It is no exaggeration to say that the death of an 'interesting' murderer will often arouse much stronger feelings than were ever excited by the death of his victim; or by the deaths of brave soldiers who perished by disease or by the sword in some obscure expedition in a remote country. This mode of judgment acts promptly upon conduct. The humanitarian spirit which mitigates the penal code and makes the reclamation of the criminal a main object is a perfectly right thing as long as it does not so far diminish the deterrent power of punishment as to increase crime, and as long as it does not place the criminal in a better position of comfort than the blameless poor, but when these conditions are not fulfilled it is much more an evil than a good. The remote, indirect and unrealised consequences of our acts are often far more important than those which are manifest and direct, and it continually happens that in extirpating some concentrated and obtrusive evil, men increase or engender a diffused malady which operates over a far wider area. How few, for example, who share the prevailing tendency to deal with every evil that appears in Society by coercive legislation adequately realise the danger of weakening the robust, self-reliant, resourceful habits on which the happiness of Society so largely depends, and at the same time, by multiplying the functions and therefore increasing the expenses of government, throwing new and crushing burdens on struggling industry! How often have philanthropists, through a genuine interest for some suffering class or people, advocated measures which by kindling, prolonging, or enlarging a great war would infallibly create calamities far greater than those which they would redress! How often might great outbursts of savage crime or grave and lasting disorders in the State, or international conflicts that have cost thousands of lives, have been averted by a prompt and unflinching severity from which an ill-judged humanity recoiled! If in the February of 1848 Louis Philippe had permitted Marshal Bugeaud to fire on the Revolutionary mob at a time when there was no real and widespread desire for revolution in France, how many bloody pages of French and European history might have been spared!

Measures guaranteeing men, and still more women, from excessive labour, and surrounding them with costly sanitary precautions, may easily, if they are injudiciously framed, so handicap a sex or a people in the competition of industry as to drive them out of great fields of industry, restrict their means of livelihood, lower their standard of wages and comfort, and thus seriously diminish the happiness of their lives. Injudicious suppressions of amusements that are not wholly good, but which afford keen enjoyment to great masses, seldom fail to give an impulse to other pleasures more secret and probably more vicious. Injudicious charities, or an extravagant and too indulgent poor law administration, inevitably discourage industry and thrift, and usually increase the poverty they were intended to cure. The parent who shrinks from inflicting any suffering on his child, or withholding from him any pleasure that he desires, is not laying the foundation of a happy life, and the benevolence which counteracts or obscures the law of nature that extravagance, improvidence and vice lead naturally to ruin, is no real kindness either to the upright man who has resisted temptation or to the weak man whose virtue is trembling doubtfully in the balance. Nor is it in the long run for the benefit of the world that superior ability or superior energy or industry should be handicapped in the race of life, forbidden to encounter exceptional risks for the sake of exceptional rewards, reduced by regulations to measures of work and gain intended for the benefit of inferior characters or powers.

The fatal vice of ill-considered benevolence is that it looks only to proximate and immediate results without considering either alternatives or distant and indirect consequences. A large and highly respectable form of benevolence is that connected with the animal world, and in England it is carried in some respects to a point which is unknown on the Continent. But what a strange form of compassion is that which long made it impossible to establish a Pasteur Institute in England, obliging patients threatened with one of the most horrible diseases that can afflict mankind to go—as they are always ready to do—to Paris, in order to undergo a treatment which what is called the humane sentiment of Englishmen forbid them to receive at home! What a strange form of benevolence is that which in a country where field sports are the habitual amusement of the higher ranks of Society denounces as criminal even the most carefully limited and supervised experiments on living animals, and would thus close the best hope of finding remedies for some of the worst forms of human suffering, the one sure method of testing supposed remedies which may be fatal or which may be of incalculable benefit to mankind! Foreign critics, indeed, often go much further and believe that in other forms connected with this subject public opinion in England is strangely capricious and inconsistent. They compare with astonishment the sentences that are sometimes passed for the ill-treatment of a woman and for the ill-treatment of a cat; they ask whether the real sufferings caused by many things that are in England punished by law or reprobated by opinion are greater than those caused by sports which are constantly practised without reproach; and they are apt to find much that is exaggerated or even fantastic in the great popularity and elaboration of some animal charities.[10] At the same time in our own country the

---

[10] As I am writing these pages I find the following paragraph in a newspaper which may illustrate my meaning:— 'DOGS' NURSING. A case was heard at the Brompton County Court on Friday in which some suggestive evidence was given of the medical treatment of dogs. The proprietor of a dogs' infirmary at Tattersall's Corner sued Mr. Harding Cox for the board and lodging of seven dogs, and the *régime* was explained. They are fed on essence of meat, washed down with port wine, and have as a digestive eggs beaten up in milk and arrowroot. Medicated baths and tonics are also supplied, and occasionally the animals are treated to a day in the country. This course of hygiene necessitated an

more recognised field sports greatly trouble many benevolent natures. I will here only say that while the positive benefits they produce are great and manifest, those who condemn them constantly forget what would be the fate of the animals that are slaughtered if such sports did not exist, and how little the balance of suffering is increased or altered by the destruction of beings which themselves live by destroying. As a poet says—

The fish exult whene'er the seagull dies,

The salmon's death preserves a thousand flies.

On most of these questions the effect on human character is a more important consideration than the effect on animal happiness. The best thing that legislation can do for wild animals is to extend as far as possible to harmless classes a close time, securing them immunity while they are producing and supporting their young. This is the truest kindness, and on quite other grounds it is peculiarly needed, as the improvement of firearms and the increase of population have completely altered, as far as man is concerned, the old balance between production and destruction, and threaten, if unchecked, to lead to an almost complete extirpation of great classes of the animal world. It is melancholy to observe how often sensitive women who object to field sports and who denounce all experiments on living animals will be found supporting with perfect callousness fashions that are leading to the wholesale destruction of some of the most beautiful species of birds, and are in some cases dependent upon acts of very aggravated cruelty.

---

expenditure of ten shillings a week. The defendant pleaded that the charges were excessive, but the judge awarded the plaintiff £25. How many hospital patients receive such treatment?'—*Daily Express*, February 16, 1897.

CHAPTER V

The illustrations given in the last chapter will be sufficient to show the danger of permitting the unselfish side of human nature to run wild without serious control by the reason and by the will. To see things in their true proportion, to escape the magnifying influence of a morbid imagination, should be one of the chief aims of life, and in no fields is it more needed than in those we have been reviewing. At the same time every age has its own ideal moral type towards which the strongest and best influences of the time converge. The history of morals is essentially a history of the changes that take place not so much in our conception of what is right and wrong as in the proportionate place and prominence we assign to different virtues and vices. There are large groups of moral qualities which in some ages of the world's history have been regarded as of supreme importance, while in other ages they are thrown into the background, and there are corresponding groups of vices which are treated in some periods as very serious and in others as very trivial. The heroic type of Paganism and the saintly type of Christianity in its purest form, consist largely of the same elements, but the proportions in which they are mixed are altogether different. There are ages when the military and civic virtues—the qualities that make good soldiers and patriotic citizens—dominate over all others. The self-sacrifice of the best men flows habitually in these channels. In such an age integrity in business relations and the domestic virtues which maintain the purity of the family may be highly valued, but they are chiefly valued because they are essential to the well-being of the State. The soldier who has attained to the highest degree the best qualities of his profession, the patriot who sacrifices to the services of the State his comforts, his ambitions and his life, is the supreme model, and the estimation in which he is held is but little lowered even though he may have been guilty, like Cato, of atrocious cruelty to his slaves, or, like some of the heroes of ancient times, of scandalous forms of private profligacy.

There are other ages in which military life is looked upon by moralists with disfavour, and in which patriotism ranks very low in the scale of virtues, while charity, gentleness, self-abnegation, devotional habits, and purity in thought, word and act are pre-eminently inculcated. The intellectual virtues, again, which deal with truth and falsehood, form a distinct group. The habit of mind which makes men love truth for its own sake as the supreme ideal, and which turns aside from all falsehood, exaggeration, party or sectarian misrepresentation and invention, is in no age a common one, but there are some ages in which it is recognised and inculcated as virtue, while there are others in which it is no exaggeration to say that the whole tendency of religious teaching has been to discourage it. During many centuries the ascetic and purely ecclesiastical standard of virtue completely dominated. The domestic virtues, though clearly recognised, held altogether a subordinate place to what were deemed the higher virtues of the ascetic celibate. Charity, though nobly cultivated and practised, was regarded mainly through a dogmatic medium and practised less for the benefit of the recipient than for the spiritual welfare of the donor.

In the eyes of multitudes the highest conception of a saintly life consisted largely if not mainly in complete detachment from secular interests and affections. No type was more admired, and no type was ever more completely severed from all active duties and all human relations than that of the saint of the desert or of the monk of one of the contemplative orders. To die to the world; to become indifferent to its aims, interests and pleasures; to measure all things by a standard wholly different from human happiness, to live habitually for another life was the constant teaching of the saints. In the stress laid on the cultivation of the spiritual life the whole sphere of active duties sank into a lower plane; and the eye of the mind was turned upwards and inwards and but little on the world around. 'Happy,' said one saint, 'is the mind which sees but two objects, God and self, one of which conceptions fills it with a sovereign delight and the other abases it to the extremest dejection.'[11] 'As much love as we give to creatures,' said another saint, 'just so much we steal from the Creator.'[12] 'Two things only do I ask,' said a third, [13] 'to suffer and to die.' 'Forsake all,' said Thomas à Kempis, 'and thou shalt find all. Leave desire and thou shalt find rest.' 'Unless a man be disengaged from the affection of all creatures he cannot with freedom of mind attend unto Divine things.'

The gradual, silent and half-unconscious modification in the type of Morals which took place after the Reformation was certainly not the least important of its results. If it may be traced in some degree to the distinctive theology of the Protestant Churches, it was perhaps still more due to the abolition of clerical celibacy which placed the religious teachers in the centre of domestic life and in close contact with a large circle of social duties. There is even now a distinct difference between the morals of a sincerely Catholic and a sincerely Protestant country, and this difference is not so much, as controversialists would tell us, in the greater and the less as in the moral type, or, in other words, in the different degrees of importance attached to different virtues and vices. Probably nowhere in the world can more beautiful and more reverent types be found than in some of the Catholic countries of Europe which are but little touched by the intellectual movements of the age, but no good observer can fail to notice how much larger is the place given to duties which rest wholly on theological considerations, and how largely even the natural duties are based on such considerations and governed, limited, and sometimes even superseded by them. The ecclesiastics who at the Council of Constance induced Sigismund to violate the safe-conduct he had given, and, in spite of his solemn promise, to condemn Huss to a death of fire,[14] and the ecclesiastics who at the Diet of Worms vainly tried to induce Charles V. to act with a similar perfidy towards Luther, represent a conception of

---

[11] St. Francis de Sales

[12] St. Philip Neri.

[13] St. Teresa

[14] 'Cum dictus Johannes Hus fidem orthodoxam pertinaciter impugnans, se ab omni con ductu et privilegio reddiderit alienum, nec aliqua sibi fides aut promissio de jure naturali divino vel humano, fuerit in præjudicium Catholicæ fidei observanda.' Declaration of the Council of Constance. See Creighton's History of the Papacy, ii. 32

morals which is abundantly prevalent in our day. It is no exaggeration to say that in Catholic countries the obligation of truthfulness in cases in which it conflicts with the interests of the Church rests wholly on the basis of honour, and not at all on the basis of religion. In the estimates of Catholic rulers no impartial observer can fail to notice how their attitude towards the interest of the Church dominates over all considerations of public and private morals.

In past ages this was much more the case. The Church filled in the minds of men a place at least equal to that of the State in the Roman Republic. Men who had made great sacrifices for it and rendered great services to it were deemed, beyond all others, the good men, and in those men things which we should regard as grossly criminal appeared mere venial frailties. Let any one who doubts this study the lives of the early Catholic saints, and the still more instructive pages in which Gregory of Tours and other ecclesiastical annalists have described the characters and acts of the more prominent figures in the secular history of their times, and he will soon feel that he has passed into a moral atmosphere and is dealing with moral measurements and perspectives wholly unlike those of our own day.[15]

In highly civilised ages the same spirit may be clearly traced. Bossuet was certainly no hypocrite or sycophant, but a man of austere virtue and undoubted courage. He did not hesitate to rebuke the gross profligacy of the life of Louis XIV., and although neither he nor any of the other Catholic divines of his age seriously protested against the wars of pure egotism and ostentation which made that sovereign the scourge of Europe and brought down upon his people calamities immeasurably greater than the faults of his private life—although, indeed, he has spoken of those wars in language of rapturous and unqualified eulogy [16]—he had at least the grace to devote a chapter of his 'Politique tirée de l'Écriture Sainte' to the theme that 'God does not love war.' But in the eyes of Bossuet the dominant fact in the life of Louis XIV. was the Revocation of the Edict of Nantes and the savage persecution of the Huguenots, and this was sufficient to place him among the best of sovereigns.[17]

To those who will candidly consider the subject there is nothing in this which need excite surprise. The doctrine that the Catholic Church is the inspired guide, representing the voice of the Divinity on earth and deciding with absolute authority all questions of right and wrong, very naturally led to the conviction that nothing which was conducive to its interests could be really criminal, and in all departments of morals it regulated the degrees of praise and blame. The doctrine which is still so

---

[15] I have collected some illustrations of this in my History of European Morals, ii. 235-242.

[16] See, e.g. his funeral oration on Marie Thérèse d'Autriche.

[17] See the enthusiastic eulogy of the persecution of the Huguenots in his funeral oration on Michel le Tellier. It concludes: 'Épanchons nos coeurs sur la piété de Louis; poussons jusqu'au ciel nos acclamations, et disons à ce nouveau Constantin, à ce nouveau Théodose, à ce nouveau Marcien, à ce nouveau Charlemagne ce que les six cent trente Pères dirent autrefois dans le Concile de Chalcédoine: "Vous avez affermi la foi; vous avez exterminé les hérétiques; c'est le digne ouvrage de votre règne; c'en est le propre caractère. Par vous l'hérésie n'est plus, Dieu seul a pu faire cette merveille. Roi du ciel, conservez le roi de la terre; c'est le voeu, des Églises; c'est le voeu des Évêques."

widely professed but now so faintly realised, that the first essential to salvation is orthodox belief, placed conduct on a lower plane of importance than dogma, while the conviction that it is in the power of man to obtain absolute certainty in religious belief, that erroneous belief is in the eyes of the Almighty a crime bringing with it eternal damnation, and that the teacher of heresy is the greatest enemy of mankind, at once justified in the eyes of the believer acts which now seem the gravest moral aberrations. Many baser motives and elements no doubt mingled with the long and hideous history of the religious persecutions of Christendom, but in the eyes of countless conscientious men this teaching seemed amply sufficient to justify them and to stifle all feeling of compassion for the victims. Much the same considerations explain the absolute indifference with which so many good men witnessed those witch persecutions which consigned thousands of old, feeble and innocent women to torture and to death.

Other illustrations of a less tragical kind might be given. Thus in cases of child-birth the physician is sometimes placed in the alternative of sacrificing the life of the mother or of the unborn child. In such cases a Protestant or freethinking physician would not hesitate to save the adult life as by far the most valuable. The Catholic doctrine is that under such circumstances the first duty of the physician is to save the life of the unbaptized child.[18] Large numbers of commercial transactions which are now universally acknowledged to be perfectly innocent and useful would during a long period have been prohibited on account of the Catholic doctrine of usury which condemned as sinful even the most moderate interest on money if it was exacted as the price of the loan.[19]

Every religious and indeed every philosophical system that has played a great part in the history of the world has a tendency either to form or to assimilate with a particular moral type, and in the eyes of a large and growing number it is upon the excellency of this type, and upon its success in producing it, that its superiority mainly depends. The superstructure or scaffolding of belief around which it is formed appears to them of comparatively little moment, and it is not uncommon to find men ardently devoted to a particular type long after they have discarded the tenets with which it was once connected. Carlyle, for example, sometimes spoke of himself as a Calvinist, and used language both in public and private as if there was no important difference between himself and the most orthodox Puritans, yet it is very evident that he disbelieved nearly all the articles of their creed. What he meant was that Calvinism had produced in all countries in which it really dominated a definite type of character and conception of morals which was in his eyes the noblest that had yet appeared in the world.

'Above all things, my brethren, swear not.' If, as is generally assumed, this refers to the custom of using profane oaths in common conversation, how remote from

---

[18] See Migne, Encyclopédie Théologique, 'Dict. de Cas de Conscience,' art. Avortement.

[19] See on this subject my History of Rationalism, ii. 250-270, and my Democracy and Liberty, ii., ch. viii

modern ideas is the place assigned to this vice, which perhaps affects human happiness as little as any other that can be mentioned, in the scale of criminality, and how curiously characteristic is the fact that the vice to which this supremacy of enormity is attributed continued to be prevalent during the ages when theological influences were most powerful, and has in all good society faded away in simple obedience to a turn of fashion which proscribes it as ungentlemanly! For a long period Acts condemning it were read at stated periods in the churches,[20] and one of these described it as likely, by provoking God's wrath, to 'increase the many calamities these nations now labour under.' How curiously characteristic is the restriction in common usage of the term 'immoral' to a single vice, so that a man who is untruthful, selfish, cruel, or intemperate might still be said to have led 'a moral life' because he was blameless in the relations of the sexes! In the estimates of the character of public men the same disproportionate judgment may be constantly found in the comparative stress placed upon private faults and the most gigantic public crimes. Errors of judgment are not errors of morals, but any public man who, through selfish, ambitious, or party motives, plunges or helps to plunge his country into an unrighteous or unnecessary war, subordinates public interest to his personal ambition, employs himself in stimulating class, national, or provincial hatreds, lowers the moral standard of public life, or supports a legislation which he knows to tend to or facilitate dishonesty, is committing a crime before which, if it be measured by its consequences, the gravest acts of mere private immorality dwindle into insignificance. Yet how differently in the case of brilliant and successful politicians are such things treated in the judgment of contemporaries, and sometimes even in the judgments of history!

It is, I think, a peculiarity of modern times that the chief moral influences are much more various and complex than in the past. There is no such absolute empire as that which was exercised over character by the State in some periods of Pagan antiquity and by the Church during the Middle Ages. Our civilisation is more than anything else an industrial civilisation, and industrial habits are probably the strongest in forming the moral type to which public opinion aspires. Slavery, which threw a deep discredit on industry and on the qualities it fosters, has passed away. The feudal system, which placed industry in an inferior position, has been abolished, and the strong modern tendency to diminish both the privileges and the exclusiveness of rank and to increase the importance of wealth is in the same direction. An industrial society has its special vices and failings, but it naturally brings into the boldest relief the moral qualities which industry is most fitted to foster and on which it most largely depends, and it also gives the whole tone of moral thinking a utilitarian character. It is not Christianity but Industrialism that has brought into the world that strong sense of the moral value of thrift, steady industry, punctuality in observing engagements, constant

---

[20] 21 James I. c. 20; 19 Geo. II. c. 21. The penalties, however, were fines, the pillory, or short periods of imprisonment. The obligation of reading the statute in churches was abolished in 1823, but the custom had before fallen into desuetude. In 1772 a vicar was (as an act of private vengeance) prosecuted and fined for having neglected to read it. (Annual Register, 1772, p. 115.)

forethought with a view to providing for the contingencies of the future, which is now so characteristic of the moral type of the most civilised nations.

Many other influences, however, have contributed to intensify, qualify, or impair the industrial type. Protestantism has disengaged primitive Christian ethics from a crowd of superstitious and artificial duties which had overlaid them, and a similar process has been going on in Catholic countries under the influence of the rationalising and sceptical spirit. The influence of dogmatic theology on Morals has declined. Out of the vast and complex religious systems of the past, an eclectic spirit is bringing into special and ever-increasing prominence those Christian virtues which are most manifestly in accordance with natural religion and most clearly conducive to the well-being of men upon the earth. Philanthropy or charity, which forms the centre of the system, has also been immensely intensified by increased knowledge and realisation of the wants and sorrows of others; by the sensitiveness to pain, by the softening of manners and the more humane and refined tastes and habits which a highly elaborated intellectual civilisation naturally produces. The sense of duty plays a great part in modern philanthropy, and lower motives of ostentation or custom mingle largely with the genuine kindliness of feeling that inspires it; but on the whole it is probable that men in our day, in doing good to others, look much more exclusively than in the past to the benefit of the recipient and much less to some reward for their acts in a future world. As long, too, as this benefit is attained, they will gladly diminish as much as possible the self-sacrifice it entails. An eminently characteristic feature of modern philanthropy is its close connection with amusements. There was a time when a great philanthropic work would be naturally supported by an issue of indulgences promising specific advantages in another world to all who took part in it. In our own generation balls, bazaars, theatrical or other amusements given for the benefit of the charity, occupy an almost corresponding place.

At the same time increasing knowledge, and especially the kind of knowledge which science gives, has in other ways largely affected our judgments of right and wrong. The mental discipline, the habits of sound and accurate reasoning, the distrust of mere authority and of untested assertions and traditions that science tends to produce, all stimulate the intellectual virtues, and science has done much to rectify the chart of life, pointing out more clearly the true conditions of human well-being and disclosing much baselessness and many errors in the teaching of the past. It cannot, however, be said that the civic or the military influences have declined. If the State does not hold altogether the same place as in Pagan antiquity, it is at least certain that in a democratic age public interests are enormously prominent in the lives of men, and there is a growing and dangerous tendency to aggrandise the influence of the State over the individual, while modern militarism is drawing the flower of Continental Europe into its circle and making military education one of the most powerful influences in the formation of characters and ideals.

I do not believe that the world will ever greatly differ about the essential elements of right and wrong. These things lie deep in human nature and in the fundamental conditions of human life. The changes that are taking place, and which seem likely to strengthen in the future, lie chiefly in the importance attached to different qualities.

What seems to be useless self-sacrifice and unnecessary suffering is as much as possible avoided. The strain of sentiment which valued suffering in itself as an expiatory thing, as a mode of following the Man of Sorrows, as a thing to be for its own sake embraced and dwelt upon, and prolonged, bears a very great part in some of the most beautiful Christian lives, and especially in those which were formed under the influence of the Catholic Church. An old legend tells how Christ once appeared as a Man of Sorrows to a Catholic Saint, and asked him what boon he would most desire. 'Lord,' was the reply, 'that I might suffer most.' This strain runs deeply through the whole ascetic literature and the whole monastic system of Catholicism, and outside Catholicism it has been sometimes shown by a reluctance to accept the aid of anæsthetics, which partially or wholly removed suffering supposed to have been sent by Providence. The history of the use of chloroform furnishes striking illustrations of this. Many of my readers may remember the French monks who devoted themselves to cultivating one of the most pestilential spots in the Roman Campagna, which was associated with an ecclesiastical legend, and who quite unnecessarily insisted on remaining there during the season when such a residence meant little less than a slow suicide. They had, as they were accustomed to say, their purgatory upon earth, and they remained till their constitutions were hopelessly shattered and they were sent to die in their own land. Touching examples might be found in modern times of men who, in the last extremes of disease or suffering, scrupled, through religious motives, about availing themselves of the simplest alleviations,[21] and something of the same feeling is shown in the desire to prolong to the last possible moment hopeless and agonising disease. All this is manifestly and rapidly disappearing. To endure with patience and resignation inevitable suffering; to encounter courageously dangers and suffering for some worthy and useful end, ranks, indeed, as high as it ever did in the ethics of the century, but suffering for its own sake is no longer valued, and it is deemed one of the first objects of a wise life to restrict and diminish it.

---

[21] The following beautiful passage from a funeral sermon by Newman is an example: 'One should have thought that a life so innocent, so active, so holy, I might say so faultless from first to last, might have been spared the visitation of any long and severe penance to bring it to an end; but in order doubtless to show us how vile and miserable the best of us are in ourselves ... and moreover to give us a pattern how to bear suffering ourselves, and to increase the merits and to hasten and brighten the crown of this faithful servant of his Lord, it pleased Almighty God to send upon him a disorder which during the last six years fought with him, mastered him, and at length has destroyed him, so far, that is, as death now has power to destroy.... It is for those who came near him year after year to store up the many words and deeds of resignation, love and humility which that long penance elicited. These meritorious acts are written in the Book of Life, and they have followed him whither he is gone. They multiplied and grew in strength and perfection as his trial proceeded; and they were never so striking as at its close. When a friend visited him in the last week, he found he had scrupled at allowing his temples to be moistened with some refreshing waters, and had with difficulty been brought to give his consent; he said he feared it was too great a luxury. When the same friend offered him some liquid to allay his distressing thirst his answer was the same.'—Sermon at the funeral of the Right Rev. Henry Weedall, pp. 19, 20

No one, I think, has seen more clearly or described more vividly than Goethe the direction in which in modern times the current of morals is flowing. His philosophy is a terrestrial philosophy, and the old theologians would have said that it allowed the second Table of the Law altogether to supersede or eclipse the first. It was said of him with much truth that 'repugnance to the supernatural was an inherent part of his mind.' To turn away from useless and barren speculations; to persistently withdraw our thoughts from the unknowable, the inevitable, and the irreparable; to concentrate them on the immediate present and on the nearest duty; to waste no moral energy on excessive introspection or self-abasement or self-reproach, but to make the cultivation and the wise use of all our powers the supreme ideal and end of our lives; to oppose labour and study to affliction and regret; to keep at a distance gloomy thoughts and exaggerated anxieties; 'to see the individual in connection and co-operation with the whole,' and to look upon effort and action as the main elements both of duty and happiness, was the lesson which he continually taught. 'The mind endowed with active powers, and keeping with a practical object to the task that lies nearest, is the worthiest there is on earth.' 'Character consists in a man steadily pursuing the things of which he feels himself capable.' 'Try to do your duty and you will know what you are worth.' 'Piety is not an end but a means; a means of attaining the highest culture by the purest tranquillity of soul.' 'We are not born to solve the problems of the world, but to find out where the problem begins and then to keep within the limits of what we can grasp.'

To cultivate sincere love of truth and clear and definite conceptions, and divest ourselves as much as possible from prejudices, fanaticisms, superstitions, and exaggeration; to take wide, sound, tolerant, many-sided views of life, stands in his eyes in the forefront of ethics. 'Let it be your earnest endeavour to use words coinciding as closely as possible with what we feel, see, think, experience, imagine, and reason;' 'remove by plain and honest purpose false, irrelevant and futile ideas.' 'The truest liberality is appreciation.' 'Love of truth shows itself in this, that a man knows how to find and value the good in everything.'[22]

In the eyes of this school of thought one of the great vices of the old theological type of ethics was that it was unduly negative. It thought much more of the avoidance of sin than of the performance of duty. The more we advance in knowledge the more we shall come to judge men in the spirit of the parable of the talents; that is by the net result of their lives, by their essential unselfishness, by the degree in which they employ and the objects to which they direct their capacities and opportunities. The staple of moral life becomes much less a matter of small scruples, of minute self-examination, of extreme stress laid upon flaws of character and conduct that have little or no bearing upon active life. A life of idleness will be regarded with much less tolerance than at present. Men will grow less introspective and more objective, and useful action will become more and more the guiding principle of morals.

---

[22] See the excellent little book of Mr. Bailey Saunders, called *The Maxims and Reflections of Goethe*.

In theory this will probably be readily admitted, but every good observer will find that it involves a considerable change in the point of view. A life of habitual languor and idleness, with no faculties really cultivated, and with no result that makes a man missed when he has passed away, may be spent without any act which the world calls vicious, and is quite compatible with much charm of temper and demeanour and with a complete freedom from violent and aggressive selfishness. Such a life, in the eyes of many moralists, would rank much higher than a life of constant, honourable self-sacrificing labour for the good of others which was at the same time flawed by some positive vice. Yet the life which seems to be comparatively blameless has in truth wholly missed, while the other life, in spite of all its defects, has largely attained what should be the main object of a human life, the full development and useful employment of whatever powers we possess. There are men, indeed, in whom an over-sensitive conscience is even a paralysing thing, which by suggesting constant petty and ingenious scruples holds them back from useful action. It is a moral infirmity corresponding to that exaggerated intellectual fastidiousness which so often makes an intellectual life almost wholly barren, or to that excessive tendency to look on all sides of a question and to realise the dangers and drawbacks of any course which not unfrequently in moments of difficulty paralyses the actions of public men. Sometimes, under the strange and subtle bias of the will, this excessive conscientiousness will be unconsciously fostered in inert and sluggish natures which are constitutionally disinclined to effort. The main lines of duty in the great relations of life are sufficiently obvious, and the casuistry which multiplies cases of conscience and invents unreal and factitious duties is apt to be rather an impediment than a furtherance to a noble life.

It is probable that as the world goes on morals will move more and more in the direction I have described. There will be at the same time a steadily increasing tendency to judge moral qualities and courses of conduct mainly by the degree in which they promote or diminish human happiness. Enthusiasm and self-sacrifice for some object which has no real bearing on the welfare of man will become rarer and will be less respected, and the condemnation that is passed on acts that are recognised as wrong will be much more proportioned than at present to the injury they inflict. Some things, such as excessive luxury of expenditure and the improvidence of bringing into the world children for whom no provision has been made, which can now scarcely be said to enter into the teaching of moralists, or at least of churches, may one day be looked upon as graver offences than some that are in the penal code.

multiplied and grew in strength and perfection as his trial proceeded; and they were

CHAPTER VI

The tendency to regard morals rather in their positive than their negative aspects, and to estimate men by the good they do in the world, is a healthy element in modern life. A strong sense of the obligation of a full, active, and useful life is the best safeguard both of individual and national morals at a time when the dissolution or enfeeblement of theological beliefs is disturbing the foundations on which most current moral teaching has been based. In the field of morals action holds a much larger place than reasoning—a larger place even in elucidating our difficulties and illuminating the path on which we should go. It is by the active pursuit of an immediate duty that the vista of future duties becomes most clear, and those who are most immersed in active duties are usually little troubled with the perplexities of life, or with minute and paralysing scruples. A public opinion which discourages idleness and places high the standard of public duty is especially valuable in an age when the tendency to value wealth, and to measure dignity by wealth, has greatly increased, and when wealth in some of its most important forms has become wholly dissociated from special duties. The duties of the landlord who is surrounded by a poor and in some measure dependent tenantry, the duties of the head of a great factory or shop who has a large number of workmen or dependents in his employment, are sufficiently obvious, though even in these spheres the tie of duty has been greatly relaxed by the growing spirit of independence, which makes each class increasingly jealous of the interference of others, and by the growing tendency of legislation to regulate all relations of business and contracts by definite law instead of leaving them, as in the past, to voluntary action. But there are large classes of fortunes which are wholly, or almost wholly, dissociated from special and definite duties. The vast and ever-increasing multitude whose incomes are derived from national, or provincial, or municipal debts, or who are shareholders or debenture-holders in great commercial and industrial undertakings, have little or no practical control over, or interest in, those from whom their fortunes are derived. The multiplication of such fortunes is one of the great characteristics of our time, and it brings with it grave dangers. Such fortunes give unrivalled opportunities of luxurious idleness, and as in themselves they bring little or no social influence or position, those who possess them are peculiarly tempted to seek such a position by an ostentation of wealth and luxury which has a profoundly vulgarising and demoralising influence upon Society. The tendency of idleness to lead to immorality has long been a commonplace of moralists. Perhaps our own age has seen more clearly than those that preceded it that complete and habitual idleness *is* immorality, and that when the circumstances of his life do not assign to a man a definite sphere of work it is his first duty to find it for himself. It has been happily said that in the beginning of the reign of Queen Victoria young men in England who were really busy affected idleness, and at the close of the reign young men who are really idle pretend to be busy. In my own opinion, a disproportionate amount of English energy takes political forms, and there is a dangerous exaggeration in the prevailing tendency to combat all social and moral abuses by Acts of

Parliament. But there are multitudes of other and less obtrusive spheres of work adapted to all grades of intellect and to many types of character, in which men who possess the inestimable boon of leisure can find abundant and useful fields for the exercise of their powers.

The rectification of moral judgments is one of the most important elements of civilisation; it is upon this that the possibility of moral progress on a large scale chiefly depends. Few things pervert men more than the habit of regarding as enviable persons or qualities injurious to Society. The most obvious example is the passionate admiration bestowed on a brilliant conqueror, which is often quite irrespective of the justice of his wars and of the motives that actuated him. This false moral feeling has acquired such a strength that overwhelming military power almost certainly leads to a career of ambition. Perverted public opinion is the main cause. Glory, not interest, is the lure, or at least the latter would be powerless if it were not accompanied by the former—if the execration of mankind naturally followed unscrupulous aggression.

Another and scarcely less flagrant instance of the worship of false ideals is to be found in the fierce competition of luxury and ostentation which characterises the more wealthy cities of Europe and America. It is no exaggeration to say that in a single festival in London or New York sums are often expended in the idlest and most ephemeral ostentation which might have revived industry, or extinguished pauperism, or alleviated suffering over a vast area. The question of expenditure on luxuries is no doubt a question of degree which cannot be reduced to strict rule, and there are many who will try to justify the most ostentatious expenditure on the ground of the employment it gives and of other incidental advantages it is supposed to produce. But nothing in political economy is more certain than that the vast and ever-increasing expenditure on the luxury of ostentation in modern societies, by withdrawing great masses of capital from productive labour, is a grave economical evil, and there is probably no other form of expenditure which, in proportion to its amount, gives so little real pleasure and confers so little real good. Its evil in setting up material and base standards of excellence, in stimulating the worst passions that grow out of an immoderate love of wealth, in ruining many who are tempted into a competition which they are unable to support, can hardly be overrated. It is felt in every rank in raising the standard of conventional expenses, excluding from much social intercourse many who are admirably fitted to adorn it, and introducing into all society a lower and more material tone. Nor are these its only consequences. Wealth which is expended in multiplying and elaborating real comforts, or even in pleasures which produce enjoyment at all proportionate to their cost, will never excite serious indignation. It is the colossal waste of the means of human happiness in the most selfish and most vulgar forms of social advertisement and competition that gives a force and almost a justification to anarchical passions which menace the whole future of our civilisation. It is such things that stimulate class hatreds and deepen class divisions, and if the law of opinion does not interfere to check them they will one day bring down upon the society that encourages them a signal and well-merited retribution.

A more recognised, though probably not really more pernicious example of false ideals, is to be found in the glorification of the demi-monde, which is so conspicuous in some societies and literatures. In a healthy state of opinion, the public, ostentatious appearance of such persons, without any concealment of their character, in the great concourse of fashion and among the notabilities of the State, would appear an intolerable scandal, and it becomes much worse when they give the tone to fashion and become the centres and the models of large and by no means undistinguished sections of Society. The evils springing from this public glorification of the class are immeasurably greater than the evils arising from its existence. The standard of popular morals is debased. Temptation in its most seductive form is forced upon inflammable natures, and the most pernicious of all lessons is taught to poor, honest, hard-working women. It is indeed wonderful that in societies where this evil prevails so much virtue should still exist among graceful, attractive women of the shopkeeping and servant class when they continually see before them members of their own class, by preferring vice to virtue, rising at once to wealth, luxury and idleness, and even held up as objects of admiration or imitation.

In judging wisely the characters of men, one of the first things to be done is to understand their ideals. Try to find out what kind of men or of life; what qualities, what positions seem to them the most desirable. Men do not always fully recognise their own ideals, for education and the conventionalities of Society oblige them to assert a preference for that which may really have no root in their minds. But by a careful examination it is usually possible to ascertain what persons or qualities or circumstances or gifts exercise a genuine, spontaneous, magnetic power over them— whether they really value supremely rank or position, or money, or beauty, or intellect, or superiority of character. If you know the ideal of a man you have obtained a true key to his nature. The broad lines of his character, the permanent tendencies of his imagination, his essential nobility or meanness, are thus disclosed more effectually than by any other means. A man with high ideals, who admires wisely and nobly, is never wholly base though he may fall into great vices. A man who worships the baser elements is in truth an idolater though he may have never bowed before an image of stone.

The human mind has much more power of distinguishing between right and wrong, and between true and false, than of estimating with accuracy the comparative gravity of opposite evils. It is nearly always right in judging between right and wrong. It is generally wrong in estimating degrees of guilt, and the root of its error lies in the extreme difficulty of putting ourselves into the place of those whose characters or circumstances are radically different from our own. This want of imagination acts widely on our judgment of what is good as well as of what is bad. Few men have enough imagination to realise types of excellence altogether differing from their own. It is this, much more than vanity, that leads them to esteem the types of excellence to which they themselves approximate as the best, and tastes and habits that are altogether incongruous with their own as futile and contemptible. It is, perhaps, most difficult of all to realise the difference of character and especially of moral sensibility produced by a profound difference of circumstances. This difficulty largely falsifies our judgments of the past, and it is the reason why a powerful imagination enabling us to realise very various characters and very remote circumstances is one of the first necessities of a great historian. Historians rarely make sufficient allowance for the degree in which the judgments and dispositions even of the best men are coloured by the moral tone of the time, society and profession in which they lived. Yet it is probable that on the whole we estimate more justly the characters of the past than of the present. No one would judge the actions of Charlemagne or of his contemporaries by the strict rules of nineteenth-century ethics. We feel that though they committed undoubted crimes, these crimes are at least indefinitely less heinous than they would have been under the wholly different circumstances and moral atmosphere of our own day. Yet we seldom apply this method of reasoning to the different strata of the same society. Men who have been themselves brought up amid all the comforts and all the moralising and restraining influences of a refined society, will often judge the crimes of the wretched pariahs of civilisation as if their acts were in no degree palliated by their position. They say to themselves 'How guilty should I have been if I had done this thing,' and their verdict is quite just according to this statement of the case. They realise the nature of the act. They utterly fail to realise the character and circumstances of the actor.

And yet it is scarcely possible to exaggerate the difference between the position of such a critic and that of the children of drunken, ignorant and profligate parents, born to abject poverty in the slums of our great cities. From their earliest childhood drunkenness, blasphemy, dishonesty, prostitution, indecency of every form are their most familiar experiences. All the social influences, such as they are, are influences of vice. As they grow up Life seems to them to present little more than the alternative of hard, ill-paid, and at the same time precarious labour, probably ending in the poor-house, or crime with its larger and swifter gains, and its intervals of coarse pleasure probably, though not certainly, followed by the prison or an early death. They see indeed, like figures in a dream, or like beings of another world, the wealthy and the luxurious spending their wealth and their time in many kinds of enjoyment, but to the very poor pleasure scarcely comes except in the form of the gin palace or perhaps the low music hall. And in many cases they have come into this reeking atmosphere of temptation and vice with natures debased and enfeebled by a long succession of vicious hereditary influences, with weak wills, with no faculties of mind or character that can respond to any healthy ambition; with powerful inborn predispositions to evil. The very mould of their features, the very shape of their skulls, marks them out as destined members of the criminal class. Even here, no doubt, there is a difference between right and wrong; there is scope for the action of free will; there are just causes of praise and blame, and Society rightly protects itself by severe penalties against the crimes that are most natural; but what human judge can duly measure the scale of moral guilt? or what comparison can there be between the crimes that are engendered by such circumstances and those which spring up in the homes of refined and well-regulated comfort?

Nor indeed even in this latter case is a really accurate judgment possible. Men are born into the world with both wills and passions of varying strength, though in mature life the strength or weakness of each is largely due to their own conduct. With different characters the same temptation, operating under the same external circumstances, has enormously different strength, and very few men can fully realise the strength of a passion which they have never themselves experienced. To repeat an illustration I have already used, how difficult is it for a constitutionally sober man to form in his own mind an adequate conception of the force of the temptation of drink to a dipsomaniac, or for a passionless man to conceive rightly the temptations of a profoundly sensual nature! I have spoken in a former chapter of the force with which bodily conditions act upon happiness. Their influence on morals is not less terrible. There are diseases well known to physicians which make the most placid temper habitually irritable; give a morbid turn to the healthiest disposition; fill the purest mind with unholy thoughts. There are others which destroy the force of the strongest will and take from character all balance and self-control.[23] It often happens that we have long been blaming a man for manifest faults of character till at last suicide, or the disclosure of some grave bodily or mental disease which has long been working unperceived, explains his faults and turns our blame into pity. In madness the whole moral character is sometimes reversed, and tendencies which have been in sane life dormant or repressed become suddenly supreme. In such cases we all acknowledge that there is no moral responsibility, but madness, with its illusions and irresistible impulses, and idiocy with its complete suspension of the will and of the judgment, are neither of them, as lawyers would pretend, clearly defined states, marked out by sharp and well-cut boundaries, wholly distinct from sanity. There are incipient stages; there are gradual approximations; there are twilight states between sanity and insanity which are clearly recognised not only by experts but by all sagacious men of the world. There are many who are not sufficiently mad to be shut up, or to be deprived of the management of their properties, or to be exempted from punishment if they have committed a crime, but who, in the common expressive phrase, 'are not all there'— whose eccentricities, illusions and caprices are on the verge of madness, whose judgments are hopelessly disordered; whose wills, though not completely atrophied, are manifestly diseased. In questions of property, in questions of crime, in questions of family arrangements, such persons cause the gravest perplexity, nor will any wise man judge them by the same moral standard as well-balanced and well-developed natures.

The inference to be drawn from such facts is certainly not that there is no such thing as free will and personal responsibility, nor yet that we have no power of judging the acts of others and distinguishing among our fellowmen between the good and the bad. The true lesson is the extreme fallibility of our moral judgments whenever we attempt to measure degrees of guilt. Sometimes men are even unjust to their own past from their incapacity in age of realising the force of the temptations they had

---

[23] Ribot, *Les Maladies de la Volonté*, pp. 92, 116-119.

experienced in youth. On the other hand, increased knowledge of the world tends to make us more sensible of the vast differences between the moral circumstances of men, and therefore less confident and more indulgent in our judgments of others. There are men whose cards in life are so bad, whose temptations to vice, either from circumstances or inborn character, seem so overwhelming, that, though we may punish, and in a certain sense blame, we can scarcely look on them as more responsible than some noxious wild beast. Among the terrible facts of life none is indeed more terrible than this. Every believer in the wise government of the world must have sometimes realised with a crushing or at least a staggering force the appalling injustices of life as shown in the enormous differences in the distribution of unmerited happiness and misery. But the disparity of moral circumstances is not less. It has shaken the faith of many. It has even led some to dream of a possible Heaven for the vicious where those who are born into the world with a physical constitution rendering them fierce or cruel, or sensual, or cowardly, may be freed from the nature which was the cause of their vice and their suffering upon earth; where due allowance may be made for the differences of circumstances which have plunged one man deeper and ever deeper into crime, and enabled another, who was not really better or worse, to pass through life with no serious blemish, and to rise higher and higher in the moral scale.

Imperfect, however, as is our power of judging others, it is a power we are all obliged to exercise. It is impossible to exclude the considerations of moral guilt and of palliating or aggravating circumstances from the penal code, and from the administration of justice, though it cannot be too clearly maintained that the criminal code is not coextensive with the moral code, and that many things which are profoundly immoral lie beyond its scope. On the whole it should be as much as possible confined to acts by which men directly injure others. In the case of adult men, private vices, vices by which no one is directly affected, except by his own free will, and in which the elements of force or fraud are not present, should not be brought within its range. This ideal, it is true, cannot be fully attained. The legislator must take into account the strong pressure of public opinion. It is sometimes true that a penal law may arrest, restrict, or prevent the revival of some private vice without producing any countervailing evil. But the presumption is against all laws which punish the voluntary acts of adult men when those acts injure no one except themselves. The social censure, or the judgment of opinion, rightly extends much further, though it is often based on very imperfect knowledge or realisation. It is probable that, on the whole, opinion judges too severely the crimes of passion and of drink, as well as those which spring from the pressure of great poverty and are accompanied by great ignorance. The causes of domestic anarchy are usually of such an intimate nature and involve so many unknown or imperfectly realised elements of aggravation or palliation that in most cases the less men attempt to judge them the better. On the other hand, public opinion is usually far too lenient in judging crimes of ambition, cupidity, envy, malevolence, and callous selfishness; the crimes of ill-gotten and ill-used wealth, especially in the many cases in which those crimes are unpunished by law.

It is a mere commonplace of morals that in the path of evil it is the first step that costs the most. The shame, the repugnance, and the remorse which attend the first crime speedily fade, and on every repetition the habit of evil grows stronger. A process of the same kind passes over our judgments. Few things are more curious than to observe how the eye accommodates itself to a new fashion of dress, however unbecoming; how speedily men, or at least women, will adopt a new and artificial standard and instinctively and unconsciously admire or blame according to this standard and not according to any genuine sense of beauty or the reverse. Few persons, however pure may be their natural taste, can live long amid vulgar and vulgarising surroundings without losing something of the delicacy of their taste and learning to accept—if not with pleasure, at least with acquiescence—things from which under other circumstances they would have recoiled. In the same way, both individuals and societies accommodate themselves but too readily to lower moral levels, and a constant vigilance is needed to detect the forms or directions in which individual and national character insensibly deteriorate.

CHAPTER VII

It is impossible for a physician to prescribe a rational regimen for a patient unless he has formed some clear conception of the nature of his constitution and of the morbid influences to which it is inclined; and in judging the wisdom of various proposals for the management of character we are at once met by the initial controversy about the goodness or the depravity of human nature. It is a subject on which extreme exaggerations have prevailed. The school of Rousseau, which dominated on the Continent in the last half of the eighteenth century, represented mankind as a being who comes into existence essentially good, and it attributed all the moral evils of the world, not to any innate tendencies to vice, but to superstition, vicious institutions, misleading education, a badly organised society. It is an obvious criticism that if human nature had been as good as such writers imagined, these corrupt and corrupting influences could never have grown up, or at least could never have obtained a controlling influence, and this philosophy became greatly discredited when the French Revolution, which it did so much to produce, ended in the unspeakable horrors of the Reign of Terror and in the gigantic carnage of the Napoleonic wars. On the other hand, there are large schools of theologians who represent man as utterly and fundamentally depraved, 'born in corruption, inclined to evil, incapable by himself of doing good;' totally wrecked and ruined as a moral being by the catastrophe in Eden. There are also moral philosophers—usually very unconnected with theology—who deny or explain away all unselfish elements in human nature, represent man as simply governed by self-interest, and maintain that the whole art of education and government consists of a judicious arrangement of selfish motives, making the interests of the individual coincident with those of his neighbours. It is not too much to say that Society never could have subsisted if this view of human nature had been a just one. The world would have been like a cage-full of wild beasts, and mankind would have soon perished in constant internecine war.

It is indeed one of the plainest facts of human nature that such a view of mankind is an untrue one. Jealousy, envy, animosities and selfishness no doubt play a great part in life and disguise themselves under many specious forms, and the cynical moralist was not wholly wrong when he declared that 'Virtue would not go so far if Vanity did not keep her company,' and that not only our crimes but even many of what are deemed our best acts may be traced to selfish motives. But he must have had a strangely unfortunate experience of the world who does not recognise the enormous exaggeration of the pictures of human nature that are conveyed in some of the maxims of La Rochefoucauld and Schopenhauer. They tell us that friendship is a mere exchange of interests in which each man only seeks to gain something from the other; that most women are only pure because they are untempted and regret that the temptation does not come; that if we acknowledge some faults it is in order to persuade ourselves that we have no greater ones, or in order, by our confession, to regain the good opinion of our neighbours; that if we praise another it is merely that we may ourselves in turn be praised; that the tears we shed over a deathbed, if they are not hypocritical tears intended only to impress our neighbours, are only due to our conviction that we have ourselves lost a source of pleasure or of gain; that envy so predominates in the world that it is only men of inferior intellect or women of inferior beauty who are sincerely liked by those about them; that all virtue is an egotistic calculation, conscious or unconscious.

Such views are at least as far removed from truth as the roseate pictures of Rousseau and St. Pierre. No one can look with an unjaundiced eye upon the world without perceiving the enormous amount of disinterested, self-sacrificing benevolence that pervades it; the countless lives that are spent not only harmlessly and inoffensively but also in the constant discharge of duties; in constant and often painful labour for the good of others. The better section of the Utilitarian school has fully recognised the truth that human nature is so constituted that a great proportion of its enjoyment depends on sympathy; or, in other words, on the power we possess of entering into and sharing the happiness of others. The spectacle of suffering naturally elicits compassion. Kindness naturally produces gratitude. The sympathies of men naturally move on the side of the good rather than of the bad. This is true not only of the things that immediately concern us, but also in the perfectly disinterested judgments we form of the events of history or of the characters in fiction and poetry. Great exhibitions of heroism and self-sacrifice touch a genuine chord of enthusiasm. The affections of the domestic circle are the rule and not the exception; patriotism can elicit great outbursts of purely unselfish generosity and induce multitudes to risk or sacrifice their lives for causes which are quite other than their own selfish interests. Human nature indeed has its moral as well as its physical needs, and naturally and instinctively seeks some object of interest and enthusiasm outside itself.

If we look again into the vice and sin that undoubtedly disfigure the world we shall find much reason to believe that what is exceptional in human nature is not the evil tendency but the restraining conscience, and that it is chiefly the weakness of the distinctively human quality that is the origin of the evil. It is impossible indeed, with the knowledge we now possess, to deny to animals some measure both of reason and of the moral sense. In addition to the higher instincts of parental affection and devotion which are so clearly developed we find among some animals undoubted signs of remorse, gratitude, affection, self-sacrifice. Even the point of honour which attaches shame to some things and pride to others may be clearly distinguished. No one who has watched the more intelligent dog can question this, and many will maintain that in some animals, though both good and bad qualities are less widely developed than in man, the proportion of the good to the evil is more favourable in the animal than in the man. At the same time in the animal world desire is usually followed without any other restraint than fear, while in man it is largely though no doubt very imperfectly limited by moral self-control. Most crimes spring not from anything wrong in the original and primal desire but from the imperfection of this higher, distinct or superadded element in our nature. The crimes of dishonesty and envy, when duly analysed, have at their basis simply a desire for the desirable—a natural and inevitable feeling. What is absent is the restraint which makes men refrain from taking or trying to take desirable things that belong to another. Sensual faults spring from a perfectly natural impulse, but the restraint which confines the action of that impulse to defined circumstances is wanting. Much, too, of the insensibility and hardness of the world is due to a simple want of imagination which prevents us from adequately realising the sufferings of others. The predatory, envious and ferocious feelings that disturb mankind operate unrestrained through the animal world, though man's superior intelligence gives his desires a special character and a greatly increased scope, and introduces them into spheres inconceivable to the animal. Immoderate and uncontrolled desires are the root of most human crimes, but at the same time the self-restraint that limits desire, or self-seeking, by the rights of others, seems to be mainly, though not wholly, the prerogative of man.

Considerations of this kind are sufficient to remedy the extreme exaggeration of human corruption that may often be heard, but they are not inconsistent with the truth that human nature is so far depraved that it can never be safely left to develop unimpeded without strong legal and social restraint. It is not necessary to seek examples of its depravity within the precincts of a prison or in the many instances that may be found outside the criminal population of morbid moral taints which are often as clearly marked as physical disease. On a large scale and in the actions of great bodies of men the melancholy truth is abundantly displayed. On the whole Christianity has been far more successful in influencing individuals than societies. The mere spectacle of a battle-field with the appalling mass of hideous suffering deliberately and ingeniously inflicted by man upon man should be sufficient to scatter all idyllic pictures of human nature. It was once the custom of a large school of writers to attribute unjust wars solely to the rulers of the world, who for their own selfish ambitions remorselessly sacrificed the lives of tens of thousands of their subjects. Their guilt has been very great, but they would never have pursued the course of ambitious conquest if the applause of nations had not followed and encouraged them, and there are no signs that democracy, which has enthroned the masses, has any real tendency to diminish war.

In modern times the danger of war lies less in the intrigues of statesmen than in deeply seated international jealousies and antipathies; in sudden, volcanic outbursts of popular passion. After eighteen hundred years' profession of the creed of peace, Christendom is an armed camp. Never, or hardly ever, in times of peace had the mere preparations of war absorbed so large a proportion of its population and resources, and very seldom has so large an amount of its ability been mainly employed in inventing and in perfecting instruments of destruction. Those who will look on the world without illusion will be compelled to admit that the chief guarantees for its peace are to be found much less in moral than in purely selfish motives. The financial embarrassments of the great nations; their profound distrust of one another; the vast cost of modern war; the gigantic commercial disasters it inevitably entails; the extreme uncertainty of its issue; the utter ruin that may follow defeat—these are the real influences that restrain the tiger passions and the avaricious cravings of mankind. It is also one of the advantages that accompany the many evils of universal service, that great citizen armies who in time of war are drawn from their homes, their families, and their peaceful occupations have not the same thirst for battle that grows up among purely professional soldiers, voluntarily enlisted and making a military life their whole career. Yet, in spite of all this, what trust could be placed in the forbearance of Christian nations if the path of aggression was at once easy, lucrative and safe? The judgments of nations in dealing with the aggressions of their neighbours are, it is true, very different from those which they form of aggressions by their own statesmen or for their own benefit. But no great nation is blameless, and there is probably no nation that could not speedily catch the infection of the warlike spirit if a conqueror and a few splendid victories obscured, as they nearly always do, the moral issues of the contest.

War, it is true, is not always or wholly evil. Sometimes it is justifiable and necessary. Sometimes it is professedly and in part really due to some strong wave of philanthropic feeling produced by great acts of wrong, though of all forms of philanthropy it is that which most naturally defeats itself. Even when unjustifiable, it calls into action splendid qualities of courage, self-sacrifice, and endurance which cast a dazzling and deceptive glamour over its horrors and its criminality. It appeals too, beyond all other things, to that craving for excitement, adventure, and danger which is an essential and imperious element in human nature, and which, while it is in itself neither a virtue nor a vice, blends powerfully with some of the best as well as with some of the worst actions of mankind. It is indeed a strange thing to observe how many men in every age have been ready to risk or sacrifice their lives for causes which they have never clearly understood and which they would find it difficult in plain words to describe.

But the amount of pure and almost spontaneous malevolence in the world is probably far greater than we at first imagine. In public life the workings of this side of human nature are at once disclosed and magnified, like the figures thrown by a magic lantern on a screen, to a scale which it is impossible to overlook. No one, for example, can study the anonymous press without perceiving how large a part of it is employed systematically, persistently and deliberately in fostering class, or race, or international hatreds, and often in circulating falsehoods to attain this end. Many newspapers notoriously depend for their existence on such appeals, and more than any other instruments they inflame and perpetuate those permanent animosities which most endanger the peace of mankind. The fact that such newspapers are becoming in many countries the main and almost exclusive reading of the poor forms the most serious deduction from the value of popular education. How many books have attained popularity, how many seats in Parliament have been won, how many posts of influence and profit have been attained, how many party victories have been achieved, by appealing to such passions! Often they disguise themselves under the lofty names of patriotism and nationality, and men whose whole lives have been spent in sowing class hatreds and dividing kindred nations may be found masquerading under the name of patriots, and have played no small part on the stage of politics. The deep-seated sedition, the fierce class and national hatreds that run through European life would have a very different intensity from what they now unfortunately have if they had not been artificially stimulated and fostered through purely selfish motives by demagogues, political adventurers and public writers.

Some of the very worst acts of which man can be guilty are acts which are commonly untouched by law and only faintly censured by opinion. Political crimes which a false and sickly sentiment so readily condones are conspicuous among them. Men who have been gambling for wealth and power with the lives and fortunes of multitudes; men who for their own personal ambition are prepared to sacrifice the most vital interests of their country; men who in time of great national danger and excitement deliberately launch falsehood after falsehood in the public press in the well-founded conviction that they will do their evil work before they can be contradicted, may be met shameless, and almost uncensured, in Parliaments and drawing-rooms. The amount of false statement in the world which cannot be attributed to mere carelessness, inaccuracy, or exaggeration, but which is plainly both deliberate and malevolent, can hardly be overrated. Sometimes it is due to a mere desire to create a lucrative sensation, or to gratify a personal dislike, or even to an unprovoked malevolence which takes pleasure in inflicting pain.

Very often it is intended for purposes of stockjobbing. The financial world is percolated with it. It is the common method of raising or depreciating securities, attracting investors, preying upon the ignorant and credulous, and enabling dishonest men to rise rapidly to fortune. When the prospect of speedy wealth is in sight, there are always numbers who are perfectly prepared to pursue courses involving the utter ruin of multitudes, endangering the most serious international interests, perhaps bringing down upon the world all the calamities of war. It is no doubt true that such men are only a minority, though it is less certain that they would be a minority if the opportunity of obtaining sudden riches by immoral means was open to all, and it is no small minority who are accustomed to condone these crimes when they have succeeded. It is much to be questioned whether the greatest criminals are to be found within the walls of prisons. Dishonesty on a small scale nearly always finds its punishment. Dishonesty on a gigantic scale continually escapes. The pickpocket and the burglar seldom fail to meet with their merited punishment, but in the management of companies, in the great fields of industrial enterprise and speculation, gigantic fortunes are acquired by the ruin of multitudes and by methods which, though they evade legal penalties, are essentially fraudulent. In the majority of cases these crimes are perpetrated by educated men who are in possession of all the necessaries, of most of the comforts, and of many of the luxuries of life, and some of the worst of them are powerfully favoured by the conditions of modern civilisation. There is no greater scandal or moral evil in our time than the readiness with which public opinion excuses them, and the influence and social position it accords to mere wealth, even when it has been acquired by notorious dishonesty or when it is expended with absolute selfishness or in ways that are positively demoralising. In many respects the moral progress of mankind seems to me incontestable, but it is extremely doubtful whether in this respect social morality, especially in England and America, has not seriously retrograded.

In truth, while it is a gross libel upon human nature to deny the vast amount of genuine kindness, self-sacrifice and even heroism that exists in the world, it is equally idle to deny the deplorable weakness of self-restraint, the great force and the widespread influence of purely evil passions in the affairs of men. The distrust of human character which the experience of life tends to produce is one great cause of the Conservatism which so commonly strengthens with age. It is more and more felt that all the restraints of law, custom, and religion are essential to hold together in peaceful co-operation the elements of society, and men learn to look with increasing tolerance on both institutions and opinions which cannot stand the test of pure reason and may be largely mixed with delusions if only they deepen the better habits and give an additional strength to moral restraints. They learn also to appreciate the danger of pitching their ideals too high, and endeavouring to enforce lines of conduct greatly above the average level of human goodness. Such attempts, when they take the form of coercive action, seldom fail to produce a recoil which is very detrimental to morals. In this, as in all other spheres, the importance of compromise in practical life is one of the great lessons which experience teaches.

CHAPTER VIII

The phrase Moral Compromise has an evil sound, and it opens out questions of practical ethics which are very difficult and very dangerous, but they are questions with which, consciously or unconsciously, every one is obliged to deal. The contrasts between the rigidity of theological formulæ and actual life are on this subject very great, though in practice, and by the many ingenious subtleties that constitute the science of casuistry, many theologians have attempted to evade them. A striking passage from the pen of Cardinal Newman will bring these contrasts into the clearest light. 'The Church holds,' he writes, 'that it were better for sun and moon to drop from heaven, for the earth to fail, and for all the many millions who are upon it to die of starvation in extremest agony, so far as temporal affliction goes, than that one soul, I will not say should be lost, but should commit one single venial sin, should tell one wilful untruth, though it harmed no one, or steal one poor farthing without excuse.'[24]

It is certainly no exaggeration to say that such a doctrine would lead to consequences absolutely incompatible with any life outside a hermitage or a monastery. It would strike at the root of all civilisation, and although many may be prepared to give it their formal assent, no human being actually believes it with the kind of belief that becomes a guiding influence in life. I have dwelt on this subject in another book, and may here repeat a few lines which I then wrote. If 'an undoubted sin, even the most trivial, is a thing in its essence and its consequences so unspeakably dreadful that rather than it should be committed it would be better that any amount of calamity which did not bring with it sin should be endured, even that the whole human race should perish in agonies, it is manifest that the supreme object of humanity should be sinlessness, and it is equally manifest that the means to this end is the absolute suppression of the desires. To expand the circle of wants is necessarily to multiply temptations and therefore to increase the number of sins.' No material and intellectual advantages, no increase of human happiness, no mitigation of the suffering or dreariness of human life can, according to this theory, be other than an evil if it adds even in the smallest degree or in the most incidental manner to the sins that are committed. 'A sovereign, when calculating the consequences of a war, should reflect that a single sin occasioned by that war, a single blasphemy of a wounded soldier, the robbery of a single hen-coop, the violation of the purity of a single woman is a greater calamity than the ruin of the entire commerce of his nation, the loss of her most precious provinces, the destruction of all her power. He must believe that the evil of the increase of unchastity which invariably results from the formation of an army is an immeasurably greater calamity than any national or political disasters that army can possibly avert. He must believe that the most fearful plagues and famines that desolate his land should be regarded as a matter of rejoicing if they have but the feeblest and most transient influence in repressing vice. He must believe that if the agglomeration of his people in great cities adds but one to the number of their sins, no possible

---

[24] Newman's *Anglican Difficulties*, p. 190.

intellectual or material advantages can prevent the construction of cities being a fearful calamity. According to this principle every elaboration of life, every amusement that brings multitudes together, almost every art, every accession of wealth, that awakens or stimulates desires is an evil, for all these become the sources of some sins, and their advantages are for the most part purely terrestrial.'

Considerations of this kind, if duly realised, bring out clearly the insincerity and the unreality of much of our professed belief. Hardly any sane man would desire to suppress Bank Holidays simply because they are the occasion of a considerable number of cases of drunkenness which would not otherwise have taken place. No humane legislator would hesitate to suppress them if they produced an equal number of deaths or other great physical calamities. This manner of measuring the relative importance of things is not incompatible with a general acknowledgment of the fact that there are many amusements which produce an amount of moral evil that overbalances their advantages as sources of pleasure, or of the great truth that the moral is the higher and ought to be the ruling part of our being. But the realities of life cannot be measured by rigid theological formulæ. Life is a scene in which different kinds of interest not only blend but also modify and in some degree counterbalance one another, and it can only be carried on by constant compromises in which the lines of definition are seldom very clearly marked, and in which even the highest interest must not altogether absorb or override the others. We have to deal with good principles that cannot be pushed to their full logical results; with varying standards which cannot be brought under inflexible law.

Take, for example, the many untruths which the conventional courtesies of Society prescribe. Some of these are so purely matter of phraseology that they deceive no one. Others chiefly serve the purpose of courteous concealment, as when they enable us to refuse a request or to decline an invitation or a visit without disclosing whether disinclination or inability is the cause. Then there are falsehoods for useful purposes. Few men would shrink from a falsehood which was the only means of saving a patient from a shock which would probably produce his death. No one, I suppose, would hesitate to deceive a criminal if by no other means he could prevent him from accomplishing a crime. There are also cases of the suppression of what we believe to be true, and of tacit or open acquiescence in what we believe to be false, when a full and truthful disclosure of our own beliefs might destroy the happiness of others, or subvert beliefs which are plainly necessary for their moral well-being. Cases of this kind will continually occur in life, and a good man who deals with each case as it arises will probably find no great difficulty in steering his course. But the vague and fluctuating lines of moral compromise cannot without grave moral danger be reduced to fixed rules to be carried out to their full logical consequences. The immortal pages of Pascal are sufficient to show to what extremes of immorality the doctrine that the end justifies the means has been pushed by the casuists of the Church of which Cardinal Newman was so great an ornament.

A large and difficult field of moral compromise is opened out in the case of war, which necessarily involves a complete suspension of great portions of the moral law.

This is not merely the case in unjust wars; it applies also, though in a less degree, to those which are most necessary and most righteous. War is not, and never can be, a mere passionless discharge of a painful duty. It is in its essence, and it is a main condition of its success, to kindle into fierce exercise among great masses of men the destructive and combative passions—passions as fierce and as malevolent as that with which the hound hunts the fox to its death or the tiger springs upon its prey. Destruction is one of its chief ends. Deception is one of its chief means, and one of the great arts of skilful generalship is to deceive in order to destroy. Whatever other elements may mingle with and dignify war, this at least is never absent; and however reluctantly men may enter into war, however conscientiously they may endeavour to avoid it, they must know that when the scene of carnage has once opened these things must be not only accepted and condoned, but stimulated, encouraged and applauded. It would be difficult to conceive a disposition more remote from the morals of ordinary life, not to speak of Christian ideals, than that with which the soldiers most animated with the fire and passion that lead to victory rush forward to bayonet the foe.

War indeed, which is absolutely indispensable in our present stage of civilisation, has its own morals which are very different from those of peaceful life. Yet there are few fields in which, through the stress of moral motives, greater changes have been effected. In the early stages of human history it was simply a question of power. There was no distinction between piracy and regular war, and incursions into a neighbouring State without provocation and with the sole purpose of plunder brought with them no moral blame. To carry the inhabitants of a conquered country into slavery; to slaughter the whole population of a besieged town; to destroy over vast tracts every town, village and house, and to put to death every prisoner, were among the ordinary incidents of war. These things were done without reproach in the best periods of Greek and Roman civilisation. In many cases neither age nor sex was spared! [25] In Rome the conquered general was strangled or starved to death in the Mamertine prison. Tens of thousands of captives were condemned to perish in gladiatorial shows. Julius Cæsar, whose clemency has been so greatly extolled, 'executed the whole senate of the Veneti; permitted a massacre of the Usipetes and Tencteri; sold as slaves 40,000 natives of Genabum; and cut off the right hands of all the brave men whose only crime was that they held to the last against him their town of Uxellodunum.'[26] No slaughter in history is more terrible than that which took place at Jerusalem under the general who was called 'the delight of the human race,' and when the last spasm of resistance had ceased, Titus sent Jewish captives, both male and female, by thousands to the provincial amphitheatres to be devoured by wild beasts or slaughtered as gladiators.

---

[25] See Grotius, *de Jure*, book iii. ch. iv. On the Jewish notions on this subject, see Deut. ii. 34; vii. 2, 16; xx. 10-16; Psalm cxxxvii. 9; 1 Sam. xv. 3. I have collected some additional facts on this subject in my *History of European Morals*.

[26] Tyrrell and Purser's *Correspondence of Cicero*, vol. v. p. xlvii.

Yet from a very early period lines were drawn forming a clear though somewhat arbitrary code of military morals. In Greece a broad distinction was made between wars with Greek States and with Barbarians, the latter being regarded as almost outside the pale of moral consideration. It is a distinction which in reality was not very widely different from that which Christian nations have in practice continually made between wars within the borders of Christendom, and wars with savage or pagan nations. Greek, and perhaps still more Roman, moralists have written much on the just causes of war. Many of them condemn all unjust, aggressive, or even unnecessary wars. Some of them insist on the duty of States always endeavouring by conferences, or even by arbitration, to avert war, and although these precepts, like the corresponding precepts of Christian divines, were often violated, they were certainly not without some influence on affairs. It is probably not too much to say that in this respect Roman wars do not compare unfavourably with those of Christian periods. It is remarkable how large a part of the best Christian works on the ethics of war is based on the precepts of pagan moralists, and although in antiquity as in modern times the real cause of war was often very different from the pretexts, the sense of justice in war was as clearly marked in Roman as in most Christian periods.[27]

Great stress was laid upon the duty of a formal declaration of war preceding hostilities. Polybius mentions the reprobation that was attached in Greece to the Ætolians for having neglected this custom. It was universal in Roman times, and during the mediæval period the custom of sending a challenge to the hostile power was carefully observed. In modern times formal declaration of war has fallen greatly into desuetude. The hostilities between England and Spain under Elizabeth, and the invasion of Germany by Gustavus Adolphus, were begun without any such declaration, and there have been numerous instances in later times.[28]

The treatment of prisoners has been profoundly modified. Quarter, it is true, has been very often refused in modern wars to rebels, to soldiers in mutiny, to revolted slaves, to savages who themselves give no quarter. It has been often—perhaps generally—refused to irregular soldiers like the French Francs-tireurs in the War of 1870, who without uniforms endeavoured to defend their homes against invasion. It was long refused to soldiers who, having rejected terms of surrender, continued to defend an indefensible place, but this severity during the last three centuries has been generally condemned. But, on the whole, the treatment of the conquered soldier has steadily improved. At one time he was killed. At another he was preserved as a slave. Then he was permitted to free himself by payment of a ransom; now he is simply kept in custody till he is exchanged or released on parole, or till the termination of the war. In the latter half of the present century many elaborate and beneficent regulations for the preservation of hospitals and the good treatment of the wounded have been

---

[27] See Grotius, *de Jure Belli et Pacis.*

[28] Much information on this subject will be found in a remarkable pamphlet (said to have been corrected by Pitt) called 'An Enquiry into the Manner in which the different wars in Europe have commenced during the last two centuries, by the Author of the History and Foundation of the Law of Nations in Europe' (1805).

sanctioned by international agreement. The distinction between the civil population and combatants has been increasingly observed. As a general rule non-combatants, if they do not obstruct the enemy, are subjected to no further injury than that of paying war contributions and in other ways providing for the subsistence of the invaders. The wanton destruction of private property has been more and more avoided. Such an act as the devastation of the Palatinate under Louis XIV. would now in a European war be universally condemned, though the wholesale destruction of villages in our own Indian frontier wars and the methods employed on both sides in the civil war in Cuba appear to have borne much resemblance to it. In the treatment of merchants the rule of reciprocity which was laid down in Magna Charta is largely observed, and the Conference of Brussels in 1874 pronounced it to be contrary to the laws of war to bombard an unfortified town. The great Civil War in America probably contributed not a little to raise the standard of humanity in war; for while few long wars have been fought with such determination or at the cost of so many lives, very few have been conducted with such a scrupulous abstinence from acts of wanton barbarity.

Many restrictive rules also have been accepted tending in a small degree to mitigate the actual operations of war, and they have had some real influence in this direction, though it is not possible to justify the military code on any clear principle either of ethics or logic. Assassination and the encouragement of assassination; the use of poison or poisoned weapons; the violation of parole; the deceptive use of a flag of truce or of the red cross; the slaughter of the wounded; the infringement of terms of surrender or of other distinct agreements, are absolutely forbidden, and in 1868 the Representatives of the European Powers assembled at St. Petersburg agreed to abolish the use in war of explosive bullets below the weight of 14 ounces, and to forbid the propagation in an enemy's country of contagious disease as an instrument of war. It laid down the general principle that the object of war is confined to disabling the enemy, and that weapons calculated to inflict unnecessary suffering, beyond what is required for attaining that object, should be prohibited. At the same time explosive shells, concealed mines, torpedoes and ambuscades lie fully within the permitted agencies of war. Starvation may be employed, and the cutting off of the supply of water, or the destruction of that supply by mixing with it something not absolutely poisonous which renders it undrinkable. It is allowable to deceive an enemy by fabricated despatches purporting to come from his own side; by tampering with telegraph messages; by spreading false intelligence in newspapers; by sending pretended spies and deserters to give him untrue reports of the numbers or movements of the troops; by employing false signals to lure him into an ambuscade. On the use of the flag and uniform of an enemy for purposes of deception there has been some controversy, but it is supported by high military authority.[29] The use of

---

[29] See Tovey's *Martial Law and the Custom of War*, part 2, pp. 13, 29. A striking instance of the deceptive use of a flag occurred in 1781, when the English, having captured St. Eustatius from the Dutch, allowed the Dutch flag still to float over its harbour in order that Dutch, French, Spanish and American ships which were ignorant of the capture might

spies is fully authorised, but the spy, if discovered, is excluded from the rights of war and liable to an ignominious death.

Apart from the questions I have discussed there is another class of questions connected with war which present great difficulty. It is the right of men to abdicate their private judgment by entering into the military profession. In small nations this question is not of much importance, for in them wars are of very rare occurrence and are usually for self-defence. In a great empire it is wholly different. Hardly any one will be so confident of the virtue of his rulers as to believe that every war which his country wages in every part of its dominions, with uncivilised as well as civilised populations, is just and necessary, and it is certainly primâ facie not in accordance with an ideal morality that men should bind themselves absolutely for life or for a term of years to kill without question, at the command of their superiors, those who have personally done them no wrong. Yet this unquestioning obedience is the very essence of military discipline, and without it the efficiency of armies and the safety of nations would be hopelessly destroyed. It is necessary to the great interests of society, and therefore it is maintained, strengthened by the obligation of an oath and still more efficaciously by a code of honour which is one of the strongest binding influences by which men can be governed.

It is not, however, altogether absolute, and a variety of distinctions and compromises have been made. There is a difference between the man who enlists in the army of his own country and a man who enlists in foreign service either permanently or for the duration of a single war. If a man unnecessarily takes an active part in a struggle between two countries other than his own, it may at least be demanded that he should be actuated, not by a mere spirit of adventure or personal ambition, but by a strong and reasoned conviction that the cause which he is supporting is a righteous one. The conduct of a man who enlists in a foreign army which may possibly be used against his own country, and who at least binds himself to obey absolutely chiefs who have no natural authority over him, has been much condemned, but even here special circumstances must be taken into account. Few persons I suppose would seriously blame the Irish Catholics of the eighteenth century who filled the armies of France, Austria, Spain and Naples at a time when disqualifying laws excluded them, on account of their religion, from the British army and from almost every path of ambition at home. There is also perhaps some distinction between the position of a soldier who is obliged to serve, and a soldier in a country where enlisting is voluntary, and also between the position of an officer who can throw up his commission without infringing the law, and a private who cannot abandon his flag without committing a grave legal offence. At the beginning of the war of the American Revolution some English officers left the army rather than serve in a cause which they believed to be unrighteous. It was in their full power to do so,

---

be decoyed into the harbour and seized as prizes. Some writers on military law maintain that this was within the rights of war.

but probably none of them would have desired that private soldiers who had no legal choice in the matter should have followed their example and become deserters from the ranks.

There are, however, extreme cases in which the violation of the military oath and disobedience to military discipline are justified. More than once in French history an usurper or his agent has ordered soldiers to coerce or fire upon the representatives of the nation. In such cases it has been said 'the conscience of the soldier is the liberty of the people,' and the refusal of private soldiers to obey a plainly illegal order will be generally though not universally applauded. In all such cases, however, there is much obscurity and inconsistency of judgment. The rule that the moral responsibility falls exclusively on the person who gives the order, and that the private has no voice or responsibility, will even here be maintained by some. Ought a private soldier to have refused to take part in such an execution as that of the Duc d'Enghien, or in the Coup d'État of Napoleon III.? Ought he to refuse to fire on a mob if he doubts the legality of the order of his superior officer? In such cases there is sometimes a direct conflict between the civil and the military law, and there have been instances in which a soldier might be punishable before the first for acts which were absolutely enforced by the second.[30]

Perhaps the strongest case of justifiable disobedience that can be alleged is when a soldier is ordered to do something which involves apostasy from his faith, though even here it would be difficult to show, in the light of pure reason, that this is a graver thing than to kill innocent men in an unrighteous cause. In the Early Church there were some soldier martyrs who suffered death because they believed it inconsistent with their faith to bear arms, or because they were asked to do some acts which savoured of idolatry. The story of the Thebæan legion which was said to have been martyred under Diocletian rests on no trustworthy authority, but it illustrates the feeling of the Church on the subject. Josephus tells how Jewish soldiers refused in spite of all punishments to bring earth with the other soldiers for the reparation of the Temple of Belus at Babylon. Conflicts between military duty and religious duty must have not unfrequently arisen during the religious wars of the sixteenth century, and in our own century and in our own army there have been instances of soldiers refusing through religious motives to escort or protect idolatrous processions in India, or to present arms in Catholic countries when the Host was passing. Quaker opinions about war are absolutely inconsistent with the compulsory service which prevails in nearly all European countries, and religious scruples about conscription have been among the motives that have brought the Russian Raskolniks into collision with the civil power.

One of the most serious instances of the collision of duties in our time is furnished by the great Sepoy Mutiny of 1857. From the days of Clive, Sepoy soldiers have served under the British flag with an admirable fidelity, and the Mutiny of Vellore in 1806, which was the one exception, was due, like that of 1857, to a belief

---

[30] See Fitzjames Stephen's *History of the Criminal Law*, i. 205.

that the British Government were interfering with their faith. Few things in the history of the great Mutiny are so touching as the profound belief of the English commanders of the Sepoy regiments in the unalterable loyalty of their soldiers. Many of them lost their lives through this belief, refusing even to the last moment and in spite of all evidence to abandon it. They were deceived, and, in the fierce outburst of indignation that followed, the conduct of the Sepoy soldiers was branded as the blackest and the most unprovoked treachery.

Yet assuredly no charge was less true. Agitators for their own selfish purposes had indeed acted upon the troops, but recent researches have fully proved that the real as well as the ostensible cause of the Mutiny was the greased cartridges. It was believed that the cartridges which had been recently issued for the Sepoy regiments were smeared with a mixture of cow's fat and pig's fat, one of these ingredients being utterly impure in the eyes of the Hindoo, and the other in the eyes of the Mussulman. To bite these cartridges would destroy the caste of the Hindoo and carry with it the loss of everything that was most dear and most sacred to him both in this world and in the next. In the eyes both of the Moslem and the Hindoo it was the gravest and the most irreparable of crimes, destroying all hopes in a future world, and yet this crime, in their belief, was imposed upon them as a matter of military duty by their officers. It was as if the Puritan soldiers of the seventeenth century had been ordered by their commanders to abjure their hopes of salvation and to repudiate and insult the Christian faith.

It is true that the existence of these obnoxious ingredients in the new cartridges was solemnly denied, but the sincerity of the Sepoy belief is incontestable, and General Anson, the commander-in-chief, having examined the cartridges, was compelled to admit that it was very plausible.[31] 'I am not so much surprised,' he wrote to Lord Canning, 'at their objections to the cartridges, having seen them. I had no idea they contained, or rather are smeared with such a quantity of grease, which looks exactly like fat. After ramming down the ball, the muzzle of the musket is covered with it.'

Unfortunately this is not a complete statement of the case. It is a shameful and terrible truth that, as far as the fact was concerned, the Sepoys were perfectly right in their belief. In the words of Lord Roberts, 'The recent researches of Mr. Forrest in the records of the Government of India prove that the lubricating mixture used in preparing the cartridges was actually composed of the objectionable ingredients, cow's fat and lard, and that incredible disregard of the soldiers' religious prejudices was displayed in the manufacture of these cartridges.'[32] This was certainly not due, as the Sepoys imagined, to any desire on the part of the British authorities to destroy caste or to prepare the way for the conversion of the Sepoys to Christianity. It was simply a glaring instance of the indifference, ignorance and incapacity too often shown by British administrators in dealing with beliefs and types of character wholly unlike their

---

[31] Lord Roberts' *Forty-one Years in India*, i. 94

[32] *Ibid.* p. 431

own. They were unable to realise that a belief which seemed to them so childish could have any depth, and they accordingly produced a Mutiny that for a time shook the English power in India to its very foundation.

The horrors of Cawnpore—which were due to a single man—soon took away from the British public all power of sanely judging the conflict, and a struggle in which no quarter was given was naturally marked by extreme savageness; but in looking back upon it, English writers must acknowledge with humiliation that, if mutiny is ever justifiable, no stronger justification could be given than that of the Sepoy troops.

Many of my readers will remember an exquisite little poem called 'The Forced Recruit,' in which Mrs. Browning has described a young Venetian soldier who was forced by the conscription to serve against his fellow-countrymen in the Austrian army at Solferino, and who advanced cheerfully to die by the Italian guns, holding a musket that had never been loaded in his hand. Such a figure, such a violation of military law, will claim the sympathy of all, but a very different judgment should be passed upon those who, having voluntarily entered an army, betray their trust and their oath in the name of patriotism. In the Fenian movement in Ireland, one of the chief objects of the conspirators was to corrupt the Irish soldiers and break down that high sense of military honour for which in all times and in many armies the Irish people have been conspicuous. 'The epidemic' [of disaffection], boasts a writer who was much mixed in the conspiracies of those times, 'was not an affair of individuals, but of companies and of whole regiments. To attempt to impeach all the military Fenians before courts martial would have been to throw England into a panic, if not to precipitate an appalling mutiny and invite foreign invasion. '[33]

I do not quote these words as a true statement. They are, I believe, a gross exaggeration and a gross calumny on the Irish soldiers, nor do I doubt that most, if not all, the soldiers who may have been induced over a glass of whiskey, or through the persuasions of some cunning agitator, to take the Fenian oath would, if an actual conflict had arisen, have proved perfectly faithful soldiers of the Queen. The perversion of morals, however, which looks on such violations of military duty as praiseworthy, has not been confined to writers of the stamp of Mr. O'Brien. A striking instance of it is furnished by a recent American biography. Among the early Fenian conspirators was a young man named John Boyle O'Reilly. He was a genuine enthusiast, with a real vein of literary talent; in the closing years of his life he won the affection and admiration of very honourable men, and I should certainly have no wish to look too harshly on youthful errors which were the result of a misguided enthusiasm if they had been acknowledged as such. As a matter of fact, however, he began his career by an act which, according to every sound principle of morality, religion, and secular honour, was in the highest degree culpable. Being a sworn Fenian, he entered a regiment of hussars, assumed the uniform of the Queen, and

---

[33] *Contemporary Review*, May 1897. Article by William O'Brien, 'Was Fenianism ever Formidable?'

took the oath of allegiance for the express purpose of betraying his trust and seducing the soldiers of his regiment. He was detected and condemned to penal servitude, and he at last escaped to America, where he took an active part in the Fenian movement. After his death his biography was written in a strain of unqualified eulogy, but the biographer has honestly and fully disclosed the facts which I have related. This book has an introduction written by Cardinal Gibbons, one of the most prominent Catholic divines in the United States. The reader may be curious to see how the act of aggravated treachery and perjury which it revealed was judged by a personage who occupies all but the highest position in a Church which professes to be the supreme and inspired teacher of morals. Not a word in this Introduction implies that O'Reilly had done any act for which he should be ashamed. He is described as 'a great and good man,' and the only allusion to his crime is in the following terms: 'In youth his heart agonises over that saddest and strangest romance in all history—the wrongs and woes of his motherland—that Niobe of the Nations. In manhood, because he dared to wish her free, he finds himself a doomed felon, an exiled convict, in what he calls himself the Nether World.... The Divine faith implanted in his soul in childhood flourished there undyingly, pervaded his whole being with its blessed influences, furnished his noblest ideals of thought and conduct.... The country of his adoption vies with the land of his birth in testifying to the uprightness of his life.... With all these voices I blend my own, and in their name I say that the world is brighter for having possessed him.'[34]

I gladly accept this assurance of Cardinal Gibbons, though I am surprised that he should not have even glanced at the book which he introduced, and that he should have been absolutely ignorant of the most conspicuous event of the life which, from early youth, he held up to unqualified admiration. I regret, too, that he has not taken the opportunity of this letter to reprobate a form of moral perversion which is widely spread among his Irish co-religionists, and which his own words are only too likely to strengthen. It is but a short time since an Irish Nationalist Member of Parliament, being accused of once having served the Queen as a Volunteer, justified himself by saying that he had only worn the coat which was worn by Lord Edward Fitzgerald and Boyle O'Reilly; while another Irish Nationalist Member of Parliament, at a public meeting in Dublin, and amid the cheers of his audience, expressed his hope that in the South African war the Irish soldiers under the British flag would fire on the English instead of on the Boers.

---

[34] Roche's *Life of John Boyle O'Reilly*, with introduction by Cardinal Gibbons. Since the publication of this book Cardinal Gibbons has written a letter to the *Tablet* (Dec. 2, 1899), in which he says: 'I feel it due to myself and the interests of truth to declare that till I read Mr. Lecky's criticism I did not know that Mr. O'Reilly had ever been a Fenian or a British soldier, or that he had tried to seduce other soldiers from their allegiance. In fact, up to this moment, I have never read a line of the biography for which I wrote the introduction.... My only acquaintance with Mr. O'Reilly's history before he came to America was the vague information I had that, for some political offence, the exact nature of which I did not learn, he had been exiled from his native land to a penal colony, from which he afterwards escaped.'

CHAPTER IX

The foregoing chapter will have shown sufficiently how largely in one great and necessary profession the element of moral compromise must enter, and will show the nature of some of the moral difficulties that attend it. We find illustrations of much the same kind in the profession of an advocate. In the interests of the proper administration of justice it is of the utmost importance that every cause, however defective, and every criminal, however bad, should be fully defended, and it is therefore indispensable that there should be a class of men entrusted with this duty. It is the business of the judge and of the jury to decide on the merits of the case, but in order that they should discharge this function it is necessary that the arguments on both sides should be laid before them in the strongest form. The clear interest of society requires this, and a standard of professional honour and etiquette is formed for the purpose of regulating the action of the advocate. Misstatements of facts or of law; misquotations of documents; strong expressions of personal opinion, and some other devices by which verdicts may be won, are condemned; there are cases which an honourable lawyer will not adopt, and there are rare cases in which, in the course of a trial, he will find it his duty to throw up his brief.

But necessary and honourable as the profession may be, there are sides of it which are far from being in accordance with an austere code of ideal morals. It is idle to suppose that a master of the art of advocacy will merely confine himself to a calm, dispassionate statement of the facts and arguments of his side. He will inevitably use all his powers of rhetoric and persuasion to make the cause for which he holds a brief appear true, though he knows it to be false; he will affect a warmth which he does not feel and a conviction which he does not hold; he will skilfully avail himself of any mistake or omission of his opponent; of any technical rule that can exclude damaging evidence; of all the resources that legal subtlety and severe cross-examination can furnish to confuse dangerous issues, to obscure or minimise inconvenient facts, to discredit hostile witnesses. He will appeal to every prejudice that can help his cause; he will for the time so completely identify himself with it that he will make its success his supreme and all-absorbing object; and he will hardly fail to feel some thrill of triumph if by the force of ingenious and eloquent pleading he has saved the guilty from his punishment or snatched a verdict in defiance of evidence.

It is not surprising that a profession which inevitably leads to such things should have excited scruples among many good men. Swift very roughly described lawyers as 'a society of men bred from their youth in the art of proving by words, multiplied for the purpose, that white is black and black is white, according as they are paid.' Dr. Arnold has more than once expressed his dislike, and indeed abhorrence, of the profession of an advocate. It inevitably, he maintained, leads to moral perversion, involving, as it does, the indiscriminate defence of right and wrong, and in many cases the knowing suppression of truth. Macaulay, who can hardly be regarded as addicted to the refinements of an over-fastidious morality, reviewing the professional rules that are recognised in England, asks 'whether it be right that not merely believing, but knowing a statement to be true, he should do all that can be done by sophistry, by rhetoric, by solemn asseveration, by indignant exclamation, by gesture, by play of features, by terrifying one honest witness, by perplexing another, to cause a jury to think that statement false.' Bentham denounced in even stronger language the habitual method of 'the hireling lawyer' in cross-examining an honest but adverse witness, and he declared that there is a code of morality current in Westminster Hall generically different from the code of ordinary life, and directly calculated to destroy the love of veracity and justice. On the other hand, Paley recognised among falsehoods that are not lies because they deceive no one, the statement of 'an advocate asserting the justice or his belief of the justice of his client's cause.' Dr. Johnson, in reply to some objections of Boswell, argues at length, but, I think, with some sophistry, in favour of the profession. 'You are not,' he says, 'to deceive your client with false representations of your opinion. You are not to tell lies to the judge, but you need have no scruple about taking up a case which you believe to be bad, or affecting a warmth which you do not feel. You do not know your cause to be bad till the judge determines it.... An argument which does not convince yourself may convince the judge, and, if it does convince him, you are wrong and he is right.... Everybody knows you are paid for affecting warmth for your client, and it is therefore properly no dissimulation.' Basil Montagu, in an excellent treatise on the subject, urges that an advocate is simply an officer assisting in the administration of justice under the impression that truth is best elicited, and that difficulties are most effectually disentangled, by the opposite statements of able men. He is an indispensable part of a machine which in its net result is acting in the real interests of truth, although he 'may profess feelings which he does not feel and may support a cause which he knows to be wrong,' and although his advocacy is 'a species of acting without an avowal that it is acting.'

It is, of course, possible to adopt the principles of the Quaker and to condemn as unchristian all participation in the law courts, and although the Catholic Church has never adopted this extreme, it seems to have instinctively recognised some incompatibility between the profession of an advocate and the saintly character. Renan notices the significant fact that St. Yves, a saint of Brittany, appears to be the only advocate who has found a place in its hagiology, and the worshippers were accustomed to sing on his festival 'Advocatus et non latro—Res miranda populo.' It is indeed evident that a good deal of moral compromise must enter into this field, and the standards of right and wrong that have been adopted have varied greatly. How far, for example, may a lawyer support a cause which he believes to be wrong? In some ancient legislations advocates were compelled to swear that they would not defend causes which they thought or discovered to be unjust. [35] St. Thomas Aquinas has laid down in emphatic terms that any lawyer who undertakes the defence of an unjust cause is committing a grievous sin. It is unlawful, he contends, to co-operate with any one who is doing wrong, and an advocate clearly counsels and assists him whose cause

---

[35] O'Brien, *The Lawyer*, pp. 169, 170.

he undertakes. Modern Catholic casuists have dealt with the subject in the same spirit. They admit, indeed, that an advocate may undertake the defence of a criminal whom he knows to be guilty, in order to bring to light all extenuating circumstances, but they contend that no advocate should undertake a civil cause unless by a previous and careful examination he has convinced himself that it is a just one; that no advocate can without sin undertake a cause which he knows or strongly believes to be unjust; that if he has done so he is himself bound in conscience to make restitution to the party that has been injured by his advocacy; that if in the course of a trial he discovers that a cause which he had believed to be just is unjust he must try to persuade his client to desist, and if he fails in this must himself abandon the cause, though without informing the opposite party of the conclusion at which he had arrived; that in conducting his case he must abstain from wounding the reputation of his neighbour or endeavouring to influence the judges by bringing before them misdeeds of his opponent which are not connected with and are not essential to the case.[36] As lately as 1886 an order was issued from Rome, with the express approbation of the Pope, forbidding any Catholic, mayor or judge, to take part in a divorce case, as divorce is absolutely condemned by the Church.[37]

There have been, and perhaps still are, instances of lawyers endeavouring to limit their practice to cases which they believed to be just. Sir Matthew Hale is a conspicuous example, but he acknowledged that he considerably relaxed his rule on the subject, having found in two instances that cases which at the first blush seemed very worthless were in truth well founded. As a general rule English lawyers make no discrimination on this ground in accepting briefs unless the injustice is very flagrant, nor will they, except in very extreme cases, do their client the great injury of throwing up a brief which they have once accepted. They contend that by acting in this way the administration of justice in the long run is best served, and in this fact they find its justification.

In the conduct of a case there are rules analogous to those which distinguish between honourable and dishonourable war, but they are less clearly defined and less universally accepted. In criminal prosecutions a remarkable though very explicable distinction is drawn between the prosecutor and the defender. It is the etiquette of the profession that the former is bound to aim only at truth, neither straining any point against the prisoner nor keeping back any fact which is favourable to him, nor using any argument which he does not himself believe to be just. The defender, however, is not bound, according to professional etiquette, by such rules. He may use arguments which he knows to be bad, conceal or shut out by technical objections facts that will tell against his clients, and, subject to some wide and vague restrictions, he must make the acquittal of his client his first object.[38]

---

[36] *Dictionnaire de Cas de Conscience*, Art. 'Avocat;' Migne, *Encyclopédie Théologique*, i. serie, tome xviii.

[37] *Revue de Droit International*, xxi. 615.

[38]] See Sir James Stephen's *General View of the Criminal Law of England*, pp. 167, 168.

Sometimes cases of extreme difficulty arise. Probably the best known is the case of Courvoisier, the Swiss valet, who murdered Lord William Russell in 1840. In the course of the trial Courvoisier informed his advocate, Phillips, that he was guilty of the murder, but at the same time directed Phillips to continue to defend him to the last extremity. As there was overwhelming evidence that the murder must have been committed by some one who slept in the house, the only possible defence was that an equal amount of suspicion attached to the housemaid and cook who were its other occupants. On the first day of the trial, before he knew the guilt of his client from his own lips, Phillips had cross-examined the housemaid, who first discovered the murder, with great severity and with the evident object of throwing suspicion upon her. What course ought he now to pursue? It happened that an eminent judge was sitting on the bench with the judge who was to try the case, and Phillips took this judge into his confidence, stated privately to him the facts that had arisen, and asked for his advice. The judge declared that Phillips was bound to continue to defend the prisoner, whose case would have been hopeless if his own counsel abandoned him, and in defending him he was bound to use all fair arguments arising out of the evidence. The speech of Phillips was a masterpiece of eloquence under circumstances of extraordinary difficulty. Much of it was devoted to impugning the veracity of the witnesses for the prosecution. He solemnly declared that it was not his business to say who committed the murder, and that he had no desire to throw any imputation on the other servants in the house, and he abstained scrupulously from giving any personal opinion on the matter; but the drift of his argument was that Courvoisier was the victim of a conspiracy, the police having concealed compromising articles among his clothes, and that there was no clear circumstance distinguishing the suspicion against him from that against the other servants.[39]

The conduct of Phillips in this case has, I believe, been justified by the preponderance of professional opinion, though when the facts were known public opinion outside the profession generally condemned it. Some lawyers have pushed the duty of defence to a point which has aroused much protest even in their own profession. 'The Advocate,' said Lord Brougham in his great speech before the House of Lords in defence of Queen Caroline, 'by the sacred duty which he owes his client, knows in the discharge of that office but one person in the world—that client and none other. To save that client by all expedient means, to protect that client at all hazards and costs to all others, and among others to himself, is the highest and most unquestioned of his duties; and he must not regard the alarm, the suffering, the torment, the destruction which he may bring upon any other. Nay, separating even the duties of a patriot from those of an advocate, and casting them, if need be, to the

---

[39] Phillips's defence of his own conduct will be found in a pamphlet called 'Correspondence of S. Warren and C. Phillips relating to the Courvoisier trial.' It has often been said that Phillips had asserted in his speech his full belief in the innocence of his client, but this is disproved by the statement of C. J. Tindal, who tried the case, and of Baron Parke, who sat on the bench. C. J. Denman also pronounced Phillips's speech to be unexceptionable. An able and interesting article on this case by Mr. Atlay will be found in the *Cornhill Magazine*, May, 1897.

wind, he must go on, reckless of consequences, if his fate it should unhappily be to involve his country in confusion for his client's protection.'

This doctrine has been emphatically repudiated by some eminent English lawyers, but both in practice and theory the profession have differed widely in different courts, times and countries. How far, for example, is it permissible in cross-examination to browbeat or confuse an honest but timid and unskilful witness; to attempt to discredit the evidence of a witness on a plain matter of fact about which he had no interest in concealment by exhuming against him some moral scandal of early youth which was totally unconnected with the subject of the trial; or, by pursuing such a line of cross-examination, to keep out of the witness-box material witnesses who are conscious that their past lives are not beyond reproach? How far is it right or permissible to press legal technicalities as opposed to substantial justice? Probably most lawyers, if they are perfectly candid, will agree that these things are in some measure inevitable in their profession, and that the real question is one of degree, and therefore not susceptible of positive definition. There is a kind of mind that grows so enamoured with the subtleties and technicalities of the law that it delights in the unexpected and unintended results to which they may lead. I have heard an English judge say of another long deceased that he had through this feeling a positive pleasure in injustice, and one lawyer, not of this country, once confessed to me the amusement he derived from breaking the convictions of criminals in his state by discovering technical flaws in their indictments. There is a class of mind that delights in such cases as that of the legal document which was invalidated because the letters A.D. were put before the date instead of the formula 'in the year of Our Lord,' or that of a swindler who was suffered to escape with his booty because, in the writ that was issued for his arrest, by a copyist's error the word 'sheriff' was written instead of 'sheriffs,' or that of a lady who was deprived of an estate of £14,000 a year because by a mere mistake of the conveyancer one material word was omitted from the will, although the clearest possible evidence was offered showing the wishes of the testator.[40] Such lawyers argue that in will cases 'the true question is not what the testator intended to do, but what is the meaning of the words of the will,' and that the balance of advantages is in favour of a strict adherence to the construction of the sentence and the technicalities of the law, even though in particular cases it may lead to grave injustice.

It must indeed be acknowledged that up to a period extending far into the nineteenth century those lawyers who adopted the most technical view of their profession were acting fully in accordance with its spirit. Few, if any, departments of English legislation and administration were till near the middle of this century so scandalously bad as those connected with the administration of the civil and the criminal law, and especially with the Court of Chancery. The whole field was covered with a network of obscure, intricate, archaic technicalities; useless except for the purpose of piling up costs, procrastinating decisions, placing the simplest legal

---

[40] See these cases in Warren's *Social and Professional Duties of an Attorney*, pp. 128-133, 195, 196.

processes wholly beyond the competence of any but trained experts, giving endless facilities for fraud and for the evasion or defeat of justice, turning a law case into a game in which chance and skill had often vastly greater influence than substantial merits. Lord Brougham probably in no degree exaggerated when he described great portions of the English law as 'a two-edged sword in the hands of craft and of oppression,' and a great authority on chancery law declared in 1839 that 'no man, as things now stand, can enter into a chancery suit with any reasonable hope of being alive at its termination if he has a determined adversary.'[41]

The moral difficulties of administering such a system were very great, and in many cases English juries, in dealing with it, adopted a rough and ready code of morals of their own. Though they had sworn to decide every case according to the law as it was stated to them, and according to the evidence that was laid before them, they frequently refused to follow legal technicalities which would lead to substantial injustice, and they still more frequently refused to bring in verdicts according to evidence when by doing so they would consign a prisoner to a savage, excessive, or unjust punishment. Some of the worst abuses of the English law were mitigated by the perjuries of juries who refused to put them in force.

The great legal reforms of the past half-century have removed most of these abuses, and have at the same time introduced a wider and juster spirit into the practical administration of the law. Yet even now different judges sometimes differ widely in the importance they attach to substantial justice and to legal technicalities; and even now one of the advantages of trial by jury is that it brings the masculine common sense and the unsophisticated sense of justice of unprofessional men into fields that would otherwise be often distorted by ingenious subtleties. It is, however, far less in the position of the judge than in the position of an advocate that the most difficult moral questions of the legal profession arise. The difference between an unscrupulous advocate and an advocate who is governed by a high sense of honour and morality is very manifest, but at best there must be many things in the profession from which a very sensitive conscience would recoil, and things must be said and done which can hardly be justified except on the ground that the existence of this profession and the prescribed methods of its action are in the long run indispensable to the honest administration of justice.

The same method of reasoning applies to other great departments of life. In politics it is especially needed. In free countries party government is the best if not the only way of conducting public affairs, but it is impossible to conduct it without a large amount of moral compromise; without a frequent surrender of private judgment and will. A good man will choose his party through disinterested motives, and with a firm and honest conviction that it represents the cast of policy most beneficial to the country. He will on grave occasions assert his independence of party, but in the large

---

[41] See the admirable article by Lord Justice Bowen on 'The Administration of the Law' in Ward's *Reign of Queen Victoria*, vol. i.

majority of cases he must act with his party even if they are pursuing courses in some degree contrary to his own judgment.

Every one who is actively engaged in politics—every one especially who is a member of the House of Commons—must soon learn that if the absolute independence of individual judgment were pushed to its extreme, political anarchy would ensue. The complete concurrence of a large number of independent judgments in a complicated measure is impossible. If party government is to be carried on, there must be, both in the Cabinet and in Parliament, perpetual compromise. The first condition of its success is that the Government should have a stable, permanent, disciplined support behind it, and in order that this should be attained the individual member must in most cases vote with his party. Sometimes he must support a measure which he knows to be bad, because its rejection would involve a change of government which he believes would be a still greater evil than its acceptance, and in order to prevent this evil he may have to vote a direct negative to some resolution containing a statement which he believes to be true. At the same time, if he is an honest man, he will not be a mere slave of party. Sometimes a question arises which he considers so supremely important that he will break away from his party and endeavour at all hazards to carry or to defeat it. Much more frequently he will either abstain from voting, or will vote against the Government on a particular question, but only when he knows that by taking this course he is simply making a protest which will produce no serious political complication. On most great measures there is a dissentient minority in the Government party, and it often exercises a most useful influence in representing independent opinion, and bringing into the measure modifications and compromises which allay opposition, gratify minorities, and soften differences. But the action of that party will be governed by many motives other than a simple consideration of the merits of the case. It is not sufficient to say that they must vote for every resolution which they believe to be true, for every bill or clause of a bill which they believe to be right, and must vote against every bill or clause or resolution about which they form an opposite judgment. Sometimes they will try in private to prevent the introduction of a measure, but when it is introduced they will feel it their duty either positively to support it or at least to abstain from protesting against it. Sometimes they will either vote against it or abstain from voting at all, but only when the majority is so large that it is sure to be carried. Sometimes their conduct will be the result of a bargain—they will vote for one portion of a bill of which they disapprove because they have obtained from the Government a concession on another which they think more important. The nature of their opposition will depend largely upon the strength or weakness of the Government, upon the size of the majority, upon the degree in which a change of ministry would affect the general policy of the country, upon the probability of the measure they object to being finally extinguished, or returning in another year either in an improved or in a more dangerous form. Questions of proportion and degree and ulterior consequences will continually sway them. Measures are often opposed, not on their own intrinsic merits, but on account of precedents they might establish; of other measures which might grow out of them or be justified by them.

Not unfrequently it happens that a section of the dominant party is profoundly discontented with the policy of the Government on some question which they deem of great importance. They find themselves incapable of offering any direct and successful opposition, but their discontent will show itself on some other Government measure on which votes are more evenly divided. Possibly they may oppose that measure. More probably they will fail to attend regularly at the divisions, or will exercise their independent judgments on its clauses in a manner they would not have done if their party allegiance had been unshaken. And this conduct is not mere revenge. It is a method of putting pressure on the Government in order to obtain concessions on matters which they deem of paramount importance. In the same way they will seek to gain supporters by political alliances. Few things in parliamentary government are more dangerous or more apt to lead to corruption than the bargains which the Americans call log-rolling; but it is inevitable that a member who has received from a colleague, or perhaps from an opponent, assistance on a question which he believes to be of the highest importance, will be disposed to return that assistance in some case in which his own feelings and opinions are not strongly enlisted.

Then, too, we have to consider the great place which obstruction plays in parliamentary government. It constantly happens that a measure to which scarcely any one objects is debated at inordinate length for no other reason than to prevent a measure which is much objected to from being discussed. Measures may be opposed by hostile votes, but they are often much more efficaciously opposed by calculated delays, by multiplied amendments or speeches, by some of the many devices that can be employed to clog the legislative machine. There are large classes of measures on which governments or parliaments think it desirable to give no opinion, or at least no immediate opinion, though they cannot prevent their introduction, and many methods are employed with the real, though not avowed and ostensible object of preventing a vote or even a ministerial declaration upon them. Sometimes Parliament is quite ready to acknowledge the abstract justice of a proposal, but does not think it ripe for legislation. In such cases the second reading of the bill will probably be accepted, but, to the indignation and astonishment of its supporters outside the House, it will be obstructed, delayed or defeated in committee with the acquiescence, or connivance, or even actual assistance of some of those who had voted for it. Some measures in the eyes of some members involve questions of principle so sacred that they will admit of no compromise of expediency, but most measures are deemed open to compromise and are accepted, rejected, or modified under some of the many motives I have described.

All this curious and indispensable mechanism of party government is compatible with a high and genuine sense of public duty, and unless such a sense at the last resort dominates over all other considerations, political life will inevitably decline. At the same time it is obvious that many things have to be done from which a very rigid and austere nature would recoil. To support a Government when he believes it to be wrong, or to oppose a measure which he believes to be right; to connive at evasions which are mere pretexts, and at delays which rest upon grounds that are not openly avowed,—is sometimes, and indeed not unfrequently, a parliamentary duty. A member of Parliament must often feel himself in the position of a private in an army, or a player in a game, or an advocate in a law case. On many questions each party represents and defends the special interests of some particular classes in the country. When there are two plausible alternative courses to be pursued which divide public opinion, the Opposition is almost bound by its position to enforce the merits of the course opposed to that adopted by the Government. In theory nothing could seem more absurd than a system of government in which, as it has been said, the ablest men in Parliament are divided into two classes, one side being charged with the duty of carrying on the government and the other with that of obstructing and opposing them in their task, and in which, on a vast multitude of unconnected questions, these two great bodies of very competent men, with the same facts and arguments before them, habitually go into opposite lobbies. In practice, however, parliamentary government by great parties, in countries where it is fully understood and practised, is found to be admirably efficacious in representing every variety of political opinion; in securing a constant supervision and criticism of men and measures; and in forming a safety valve through which the dangerous humours of society can expand without evil to the community.

This, however, is only accomplished by constant compromises which are seldom successfully carried out without a long national experience. Party must exist. It must be maintained as an essential condition of good government, but it must be subordinated to the public interests, and in the public interests it must be in many cases suspended. There are subjects which cannot be introduced without the gravest danger into the arena of party controversy. Indian politics are a conspicuous example, and, although foreign policy cannot be kept wholly outside it, the dangers connected with its party treatment are extremely great. Many measures of a different kind are conducted with the concurrence of the two front benches. A cordial union on large classes of questions between the heads of the rival parties is one of the first conditions of successful parliamentary government. The Opposition leader must have a voice in the conduct of business, on the questions that should be brought forward, and on the questions that it is for the public interest to keep back. He is the official leader of systematic, organised opposition to the Government, yet he is on a large number of questions their most powerful ally. He must frequently have confidential relations with them, and one of his most useful functions is to prevent sections of his party from endeavouring to snatch party advantages by courses which might endanger public interests. If the country is to be well governed there must be a large amount of continuity in its policy; certain conditions and principles of administration must be inflexibly maintained, and in great national emergencies all parties must unite.

In questions which lie at the heart of party politics, also some amount of compromise is usually effected. Debate not only elicits opinions but also suggests alternatives and compromises, and very few measures are carried by a majority which do not bear clear traces of the action of the minority. The line is constantly deflected now on one side and now on the other, and (usually without much regard to logical consistency) various and opposing sentiments are in some measure gratified. If the lines of party are drawn with an inflexible rigidity; and if the majority insist on the full exercise of their powers, parliamentary government may become a despotism as crushing as the worst autocracy—a despotism which is perhaps even more dangerous as the sense of responsibility is diminished by being divided. If, on the other hand, the latitude conceded to individual opinion is excessive, Parliament inevitably breaks into groups, and parliamentary government loses much of its virtue. When coalitions of minorities can at any time overthrow a ministry, the whole force of Government is lost. The temptation to corrupt bargains with particular sections is enormously increased, and the declining control of the two front benches will be speedily followed by a diminished sense of responsibility, and by the increased influence of violent, eccentric, exaggerated opinions. It is of the utmost moment that the policy of an Opposition should be guided by its most important men, and especially by men who have had the experience and the responsibility of office, and who know that they may have that responsibility again. But the healthy latitude of individual opinion and expression in a party is like most of those things we are now considering, a question of degree, and not susceptible of clear and sharp definition.

Other questions of a somewhat different nature, but involving grave moral considerations, arise out of the relations between a member and his constituents. In the days when small boroughs were openly bought in the market, this was sometimes defended on the ground of the complete independence of judgment which it gave to the purchasing member. Romilly and Henry Flood are said to have both purchased their seats with the express object of securing such independence. In the political philosophy of Burke, no doctrine is more emphatically enforced than that a member of Parliament is a representative but not a delegate; that he owes to his constituents not only his time and his services, but also the exercise of his independent and unfettered judgment; that, while reflecting the general cast of their politics, he must never suffer himself to be reduced to a mere mouthpiece, or accept binding instructions prescribing on each particular measure the course he may pursue; that after his election he must consider himself a member of an Imperial Parliament rather than the representative of a particular locality, and must subordinate local and special interests to the wider and more general interests of the whole nation.

The conditions of modern political life have greatly narrowed this liberty of judgment. In most constituencies a member can only enter Parliament fettered by many pledges relating to specific measures, and in every turn of policy sections of his constituents will attempt to dictate his course of action. Certain large and general pledges naturally and properly precede his election. He is chosen as a supporter or opponent of the Government; he avows himself an adherent of certain broad lines of policy, and he also represents in a special degree the interests and the distinctive type of opinion of the class or industry which is dominant in his constituency. But even at the time of election he often finds that on some particular question in which his electors are much interested he differs from them, though they consent, in spite of it, to elect him; and, in the course of a long Parliament, others are very apt unexpectedly to arise. Political changes take place which bring into the foreground matters which at the time of the election seemed very remote, or produce new questions, or give rise to unforeseen party combinations, developments, and tendencies. It will often happen that on these occasions a member will think differently from the majority of his electors, and he must meet the question how far he must sacrifice his judgment to theirs, and how far he may use the influence which their votes have given him to act in opposition to their wishes and perhaps even to their interests. Burke, for example, found himself in this position when, being member for Bristol, he considered it his duty to support the concession of Free-trade to Ireland, although his constituents had, or thought they had, a strong interest in commercial restrictions and monopoly. In our own day it has happened that members representing manufacturing districts of Lancashire have found themselves unexpectedly called upon to vote upon some measure for crippling or extending rival manufactures in India; for opening new markets by some very dubious aggression in a distant land; or for limiting the child labour employed in the local manufacture; and these members have often believed that the right course was a course which was exceedingly repugnant to great sections of their electors.

Sometimes, too, a member is elected on purely secular issues, but in the course of the Parliament one of those fierce, sudden storms of religious sentiment, to which England is occasionally liable, sweeps over the land, and he finds himself wholly out of sympathy with a great portion of his constituency. In other cases the party which he entered Parliament to support, pursues, on some grave question, a line of policy which he believes to be seriously wrong, and he goes into partial or even complete and bitter opposition. Differences of this kind have frequently arisen when there is no question of any interested motive having influenced the member. Sometimes in such cases he has resigned his seat and gone to his electors for re-election. In other cases he remains in Parliament till the next election. Each case, however, must be left to individual judgment, and no clear, definite, unwavering moral line can be drawn. The member will consider the magnitude of the disputed question, both in his own eyes and in the eyes of those whom he represents; its permanent or transitory character, the amount and importance of the majority opposed to his views, the length of time that is likely to elapse before a dissolution will bring him face to face with his constituents. In matters which he does not consider very urgent or important, he will probably sacrifice his own judgment to that of his electors, at least so far as to abstain from voting or from pressing his own views. In graver matters it is his duty boldly to face unpopularity, or perhaps even take the extreme step of resigning his seat.

The cases in which a member of Parliament finds it his duty to support a measure which he believes to be positively bad, on the ground that greater evils would follow its rejection, are happily not very numerous. He can extricate himself from many moral difficulties by sometimes abstaining from voting or from the expression of his real opinions, and most measures are of a composite character in which good and evil elements combine, and may in some degree be separated. In such measures it is often possible to accept the general principle while opposing particular details, and there is considerable scope for compromise and modification. But the cases in which a member of Parliament is compelled to vote for measures about which he has no real knowledge or conviction are very many. Crowds of measures of a highly complex and technical character, affecting departments of life with which he has had no experience, relating to the multitudinous industries, interests and conditions of a great people, are brought before him at very short notice; and no intellect, however powerful, no industry, however great, can master them. It is utterly impossible that mere extemporised knowledge, the listening to a short debate, the brief study which a member of Parliament can give to a new subject, can place him on a real level of competence with those who can bring to it a lifelong knowledge or experience.

A member of Parliament will soon find that he must select a class of subjects which he can himself master, while on many others he must vote blindly with his party. The two or three capital measures in a session are debated with such a fulness that both the House and the country become thoroughly competent to judge them, and in those cases the preponderance of argument will have great weight. A powerful ministry and a strongly organised party may carry such a measure in spite of it, but they will be obliged to accept amendments and modifications, and if they persist in their policy their position both in the House and in the country will sooner or later be inevitably changed. But a large number of measures have a more restricted interest, and are far less widely understood. The House of Commons is rich in expert knowledge, and few subjects are brought before it which some of its members do not thoroughly understand; but in a vast number of cases the majority who decide the question are obliged to do so on the most superficial knowledge. Very often it is physically impossible for a member to obtain the knowledge he requires. The most important and detailed investigation has taken place in a committee upstairs to which he did not belong, or he is detained elsewhere on important parliamentary business while the debate is going on. Even when this is not the case, scarcely any one has the physical or mental power which would enable him to sit intelligently through all the debates. Every member of Parliament is familiar with the scene, when, after a debate, carried on before nearly empty benches, the division bell rings, and the members stream in to decide the issue. There is a moment of uncertainty. The questions 'Which side are we?' 'What is it about?' may be heard again and again. Then the Speaker rises, and with one magical sentence clears the situation. It is the sentence in which he announces that the tellers for the Ayes or Noes, as the case may be, are the Government whips. It is not argument, it is not eloquence, it is this single sentence which in countless cases determines the result and moulds the legislation of the country. Many members, it is true, are not present in the division lobby, but they are usually paired—that is to say, they have taken their sides before the discussion began; perhaps without even knowing what subject is to be discussed, perhaps for all the many foreseen and unforeseen questions that may arise during long periods of the session.

It is a strange process, and to a new member who has been endeavouring through his life to weigh arguments and evidence with scrupulous care, and treat the formation and expression of opinions as a matter of serious duty, it is at first very painful. He finds that he is required again and again to give an effective voice in the great council of the nation, on questions of grave importance, with a levity of conviction upon which he would not act in the most trivial affairs of private life. No doctor would prescribe for the slightest malady; no lawyer would advise in the easiest case; no wise man would act in the simplest transactions of private business, or would even give an opinion to his neighbour at a dinner party without more knowledge of the subject than that on which a member of Parliament is often obliged to vote. But he soon finds that for good or evil this system is absolutely indispensable to the working of the machine. If no one voted except on matters he really understood and cared for, four-fifths of the questions that are determined by the House of Commons would be determined by mere fractions of its members, and in that case parliamentary government under the party system would be impossible. The stable, disciplined majorities without which it can never be efficiently conducted would be at an end. Those who refuse to accept the conditions of parliamentary life should abstain from entering into it.

It is obvious that the one justification of this system is to be found in the belief that parliamentary government, as it is worked in England, is on the whole a good thing, and that this is the indispensable condition of its existence. Probably also with most men it strengthens the disposition to support the Government on matters which they do not understand and in which grave party issues are not involved. They know that these minor questions have at least been carefully examined on their merits by responsible men, and with the assistance of the best available expert knowledge.

This fact goes far to reconcile us to the tendency to give governments an almost complete monopoly in the initiation of legislation which is so evident in modern parliamentary life. Much useful legislation in the past has been due to private and independent members, but the chance of bills introduced by such members ever becoming law is steadily diminishing. This is not due to any recognised constitutional change, but to the constantly increasing pressure of government business on the time of the House, and especially to what is called the twelve o'clock rule, terminating debates at midnight.

It is a rule which is manifestly wise, for it limits on ordinary occasions the hours of parliamentary work to a period within the strength of an average man. Parliamentary government has many dubious aspects, but it never appears worse than in the cases which may still sometimes be seen when a Government thinks fit to force through an important measure by all-night sittings, and when a weary and irritated House which has been sitting since three or four in the afternoon is called upon at a corresponding hour of the early morning to pronounce upon grave and difficult questions of principle, and to deal with the serious interests of large classes. The utter and most natural incapacity of the House at such an hour for sustained argument; its anxiety that each successive amendment should be despatched in five minutes; the readiness with which in that tired, feverish atmosphere, surprises and coalitions may be effected and solutions accepted, to which the House in its normal state would scarcely have listened, must be evident to every observer. Scenes of this kind are among the greatest scandals of Parliament, and the rule which makes them impossible except in the closing weeks of the Session has been one of the greatest improvements in modern parliamentary work. But its drawback is that it has greatly limited the possibility of private member legislation. It is in late and rapid sittings that most measures of this kind passed through their final stages, and since the twelve o'clock rule has been adopted a much smaller number of bills introduced by private members find their way to the statute book.

CHAPTER X

It is obvious from the considerations that have been adduced in the last chapter that the moral limitations and conditions under which an ordinary member of Parliament is compelled to work are far from ideal. An upright man will try conscientiously, under these conditions, to do his best for the cause of honesty and for the benefit of his country, but he cannot essentially alter them, and they present many temptations and tend in many ways to blur the outlines separating good from evil. He will find himself practically pledged to support his party in measures which he has never seen and in policies that are not yet developed; to vote in some cases contrary to his genuine belief and in many cases without real knowledge; to act throughout his political career on many motives other than a reasoned conviction of the substantial merits of the question at issue.

I have dwelt on the difficult questions which arise when the wishes of his constituents are at variance with his own genuine opinions. Another and a wider question is how far he is bound to make what he considers the interests of the nation his guiding light, and how far he should subordinate what he believes to be their interests to their prejudices and wishes. One of the first lessons that every active politician has to learn is that he is a trustee bound to act for men whose opinions, aims, desires and ideals are often very different from his own. No man who holds the position of member of Parliament should divest himself of this consideration, though it applies to different classes of members in different degrees. A private member should not forget it, but at the same time, being elected primarily and specially to represent one particular element in the national life, he will concentrate his attention more exclusively on a narrow circle, though he has at the same time more latitude of expressing unpopular opinions and pushing unripe and unpopular causes than a member who is taking a large and official part in the government of the nation. The opposition front bench occupies a somewhat different position. They are the special and organised representatives of a particular party and its ideas, but the fact that they may be called upon at any time to undertake the government of the nation as a whole, and that even while in opposition they take a great part in moulding its general policy, imposes on them limitations and restrictions from which a mere private member is in a great degree exempt. When a party comes into power its position is again slightly altered. Its leaders are certainly not detached from the party policy they had advocated in opposition. One of the main objects of party is to incorporate certain political opinions and the interests of certain sections of the community in an organised body which will be a steady and permanent force in politics. It is by this means that political opinions are most likely to triumph; that class interests are most effectually protected. But a Government cannot govern merely in the interests of a party. It is a trustee for the whole nation, and one of its first duties is to ascertain and respect as far as possible the wishes as well as the interests of all sections.

Concrete examples may perhaps show more clearly than abstract statements the kind of difficulties that I am describing. Take, for example, the large class of proposals for limiting the sale of strong drink by such methods as local veto or Sunday closing of public-houses. One class of politicians take up the position of uncompromising opponents of the drink trade. They argue that strong drink is beyond all question in England the chief source of the misery, the vice, the degradation of the poor; that it not only directly ruins tens of thousands, body and soul, but also brings a mass of wretchedness that it is difficult to overrate on their innocent families; that the drunkard's craving for drink often reproduces itself as an hereditary disease in his children; and that a legislator can have no higher object and no plainer duty than by all available means to put down the chief obstacle to the moral and material well-being of the people. The principle of compulsion, as they truly say, is more and more pervading all departments of industry. It is idle to contend that the State which, while prohibiting other forms of Sunday trading, gives a special privilege to the most pernicious of all, has not the right to limit or to withdraw it, and the legislature which levies vast sums upon the whole community for the maintenance of the police as well as for poor-houses, prisons and criminal administration, ought surely, in the interests of the whole community, to do all that is in its power to suppress the main cause of pauperism, disorder and crime.

Another class of politicians approach the question from a wholly different point of view. They emphatically object to imposing upon grown-up men a system of moral restriction which is very properly imposed upon children. They contend that adult men who have assumed all the duties and responsibilities of life, and have even a voice in the government of the country, should regulate their own conduct, as far as they do not directly interfere with their neighbours, without legal restraint, bearing themselves the consequences of their mistakes or excesses. This, they say, is the first principle of freedom, the first condition in the formation of strong and manly characters. A poor man, who desires on his Sunday excursion to obtain moderate refreshment such as he likes for himself or his family, and who goes to the public-house—probably in most cases to meet his friends and discuss the village gossip over a glass of beer—is in no degree interfering with the liberty of his neighbours. He is doing nothing that is wrong; nothing that he has not a perfect right to do. No one denies the rich man access to his club on Sunday, and it should be remembered that the poor man has neither the private cellars nor the comfortable and roomy homes of the rich, and has infinitely fewer opportunities of recreation. Because some men abuse this right and are unable to drink alcohol in moderation, are all men to be prevented from drinking it at all, or at least from drinking it on Sunday? Because two men agree not to drink it, have they a right to impose the same obligation on an unwilling third? Have those who never enter a public-house, and by their position in life never need to enter it, a right, if they are in a majority, to close its doors against those who use it? On such grounds these politicians look with extreme disfavour on all this restrictive legislation as unjust, partial and inconsistent with freedom.

Very few, however, would carry either set of arguments to their full logical consequences. Not many men who have had any practical experience in the management of men would advocate a complete suppression of the drink trade, and still fewer would put it on the basis of complete free trade, altogether exempt from special legislative restriction. To responsible politicians the course to be pursued will depend mainly on fluctuating conditions of public opinion. Restrictions will be imposed, but only when and as far as they are supported by a genuine public opinion. It must not be a mere majority, but a large majority; a steady majority; a genuine majority representing a real and earnest desire, and especially in the classes who are most directly affected; not a mere factitious majority such as is often created by skilful organisation and agitation; by the enthusiasm of the few confronting the indifference of the many. In free and democratic States one of the most necessary but also one of the most difficult arts of statesmanship is that of testing public opinion, discriminating between what is real, growing and permanent and what is transient, artificial and declining. As a French writer has said, 'The great art in politics consists not in hearing those who speak, but in hearing those who are silent.' On such questions as those I have mentioned we may find the same statesman without any real inconsistency supporting the same measures in one part of the kingdom and opposing them in another; supporting them at one time because public opinion runs strongly in their favour; opposing them at another because that public opinion has grown weak.

One of the worst moral evils that grow up in democratic countries is the excessive tendency to time-serving and popularity hunting, and the danger is all the greater because in a certain sense both of these things are a necessity and even a duty. Their moral quality depends mainly on their motive. The question to be asked is whether a politician is acting from personal or merely party objects or from honourable public ones. Every statesman must form in his own mind a conception whether a prevailing tendency is favourable or opposed to the real interests of the country. It will depend upon this judgment whether he will endeavour to accelerate or retard it; whether he will yield slowly or readily to its pressure, and there are cases in which, at all hazards of popularity and influence, he should inexorably oppose it. But in the long run, under free governments, political systems and measures must be adjusted to the wishes of the various sections of the people, and this adjustment is the great work of statesmanship. In judging a proposed measure a statesman must continually ask himself whether the country is ripe for it—whether its introduction, however desirable it might be, would not be premature, as public opinion is not yet prepared for it?—whether, even though it be a bad measure, it is not on the whole better to vote for it, as the nation manifestly desires it?

The same kind of reasoning applies to the difficult question of education, and especially of religious education. Every one who is interested in the subject has his own conviction about the kind of education which is in itself the best for the people, and also the best for the Government to undertake. He may prefer that the State should confine itself to purely secular education, leaving all religious teaching to voluntary agencies; or he may approve of the kind of undenominational religious teaching of the English School Board; or he may be a strong partisan of one of the many forms of distinctly accentuated denominational education. But when he comes to act as a responsible legislator, he should feel that the question is not merely what *he* considers the best, but also what the parents of the children most desire. It is true that the authority of parents is not absolutely recognised. The conviction that certain things are essential to the children, and to the well-being and vigour of the State, and the conviction that parents are often by no means the best judges of this, make legislators, on some important subjects, override the wishes of the parents. The severe restrictions imposed on child labour; the measure—unhappily now greatly relaxed—providing for children's vaccination; and the legislation protecting children from ill treatment by their parents, are illustrations, and the most extensive and far-reaching of all exceptions is education. After much misgiving, both parties in the State have arrived at the conclusion that it is essential to the future of the children, and essential also to the maintenance of the relative position of England in the great competition of nations, that at least the rudiments of education should be made universal, and they are also convinced that this is one of the truths which perfectly ignorant parents are least competent to understand. Hence the system which of late years has so rapidly extended of compulsory education.

Many nations have gone further, and have claimed for the State the right of prescribing absolutely the kind of education that should be permitted, or at least the kind of education which shall be exclusively supported by State funds. In England this is not the case. A great variety of forms of education corresponding to the wishes and opinions of different classes of parents receive assistance from the State, subject to the conditions of submitting to certain tests of educational efficiency, and to a conscience clause protecting minorities from interference with their faith.

A case which once caused much moral heart-burning among good men was the endowment, by the State, of Maynooth College, which is absolutely under the control of the Roman Catholic priesthood, and intended to educate their Divinity students in the Roman Catholic faith. The endowment dated from the period of the old Irish Protestant Parliament; and when, on the Disestablishment of the Irish Church, it came to an end, it was replaced by a large capital grant from the Irish Church Fund, and it is upon the interest of that grant that the College is still supported. This grant was denounced by many excellent men on the ground that the State was Protestant; that it had a definite religious belief upon which it was bound in conscience to act; and that it was a sinful apostasy to endow out of the public purse the teaching of what all Protestants believe to be superstition, and what many Protestants believe to be idolatrous and soul-destroying error. The strength of this kind of feeling in England is shown by the extreme difficulty there has been in persuading public opinion to acquiesce in any form of that concurrent endowment of religions which exists so widely and works so well upon the Continent.

Many, again, who have no objection to the policy of assisting by State subsidies the theological education of the priests are of opinion that it is extremely injurious both to the State and to the young that the secular education—and especially the higher secular education—of the Irish Catholic population should be placed under their complete control, and that, through their influence, the Irish Catholics should be strictly separated during the period of their education from their fellow-countrymen of other religions. No belief, in my own opinion, is better founded than this. If, however, those who hold it find that there is a great body of Catholic parents who persistently desire this control and separation; who will not be satisfied with any removal of disabilities and sectarian influence in systems of common education; who object to all mixed and undenominational education on the ground that their priests have condemned it, and that they are bound in conscience to follow the orders of their priests, and who are in consequence withholding from their children the education they would otherwise have given them, such men will in my opinion be quite justified in modifying their policy. As a matter of expediency they will argue that it is better that these Catholics should receive an indifferent university education than none at all; and that it is exceedingly desirable that what is felt to be a grievance by many honest, upright and loyal men should be removed. As a matter of principle, they contend that in a country where higher education is largely and variously endowed from public sources, it is a real grievance that there should be one large body of the people who can derive little or no benefit from those endowments. It is no sufficient answer to say that the objection of the Catholic parents is in most cases not spontaneous, but is due to the orders of their priests, since we are dealing with men who believe it to be a matter of conscience on such questions to obey their priests. Nor is it, I think, sufficient to argue—as very many enlightened men will do—that everything that could be in the smallest degree repugnant to the faith of a Catholic has been eliminated from the education which is imposed on them in existing universities; that every post of honour, emolument and power has been thrown open to them; that for generations they gladly followed the courses of Dublin University, and are even now permitted by their ecclesiastics to follow those of Oxford and Cambridge; that, the nation having adopted the broad principle of unsectarian education open to all, no single sect has a right to exceptional treatment, though every sect has an undoubted right to set up at its own expense such education as it pleases. The answer is that the objection of a certain class of Roman Catholics in Ireland is not to any abuses that may take place under the system of mixed and undenominational education, but to the system itself, and that the particular type of education of which alone one considerable class of taxpayers can conscientiously avail themselves has only been set up by voluntary effort, and is only inadequately and indirectly endowed by the State.[42] Slowly and very reluctantly governments in England have come to recognise the fact that the trend of Catholic opinion in Ireland is as clearly in the direction of denominationalism as the trend of Nonconformist English opinion is in the direction of undenominationalism, and that it is impossible to carry on the education of a priest-ridden Catholic people on the same lines as a Protestant one. Primary education has become almost absolutely

---

[42] This sentence may appear obscure to English readers. The explanation is, that by an ingenious arrangement, devised by Lord Beaconsfield, the professors of the Jesuit College in Stephen's Green are nearly all made Fellows of the Royal University, those of the Arts Faculty receiving 400*l.* a year, and three Medical Fellows 150*l.* each. By this device the Catholic college has in reality a State endowment to the amount of between 6,000*l.* and 7,000*l.* a year. This fact considerably reduces the grievance.

denominational, and, directly or indirectly, a crowd of endowments are given to exclusively Catholic institutions. On such grounds, many who entertain the strongest antipathy to the priestly control of higher education are prepared to advocate an increased endowment of some university or college which is distinctly sacerdotal, while strenuously upholding side by side with it the undenominational institutions which they believe to be incomparably better, and which are at present resorted to not only by all Protestants, but also by a not inconsiderable body of Irish Catholics.

Many of my readers will probably come to an opposite conclusion on this very difficult question. The object of what I have written is simply to show the process by which a politician may conscientiously advocate the establishment and endowment of a thing which he believes to be intrinsically bad. It is said to have been a saying of Sir Robert Inglis—an excellent representative of an old school of extreme but most conscientious Toryism—that 'he would never vote one penny of public money for any purpose which he did not think right and good.' The impossibility of carrying out such a principle must be obvious to any one who has truly grasped the nature of representative government and the duty of a member of Parliament to act as a trustee for all classes in the community. In the exercise of this function every conscientious member is obliged continually to vote money for purposes which he dislikes. In the particular instance I have just given, the process of reasoning I have described is purely disinterested, but of course it is not by such a process of pure reasoning that such a question will be determined. English and Scotch members will have to consider the effects of their vote on their own constituencies, where there are generally large sections of electors with very little knowledge of the special circumstances of Irish education, but very strong feelings about the Roman Catholic Church. Statesmen will have to consider the ulterior and various ways in which their policy may affect the whole social and political condition of Ireland, while the overwhelming majority of the Irish members are elected by small farmers and agricultural labourers who could never avail themselves of University education, and who on all matters relating to education act blindly at the dictation of their priests.

Inconsistency is no necessary condemnation of a politician, and parties as well as individual statesmen have abundantly shown it. It would lead me too far in a book in which the moral difficulties of politics form only one subdivision, to enter into the history of English parties; but those who will do so will easily convince themselves that there is hardly a principle of political action that has not in party history been abandoned, and that not unfrequently parties have come to advocate at one period of their history the very measures which at another period they most strenuously resisted. Changed circumstances, the growth or decline of intellectual tendencies, party strategy, individual influence, have all contributed to these mutations, and most of them have been due to very blended motives of patriotism and self-interest.

In judging the moral quality of the changes of party leaders, the element of time will usually be of capital importance. Violent and sudden reversals of policy are never effected by a party without a great loss of moral weight; though there are circumstances under which they have been imperatively required. No one will now dispute the integrity of the motives that induced the Duke of Wellington and Sir Robert Peel to carry Catholic Emancipation in 1829, when the Clare election had brought Ireland to the verge of revolution; and the conduct of Sir Robert Peel in carrying the repeal of the Corn Laws was certainly not due to any motive either of personal or party ambition, though it may be urged with force that at a time when he was still the leader of the Protectionist party his mind had been manifestly moving in the direction of Free trade, and that the Irish famine, though not a mere pretext, was not wholly the cause of the surrender. In each of these cases a ministry pledged to resist a particular measure introduced and carried it, and did so without any appeal to the electors. The justification was that the measure in their eyes had become absolutely necessary to the public welfare, and that the condition of politics made it impossible for them either to carry it by a dissolution or to resign the task into other hands. Had Sir Robert Peel either resigned office or dissolved Parliament after the Clare election in 1828, it is highly probable that the measure of Catholic Emancipation could not have been carried, and its postponement, in his belief, would have thrown Ireland into a dangerous rebellion. Few greater misfortunes have befallen party government than the failure of the Whigs to form a ministry in 1845. Had they done so the abolition of the Corn Laws would have been carried by statesmen who were in some measure supported by the Free-trade party, and not by statesmen who had obtained their power as the special representatives of the agricultural interests.

Another case which in a party point of view was more successful, but which should in my opinion be much more severely judged, was the Reform Bill of 1867. The Conservative party, under the guidance of Mr. Disraeli, defeated Mr. Gladstone's Reform Bill mainly on the ground that it was an excessive step in the direction of Democracy. The victory placed them in office, and they then declared that, as the question had been raised, they must deal with it themselves. They introduced a bill carrying the suffrage to a much lower point than that which the late Government had proposed, but they surrounded it with a number of provisions securing additional representation for particular classes and interests which would have materially modified its democratic character.

But for these safeguarding provisions the party would certainly not have tolerated the introduction of such a measure, yet in the face of opposition their leader dropped them one by one as of no capital importance, and, by a leadership which was a masterpiece of unscrupulous adroitness, succeeded in inducing his party to carry a measure far more democratic than that which they had a few months before denounced and defeated. It was argued that the question must be settled; that it must be placed on a permanent and lasting basis; that it must no longer be suffered to be a weapon in the hands of the Whigs, and that the Tory Reform Bill, though it was acknowledged to be a 'leap in the dark,' had at least the result of 'dishing the Whigs.' There is little doubt that it was in accordance with the genuine convictions of Disraeli. He belonged to a school of politics of which Bolingbroke, Carteret and Shelburne, and, in some periods of his career, Chatham, were earlier representatives who had no real sympathy with the preponderance of the aristocratic element in the old Tory party, who had a decided disposition to appeal frankly to democratic support, and who believed that a strong executive resting on a broad democratic basis was the true future of Toryism. He anticipated to a remarkable degree the school of political thought which has triumphed in our own day, though he did not live to witness its triumph. At the same time it cannot be denied that the Reform Bill of 1867 in the form in which it was ultimately carried was as far as possible from the wishes and policy of his party in the beginning of the session, and as inconsistent as any policy could be with their language and conduct in the session that preceded it.

A parliamentary government chosen on the party system is, as we have seen, at once the trustee of the whole nation, bound as such to make the welfare of the whole its supreme end, and also the special representative of particular classes, the special guardian of their interests, aims, wishes, and principles. The two points of view are not the same, and grave difficulties, both ethical and political, have often to be encountered in endeavouring to harmonise them. It is, of course, not true that a party object is merely a matter of place or power, and naturally a different thing from a patriotic object. The very meaning of party is that public men consider certain principles of government, certain lines of policy, the protection and development of particular interests, of capital importance to the nation, and they are therefore on purely public grounds fully justified in making it a main object to place the government of the country in the hands of their party. The importance, however, of maintaining a particular party in power varies greatly. In many, probably in most, periods of English history a change of government means no violent or far-reaching alteration in policy. It means only that one set of tendencies in legislation will for a time be somewhat relaxed, and another set somewhat intensified; that the interests of one class will be somewhat more and those of another class somewhat less attended to; that the rate of progress or change will be slightly accelerated or retarded. Sometimes it means even less than this. Opinions on the two front benches are so nearly assimilated that a change of government principally means the removal for a time from office of ministers who have made some isolated administrative blunders or incurred some individual unpopularity quite apart from their party politics. It means that ministers who are jaded and somewhat worn out by several years' continuous work, and of whom the country had grown tired, are replaced by men who can bring fresher minds and energies to the task; that patronage in all its branches having for some years gone mainly to one party, the other party are now to have their turn. There are periods when the country is well satisfied with the general policy of a government but not with the men who carry it on. Ministers of excellent principles prove inefficient, tactless, or unfortunate, or quarrels and jealousies arise among them, or difficult negotiations are going on with foreign nations which can be best brought to a successful termination if they are placed in the hands of fresh men, unpledged and unentangled by their past. The country wants a change of government but not a change of policy, and under such circumstances the task of a victorious opposition is much less to march in new directions than to mark time, to carry on the affairs of the nation on the same lines, but with greater administrative skill. In such periods the importance of party objects is much diminished and a policy which is intended merely to keep a party in power should be severely condemned.

Sometimes, however, it happens that a party has committed itself to a particular measure which its opponents believe to be in a high degree dangerous or even ruinous to the country. In that case it becomes a matter of supreme importance to keep this party out of office, or, if they are in office, to keep them in a position of permanent debility till this dangerous project is abandoned. Under such circumstances statesmen are justified in carrying party objects and purely party legislation much further than in other periods. To strengthen their own party; to gain for it the largest amount of popularity; to win the support of different factions of the House of Commons, become a great public object; and, in order to carry it out, sacrifices of policy and in some degree of principle, the acceptance of measures which the party had once opposed, and the adjournment or abandonment of measures to which it had been pledged, which would once have been very properly condemned, become justifiable. The supreme interest of the State is the end and the justification of their policy, and alliances are formed which under less pressing circumstances would have been impossible, and which, once established, sometimes profoundly change the permanent character of party politics. Here, as in nearly all political matters, an attention to proportion and degree, the sacrifice of the less for the attainment of the greater, mark the path both of wisdom and of duty.

The temptations of party politicians are of many kinds and vary greatly with different stages of political development. The worst is the temptation to war. War undertaken without necessity, or at least without serious justification, is, according to all sound ethics, the gravest of crimes, and among its causes motives of the kind I have indicated may be often detected. Many wars have been begun or have been prolonged in order to consolidate a dynasty or a party; in order to give it popularity or at least to save it from unpopularity; in order to divert the minds of men from internal questions which had become dangerous or embarrassing, or to efface the memory of past quarrels, mistakes or crimes.[43] Experience unfortunately shows only too clearly how easily the combative passions of nations can be aroused and how much popularity may be gained by a successful war. Even in this case, it is true, war usually impoverishes the country that wages it, but there are large classes to whom it is by no means a calamity. The high level of agricultural prices; the brilliant careers opened to the military and naval professions; the many special industries which are immediately

---

[43] See e.g. the death-bed counsels of Henry IV. to his son:—

       'Therefore, my Harry,

  Be it thy course to busy giddy minds

  With foreign quarrels; that action, hence borne out,

  May waste the memory of the former days.'

    Henry IV. Part II. Act IV. Sc. 4.

stimulated; the rise in the rate of interest; the opportunities of wealth that spring from violent fluctuations on the Stock Exchange; even the increased attractiveness of the newspapers,—all tend to give particular classes an interest in its continuance. Sometimes it is closely connected with party sympathies. During the French wars of Anne, the facts that Marlborough was a Whig, and that the Elector of Hanover, who was the hope of the Whig party, was in favour of the war, contributed very materially to retard the peace. A state of great internal disquietude is often a temptation to war, not because it leads to it directly, but because rulers find a foreign war the best means of turning dangerous and disturbing energies into new channels, and at the same time of strengthening the military and authoritative elements in the community. The successful transformation of the anarchy of the great French Revolution into a career of conquest is a typical example.

In aristocratic governments such as existed in England during the eighteenth century, temptations to corruption were especially strong. To build up a vast system of parliamentary influence by rotten boroughs, and, by systematically bestowing honours on those who could control them, to win the support of great corporations and professions by furthering their interests and abstaining from all efforts to reform them, was a chief part of the statecraft of the time. Class privileges in many forms were created, extended and maintained, and in some countries—though much less in England than on the Continent—the burden of taxation was most inequitably distributed, falling mainly on the poor.

In democratic governments the temptations are of a different kind. Popularity is there the chief source of power, and the supreme tribunal consists of numbers counted by the head. The well-being of the great mass of the people is the true end of politics, but it does not necessarily follow that the opinion of the least instructed majority is the best guide to obtaining it. In dwelling upon the temptations of politicians under such a system I do not now refer merely to the unscrupulous agitator or demagogue who seeks power, notoriety or popularity by exciting class envies and animosities, by setting the poor against the rich and preaching the gospel of public plunder; nor would I dilate upon the methods so largely employed in the United States of accumulating, by skilfully devised electoral machinery, great masses of voting power drawn from the most ignorant voters, and making use of them for purposes of corruption. I would dwell rather on the bias which almost inevitably obliges the party leader to measure legislation mainly by its immediate popularity, and its consequent success in adding to his voting strength. In some countries this tendency shows itself in lavish expenditure on public works which provide employment for great masses of workmen and give a great immediate popularity in a constituency, leaving to posterity a heavy burden of accumulated debt. Much of the financial embarrassment of Europe is due to this source, and in most countries extravagance in government expenditure is more popular than economy. Sometimes it shows itself in a legislation which regards only proximate or immediate effects, and wholly neglects those which are distant and obscure. A far-sighted policy sacrificing the present to a distant future becomes more difficult; measures involving new principles, but meeting present embarrassments or securing immediate popularity, are started with little consideration for the precedents they are establishing and for the more extensive changes that may follow in their train. The conditions of labour are altered for the benefit of the existing workmen, perhaps at the cost of diverting capital from some great form of industry, making it impossible to resist foreign competition, and thus in the long run restricting employment and seriously injuring the very class who were to have been benefited.

When one party has introduced a measure of this kind the other is under the strongest temptation to outbid it, and under the stress of competition and through the fear of being distanced in the race of popularity both parties often end by going much further than either had originally intended. When the rights of the few are opposed to the interests of the many there is a constant tendency to prefer the latter. It may be that the few are those who have built up an industry; who have borne all the risk and cost, who have by far the largest interest in its success. The mere fact that they are the few determines the bias of the legislators. There is a constant disposition to tamper with even clearly defined and guaranteed rights if by doing so some large class of voters can be conciliated.

Parliamentary life has many merits, but it has a manifest tendency to encourage short views. The immediate party interest becomes so absorbing that men find it difficult to look greatly beyond it. The desire of a skilful debater to use the topics that will most influence the audience before him, or the desire of a party leader to pursue the course most likely to be successful in an immediately impending contest, will often override all other considerations, and the whole tendency of parliamentary life is to concentrate attention on landmarks which are not very distant, thinking little of what is beyond.

One great cause of the inconsistency of parties lies in the absolute necessity of assimilating legislation. Many, for example, are of opinion that the existing tendency to introduce government regulations and interferences into all departments is at least greatly exaggerated, and that it would be far better if a larger sphere were left to individual action and free contract. But if large departments of industry have been brought under the system of regulation, it is practically impossible to leave analogous industries under a different system, and the men who most dislike the tendency are often themselves obliged to extend it. They cannot resist the contention that certain legislative protections or other special favours have been granted to one class of workmen, and that there is no real ground for distinguishing their case from that of others. The dominant tendency will thus naturally extend itself, and every considerable legislative movement carries others irresistibly in its train.

The pressure of this consideration is most painfully felt in the case of legislation which appears not simply inexpedient and unwise, but distinctly dishonest. In legislation relating to contracts there is a clear ethical distinction to be drawn. It is fully within the moral right of legislators to regulate the conditions of future contracts. It is a very different thing to break existing contracts, or to take the still more extreme step of altering their conditions to the benefit of one party without the assent of the other, leaving that other party bound by their restrictions.

In the American Constitution there is a special clause making it impossible for any State to pass any law violating contracts. In England, unfortunately, no such provision exists. The most glaring and undoubted instance of this kind is to be found in the Irish land legislation which was begun by the Ministry of Mr. Gladstone, but which has been largely extended by the party that originally most strenuously opposed it. Much may no doubt be said to palliate it: agricultural depression; the excessive demand for land; the fact that improvements were in Ireland usually made by the tenants (who, however, were perfectly aware of the conditions under which they made them, and whose rents were proportionately lower); the prevalence in some parts of Ireland of land customs unsanctioned by law; the existence of a great revolutionary movement which had brought the country into a condition of disgraceful anarchy. But when all this has been admitted, it remains indisputable to every clear and honest mind that English law has taken away without compensation unquestionably legal property and broken unquestionably legal contracts. A landlord placed a tenant on his farm on a yearly tenancy, but if he desired to exercise his plain legal right of resuming it at the termination of the year, he was compelled to pay a compensation 'for disturbance,' which might amount to seven times the yearly rent. A landlord let his land to a farmer for a longer period under a clear written contract bearing the government stamp, and this contract defined the rent to be paid, the conditions under which the farm was to be held, and the number of years during which it was to be alienated from its owner. The fundamental clause of the lease distinctly stipulated that at the end of the assigned term the tenant must hand back that farm to the owner from whom he received it. The law has interposed, and determined that the rent which this farmer had undertaken to pay shall be reduced by a government tribunal without the assent of the owner, and without giving the owner the option of dissolving the contract and seeking a new tenant. It has gone further, and provided that at the termination of the lease the tenant shall not hand back the land to the owner according to the terms of his contract, but shall remain for all future time the occupier, subject only to a rent fixed and periodically revised, irrespective of the wishes of the landlord, by an independent tribunal. Vast masses of property in Ireland had been sold under the Incumbered Estates Act by a government tribunal acting as the representative of the Imperial Parliament, and each purchaser obtained from this tribunal a parliamentary title making him absolute owner of the soil and of every building upon it, subject only to the existing tenancies in the schedule. No accounts of the earlier history of the property were handed to him, for except under the terms of the leases which had not yet expired he had no liability for anything in the past. The title he received was deemed so indefeasible that in one memorable case, where by mistake a portion of the property of one man had been included in the sale of the property of another man, the Court of Appeal decided that the injustice could not be remedied, as it was impossible, except in the case of intentional fraud, to go behind parliamentary titles.[44] In cases in which the land was let at low rents, and in cases where tenants held under leases which would soon expire, the facility of raising the rents was constantly specified by the authority of the Court as an inducement to purchasers.

What has become of this parliamentary title? Improvements, if they had been made, or were presumed to have been made by tenants anterior to the sale, have ceased to be the property of the purchaser, and he has at the same time been deprived of some of the plainest and most inseparable rights of property. He has lost the power of disposing of his farms in the open market, of regulating the terms and conditions on which he lets them, of removing a tenant whom he considers unsuitable, of taking the land back into his own hands when the specified term of a tenancy had expired, of availing himself of the enhanced value which a war or a period of great prosperity, or some other exceptional circumstance, may have given to his property. He has become a simple rent-charger on the land which by inheritance or purchase was incontestably his own, and the amount of his rent-charge is settled and periodically revised by a tribunal in which he has no voice, and which has been given an absolute power over his estate. He bought or inherited an exclusive right. The law has turned it into a dual ownership. A tenant right which, when he obtained his property, was wholly unknown to the law, and was only generally recognised by custom in one province, has been carved out of it. The tenant who happened to be in occupation when the law was passed can, without the consent of the owner, sell to another the right of occupying the farm at the existing rent. In numerous cases this tenant right is more valuable than the fee simple of the farm. In many cases a farmer who had eagerly begged to be a tenant at a specified rent has afterwards gone into the land court and had that rent reduced, and has then proceeded to sell the tenant right for a sum much more than equivalent to the difference between the two rents. In many cases this has happened where there could be no possible question of improvements by the tenant. The tenant right of the smaller farms has steadily risen in proportion as the rent has been reduced. In many cases, no doubt, the excessive price of tenant right may be attributed to the land hunger or passion for land speculation so common in Ireland, or to some exceptional cause inducing a farmer to give an extravagant price for the tenant right of a particular farm. But although in such instances the price of tenant right is a deceptive test, the movement, when it is a general one, is a clear proof that the reduction of rent did not represent an equivalent decline in the marketable value of the land, but was simply a gratuitous transfer, by the State, of property from one person to another. Having in the first place turned the exclusive ownership of the landlord into a simple partnership, the tribunal proceeded, in defiance of all equity, to throw the whole burden of the agricultural depression on one of the two partners. The law did, it is true, reserve to the landlord the right of pre-emption, or in other words the right of purchasing the tenant right when it was for sale, at a price to be

---

[44] Lord Lanesborough *v.* Reilly.

determined by the Court, and thus becoming once more the absolute owner of his farm. The sum specified by the Court was usually about sixteen years' purchase of the judicial rent. By the payment of this large sum he may regain the property which a few years ago was incontestably his own, which was held by him under the most secure title known to English law, and which was taken from him, not by any process of honest purchase, but by an act of simple legislative confiscation.

Whatever palliations of expediency may be alleged, the true nature of this legislation cannot reasonably be questioned, and it has established a precedent which is certain to grow. The point, however, on which I would especially dwell is that the very party which most strongly opposed it, and which most clearly exposed its gross and essential dishonesty, have found themselves, or believed themselves to be, bound not only to accept it but to extend it. They have contended that, as a matter of practical politics, it is impossible to grant such privileges to one class of agricultural tenants and to withhold it from others. The chief pretext for this legislation in its first stages was that it was for the benefit of very poor tenants who were incapable of making their own bargains, and that the fixity of tenure which the law gave to yearly tenants as long as they paid their rents had been very generally voluntarily given them by good landlords. But the measure was soon extended by a Unionist government to the leaseholders, who are the largest and most independent class of farmers, and who held their land for a definite time and under a distinct written contract. It is in truth much more the shrewder and wealthier farmers than the poor and helpless ones that this legislation has chiefly benefited.

Instances of this kind, in which strong expediency or an absolute political necessity is in apparent conflict with elementary principles of right and wrong, are among the most difficult with which a politician has to deal. He must govern the country and preserve it in a condition of tolerable order, and he sometimes persuades himself that without a capitulation to anarchy, without attacks on property and violations of contract, this is impossible. Whether the necessity is as absolute or the expediency as rightly calculated as he supposed, may indeed be open to much question, but there can be no doubt that most of the English statesmen who carried the Irish agrarian legislation sincerely believed it, and some of them imagined that they were giving a security and finality to the property which was left, that would indemnify the plundered landlords. Perhaps, under such circumstances, the most that can be said is that wise legislators will endeavour, by encouraging purchase on a large scale, gradually to restore the absolute ownership and the validity of contract which have been destroyed, and at the same time to compensate indirectly—if they cannot do it directly—the former owners for that portion of their losses which is not due to merely economical causes, but to acts of the legislature that were plainly fraudulent.

There are other temptations of a different kind with which party leaders have to deal. One of the most serious is the tendency to force questions for which there is no genuine desire, in order to restore the unity or the zeal of a divided or dispirited party. As all politicians know, the desire for an attractive programme and a popular election cry is one of the strongest in politics, and, as they also know well, there is such a thing as manufactured public opinion and artificially stimulated agitation. Questions are raised and pushed, not because they are for the advantage of the country, but simply for the purposes of party. The leaders have often little or no power of resistance. The pressure of their followers, or of a section of their followers, becomes irresistible; ill-considered hopes are held out; rash pledges are extorted, and the party as a whole is committed. Much premature and mischievous legislation may be traced to such causes.

Another very difficult question is the manner in which governments should deal with the acts of public servants which are intended for the public service, but which in some of their parts are morally indefensible. Very few of the great acquisitions of nations have been made by means that were absolutely blameless, and in a great empire which has to deal with uncivilised or semi-civilised populations acts of violence are certain to be not infrequent. Neither in our judgments of history nor in our judgments of contemporaries is it possible to apply the full stringency of private morals to the cases of men acting in posts of great responsibility and danger amid the storms of revolution, or panic, or civil war. With the vast interests confided to their care, and the terrible dangers that surround them, measures must often be taken which cannot be wholly or at least legally justified. On the other hand, men in such circumstances are only too ready to accept the principle of Macchiavelli and of Napoleon, and to treat politics as if they had absolutely no connection with morals.

Cases of this kind must be considered separately and with a careful examination of the motives of the actor and of the magnitude of the dangers he had to encounter. Allowances must be made for the moral atmosphere in which he moved, and his career must be considered as a whole, and not only in its peccant parts. In the trial of Warren Hastings, and in the judgments which historians have passed on the lives of the other great adventurers who have built up the Empire, questions of this kind continually arise.

In our own day also they have been very frequent. The Coup d'état of the 2nd of December, 1851, is an extreme example. Louis Napoleon had sworn to observe and to defend the Constitution of the French Republic, which had been established in 1848, and that Constitution, among other articles, pronounced the persons of the representatives of the people to be inviolable; declared every act of the President which dissolved the Assembly or prorogued it, or in any way trammelled it in the exercise of its functions, to be high treason, and guaranteed the fullest liberty of writing and discussion. 'The oath which I have just taken,' said the President, addressing the Assembly, 'commands my future conduct. My duty is clear; I will fulfil it as a man of honour. I shall regard as enemies of the country all those who endeavour to change by illegal means what all France has established.' In more than one subsequent speech he reiterated the same sentiments and endeavoured to persuade the country that under no possible circumstances would he break his oath or violate his conscience, or overstep the limits of his constitutional powers.

What he did is well known. Before daybreak on December 2, some of the most eminent statesmen in France, including eighteen members of the Chamber, were, by his orders, arrested in their beds and sent to prison, and many of them afterwards to exile. The Chamber was occupied by soldiers, and its members, who assembled in another place, were marched to prison. The High Court of Justice was dissolved by force. Martial law was proclaimed. Orders were given that all who resisted the usurpation in the streets were at once, and without trial, to be shot. All liberty of the press, all liberty of public meeting or discussion, were absolutely destroyed. About one hundred newspapers were suppressed and great numbers of their editors transported to Cayenne. Nothing was allowed to be published without Government authority. In order to deceive the people as to the amount of support behind the President, a 'Consultative Commission' was announced and the names were placarded in Paris. Fully half the persons whose names were placed on this list refused to serve, but in spite of their protests their names were kept there in order that they might appear to have approved of what was done.45 Orders were issued immediately after the Coup d'état that every public functionary who did not instantly give in writing his adhesion to the new Government should be dismissed. The Préfets were given the right to arrest in their departments whoever they pleased. By an ex post facto decree, issued on December 8, the Executive were enabled without trial to send to Cayenne, or to the penal settlements in Africa, any persons who had in any past time belonged to a 'secret society,' and this order placed all the numerous members of political clubs at the mercy of the Government. Parliament, when it was suffered to reassemble, was so organised and shackled that every vestige of free discussion for many years disappeared, and a despotism of almost Asiatic severity was established in France.

It may be fully conceded that the tragedy of December 4, when for more than a quarter of an hour some 3,000 French soldiers deliberately fired volley after volley without return upon the unoffending spectators on the Boulevards, broke into the houses and killed multitudes, not only of men but of women and children, till the Boulevards, in the words of an English eye-witness, were 'at some points a perfect shambles,' and the blood lay in pools round the trees that fringed them, was not ordered by the President, though it remained absolutely unpunished and uncensured by him. There is conflicting evidence on this point, but it is probable that some stray shots had been fired from the houses, and it is certain that a wild and sanguinary panic had fallen upon the soldiers. It is possible too, and not improbable, that the stories so generally believed in Paris that large batches of prisoners, who had been arrested, were brought out of prison in the dead hours of the night and deliberately shot by bodies of soldiers, may have been exaggerated or untrue. Maupas, who was Préfet of Police, and who must have known the truth, positively denied it; but the question what credence should be attached to a man of his antecedents who boasted that he had been from the first a leading agent in the whole conspiracy may be reasonably asked.[46] Evidence of these things, as has been truly said, could scarcely be

---

[45] See Tocqueville's *Memoirs* (English trans.), ii. 189, Letter to the *Times*.

[46] See Maupas, *Mémoires sur le Second Empire*, i. 511, 512. It is said that, contrary to the orders of St.-Arnaud, the soldiers, instead of immediately shooting all persons in the street who were found with arms or constructing or

obtained, for the press was absolutely gagged and all possibility of investigation was prevented. For the number of those who were transported or forcibly expelled within the few weeks after December 2, we may perhaps rely upon the historian and panegyrist of the Empire. He computes them at the enormous number of 26,500.[47] After the Plébiscite new measures of proscription were taken, and, according to Émile Ollivier, one of the most enthusiastic and skilful eulogists of the Coup d'état, in the first months of 1852 there were from 15,000 to 20,000 political prisoners in the French prisons.[48] It was by such means that Louis Napoleon attained the empire which had been the dream of his life.

Like many, however, of the great crimes of history, this was not without its palliations, and a more detailed investigation will show that those palliations were not inconsiderable. Napoleon had been elected to the presidency by 5,434,226 votes out of 7,317,344 which were given, and with his name, his antecedents, and his well-known aspirations, this overwhelming majority clearly showed what were the real wishes of the people. His power rested on universal suffrage; it was independent of the Chamber. It gave him the direction of the army, though he could not command it in person, and from the very beginning he assumed an independent and almost regal position. In the first review that took place after his election he was greeted by the soldiers with cries of 'Vive Napoléon! Vive l'Empereur!' It was soon proved that the Constitution of 1848 was exceedingly unworkable. In the words of Lord Palmerston: 'There were two great powers, each deriving its existence from the same source, almost sure to disagree, but with no umpire to decide between them, and neither able by any legal means to get rid of the other.' The President could not dissolve the Chamber, but he could impose upon it any ministry he chose. He was himself elected for only four years, and he could not be re-elected, while by a most fatuous provision the powers of the President and the Chamber were to expire in 1852 at the same time, leaving France without a government and exposed to the gravest danger of anarchy.

The Legislative Assembly, which was elected in May, 1849, was, it is true, far from being a revolutionary one. It contained a minority of desperate Socialists, it was broken into many factions, and like most democratic French Chambers it showed much weakness and inconsistency; but the vast majority of its members were Conservatives who had no kind of sympathy with revolution, and its conduct towards the President, if fairly judged, was on the whole very moderate. He soon treated it with contempt, and it was quite evident that there was no national enthusiasm behind it. The Socialist party was growing rapidly in the great towns; in June, 1849, there was an abortive Socialist insurrection in Paris, and a somewhat more formidable one at Lyons. They were easily put down, but the Socialists captured a great part of the

---

defending a barricade, made many prisoners, and it is not clear what became of them. Granier de Cassagnac, however, altogether denies the executions on the Champ de Mars (ii. 433).

[47] Granier de Cassagnac, ii. 438.

[48] *L'Empire Libéral*, ii. 526.

representation of Paris, and they succeeded in producing a wild panic throughout the country. It led to several reactionary measures, the most important being a law which by imposing new conditions of residence very considerably limited the suffrage. This law was presented to the Chamber by the Ministers of the President and with his assent, though he subsequently demanded the reestablishment of universal suffrage, and made a decree effecting this one of the chief justifications of his *Coup d'état.* The restrictive law was carried through the Chamber on May 31, 1850, by an immense majority, but it was denounced with great eloquence by some of its leading members, and it added seriously to the unpopularity of the Assembly, and greatly lowered its authority in contending with a President whose authority rested on direct universal suffrage. More than once he exercised his power of dismissing and appointing ministries absolutely irrespective of its votes and wishes, and in each case in order to fill all posts of power with creatures of his own. The newspapers supporting him continually inveighed against the Chamber, and dwelt upon the danger of anarchy to which France would be exposed in 1852 and upon the absolute necessity of 'a Saviour of Society.' In repeated journeys through France, and in more than one military review, the President gave the occasion of demonstrations in which the cries of 'Vive l'Empereur!' were often heard, and which were manifestly intended to strengthen him in his conflict with the Chamber.

The man from whom he had most to fear was Changarnier, who since the close of 1848 had been commander of the troops in Paris, and whose name, though far less popular than that of Napoleon, had much weight with the army. He was a man with strong leanings to authority, and was much courted by the monarchical parties, but was for some time in decided sympathy with Napoleon, from whom, however, in spite of large offers that had been made him, he gradually diverged. He issued peremptory orders to the troops under his command, forbidding all party cries at reviews. He declared in the Chamber that these cries had been 'not only encouraged but provoked,' and when the intention of the President to prolong his presidency became apparent, he assured Odilon Barrot that he was prepared, if ordered by the minister and authorised by the President of the Chamber, to anticipate the Coup d'état by seizing and imprisoning Louis Napoleon.[49] The President succeeded in removing him from his command, and in placing a creature of his own at the head of the Paris troops; but though Changarnier acquiesced without resistance in his dismissal, he remained an important member of the Assembly; he openly declared that his sword was at its service, and if an armed conflict broke out it was tolerably certain that he would be its representative. The President had an official salary of 48,000 *l.*—nearly five times as much as the President of the United States. The Chamber refused to increase it, though they consented by a very small majority, and at the request of Changarnier, to pay his debts.

---

[49] *Mémoires d'Odilon Barrot*, iv. 59-61

The demand for a revision of the Constitution, making it possible for the President to be re-elected, was rising rapidly through the country, and there can be but little doubt that this was generally looked forward to as the only peaceful solution, and that it represented the real wish of the great majority of the people. Petitions in favour of it, bearing an enormous number of signatures, were presented to the Chamber, and the overwhelming majority of the Conseils Généraux of which the Deputies generally formed part voted for revision. The President did not so much petition for it as demand it. In a message he sent to the Chamber, he declared that if they did not vote Revision the people would, in 1852, solemnly manifest their wishes. In a speech at Dijon, June 1, 1851, he declared that France from end to end demanded it; that he would follow the wishes of the nation, and that France would not perish in his hands. In the same speech he accused the Chamber of never seconding his wishes to ameliorate the lot of the people. He at the same time lost no opportunity of showing that his special sympathy and trust lay with the army, and he singled out with marked favour the colonels of the regiments which had shown themselves at the reviews most prominent in demonstrations in his favour.[50] The meaning of all this was hardly doubtful. Changarnier took up the gauntlet, and at a time when the question of Revision was before the Chamber he declared that no soldier would ever be induced to move against the law and the Assembly, and he called upon the Deputies to deliberate in peace.

The Revision was voted in the Chamber by 446 votes to 278, but a majority of three-fourths was required for a constitutional change, and this majority was not obtained, and in the disintegrated condition of French parties it seemed scarcely likely to be obtained. The Chamber was soon after prorogued for about two months, leaving the situation unchanged, and the tension and panic were extreme. Out of eighty-five Conseils Généraux in France, eighty passed votes in favour of Revision, three abstained, two only opposed.

The President had now fully resolved upon a Coup d'état, and before the Chamber reassembled a new ministry was constituted, St.-Arnaud being at the head of the army, and Maupas at the head of the police. His first step was to summon the Chamber to repeal the law of May 31 which abolished universal suffrage. The Chamber, after much hesitation, refused, but only by two votes. The belief that the question could only be solved by force was becoming universal, and the bolder spirits in the Chamber clearly saw that if no new measure was taken they were likely to be helpless before the military party. By a decree of 1848 the President of the Chamber had a right, if necessary, to call for troops for its protection independently of the Minister of War, and a motion was now made that he should be able to select a general to whom he might delegate this power. Such a measure, dividing the military command and enabling the Chamber to have its own general and its own army, might have proved very efficacious, but it would probably have involved France in civil war,

---

[50] Mémoires d'Odilon Barrot, iv. 56, 57.

and the President was resolved that, if the Chamber voted it, the Coup d'état should immediately take place. The vote was taken on November 17, 1851. St.-Arnaud, as Minister of War, opposed the measure on constitutional grounds, dilating on the danger of a divided military command, but during the discussion Maupas and Magnan were in the gallery of the Chamber, waiting to give orders to St.-Arnaud to call out the troops and to surround and dissolve the Chamber if the proposition was carried.

It was, however, rejected by a majority of 108, and a few troubled days of conspiracy and panic still remained before the blow was struck. The state of the public securities and the testimony of the best judges of all parties showed the genuineness of the alarm. It was not true, as the President stated in the proclamation issued when the Coup d'état was accomplished, that the Chamber had become a mere nest of conspiracies, and there was a strange audacity in his assertion that he made the Coup d'état for the purpose of maintaining the Republic against monarchical plots; but it was quite true that the conviction was general that force had become inevitable; that the chief doubt was whether the first blow would be struck by Napoleon or Changarnier, and that while the evident desire of the majority of the people was to re-elect Napoleon, there was a design among some members of the Chamber to seize him by force and to elect in his place some member of the House of Orleans.[51] On December 2 the curtain fell, and Napoleon accompanied his Coup d'état by a decree dissolving the Chamber, restoring by his own authority universal suffrage, abolishing the law of May 31, establishing a state of siege, and calling on the French people to judge his action by their vote.

It was certainly not an appeal upon which great confidence could be placed. Immediately after the Coup d'état, the army, which was wholly on his side, voted separately and openly in order that France might clearly know that the armed forces were with the President and might be able to predict the consequences of a verdict unfavourable to his pretensions. When, nearly three weeks later, the civilian Plébiscite took place, martial law was in force. Public meetings of every kind were forbidden. No newspaper hostile to the new authority was permitted. No electioneering paper or placard could be circulated which had not been sanctioned by Government officials. The terrible decree that all who had ever belonged to a secret society might be sent to die in the fevers of Africa was interpreted in the widest sense, and every political society or organisation was included in it. All the functionaries of a highly centralised country were turned into ardent electioneering agents, and the question was so put that the voters had no alternative except for or against the President, a negative vote leaving the country with no government and an almost certain prospect of anarchy

---

[51] See Lord Palmerston's statements on this subject in Ashley's Life of Palmerston, ii. 200-211. Tocqueville, however, utterly denies that the majority of the Assembly had any sympathy with these views (Tocqueville's Memoirs (Eng. trans.), ii. 177). Maupas, in his Mémoires, gives a very detailed account of the conspiracy on the Bonapartist side. It appears that the 'homme de confiance' of Changarnier was in his pay.

and civil war. Under these circumstances 7,500,000 votes were given for the President and 500,000 against him.

But after all deductions have been made there can be no real doubt that the majority of Frenchmen acquiesced in the new régime. The terror of Socialism was abroad, and it brought with it an ardent desire for strong government. The probabilities of a period of sanguinary anarchy were so great that multitudes were glad to be secured from it at almost any cost. Parliamentarism was profoundly discredited. The peasant proprietary had never cared for it, and the bourgeois class, among whom it had once been popular, were now thoroughly scared. Nothing in the contemporary accounts of the period is more striking than the indifference, the almost amused cynicism, or the sense of relief with which the great mass of Frenchmen seem to have witnessed the destruction of their Constitution and the gross insults inflicted upon a Chamber which included so many of the most illustrious of their countrymen.

We can hardly have a better authority on this point than Tocqueville. No one felt more profoundly or more bitterly the iniquity of what had been done; but he was under no illusion about the sentiments of the people. The Constitution, he says, was thoroughly unpopular. 'Louis Napoleon had the merit or the luck to discover what few suspected—the latent Bonapartism of the nation.... The memory of the Emperor, vague and undefined, but therefore the more imposing, still dwelt like an heroic legend in the imaginations of the people.' All the educated, in the opinion of Tocqueville, condemned and repudiated the Coup d'état. 'Thirty-seven years of liberty have made a free press and free parliamentary discussion necessary to us.' But the bulk of the nation was not with them. The new Government, he predicted, 'will last until it is unpopular with the mass of the people. At present the disapprobation is confined to the educated classes.' 'The reaction against democracy and even against liberty is irresistible.'[52]

There is no doubt some exaggeration on both sides of this statement. The appalling magnitude of the deportations and imprisonments by the new Government seems to show that the hatred went deeper than Tocqueville supposed, and on the other hand it can hardly be said that the educated classes wholly repudiated what had been done when we remember that the French Funds at once rose from 91 to 102, that nearly all branches of French commerce made a similar spring,[53] that some twenty generals were actively engaged in the conspiracy, and that the great body of the priests were delighted at its success. The truth seems to be that the property of France saw in the success of the Coup d'état an escape from a great danger, while two powerful professions, the army and the Church, were strongly in favour of the President. Over the army the name of Napoleon exercised a magical influence, and the expedition to Rome and the probability that the new government would be under clerical guidance were, in the eyes of the Church party, quite sufficient to justify what had been done.

---

[52] Tocqueville's *Memoirs*, ii.

[53] Ashley's *Life of Palmerston*, ii. 208.

Nothing, indeed, in this strange history is more significant than the attitude assumed by the special leaders and representatives of the Church which teaches that 'it were better for the sun and moon to drop from heaven, for the earth to fail, and for all of the many millions upon it to die of starvation in extremest agony, so far as temporal affliction goes, than that one soul ... should commit one venial sin, should tell one wilful untruth.'[54]

Three illustrious churchmen—Lacordaire, Ravignan and Dupanloup—to their immortal honour refused to give any approbation to the Coup d'état or to express any confidence in its author. But the latest panegyrist of the Empire boasts that they were almost alone in their profession. By the advice of the Papal Nuncio and of the leading French bishops, the clergy lost no time in presenting their felicitations. Veuillot, who more than any other man represented and influenced the vast majority of the French priesthood, wrote on what had been done with undisguised and unqualified exultation and delight. Even Montalembert rallied to the Government on the morrow of the Coup d'état. He described Louis Napoleon as a Prince 'who had shown a more efficacious and intelligent devotion to religious interests than any of those who had governed France during sixty years;' and it was universally admitted that the great body of the clergy, with Archbishop Sibour at their head, were in this critical moment ardent supporters of the new government.[55] Kinglake, in a page of immortal beauty, has described the scene when, thirty days after the Coup d'état, Louis Napoleon appeared in Notre Dame to receive, amid all the pomp that Catholic ceremonial could give, the solemn blessing of the Church, and to listen to the Te Deum thanking the Almighty for what had been accomplished. The time came, it is true, when the policy of the priests was changed, for they found that Louis Napoleon was more liberal and less clerical than they imagined; but in estimating the feelings with which French Liberals judge the Church, its attitude towards the perjury and violence of December 2 should never be forgotten.

To those who judge the political ethics of the Roman Catholic Church not from the deceptive pages of such writers as Newman, but from an examination of its actual conduct in the different periods of its history, it will appear in no degree inconsistent. It is but another instance added to many of the manner in which it regards all acts which appear conducive to its interests. It was the same spirit that led a Pope to offer public thanks for the massacre of St. Bartholomew, and to order Vasari to paint the murder of Coligny on the walls of the Vatican among the triumphs of the Church. No Christian sovereign of modern times has left a worse memory behind him than Ferdinand II. of Naples, who received the Pope when he fled to Gaëta in 1848. He was the sovereign whose government was described by Gladstone as 'a negation of God.' He not only destroyed the Constitution he had sworn to observe, but threw into a loathsome dungeon the Liberal ministers who had trusted him. But in the eyes of the

---

[54] Newman.

[55] See Ollivier, *L'Empire Libéral*, i. 510-512

Pope his services to the Church far outweighed all defects, and the monument erected to this 'most pious prince' may be seen in one of the chapels of St. Peter's. Every visitor to Paris may see the fresco in the Madeleine in which Napoleon I. appears seated triumphant on the clouds and surrounded by an admiring priesthood, the most prominent and glorified figure in a picture representing the history of French Christianity, with Christ above, blessing the work.

It is indeed a most significant fact that in Catholic countries the highest moral level in public life is now rarely to be found among those who specially represent the spirit and teaching of their Church, and much more frequently among men who are unconnected with it, and often with all dogmatic theology. How seldom has the distinctively Catholic press seriously censured unjust wars, unscrupulous alliances, violations of constitutional obligations, unprovoked aggressions, great outbursts of intolerance and fanaticism! It is, indeed, not too much to say that some of the worst moral perversions of modern times have been supported and stimulated by a great body of genuinely Catholic opinion both in the priesthood and in the press. The anti-Semite movement, the shameful indifference to justice shown in France in the Dreyfus case, and the countless frauds, outrages and oppressions that accompanied the domination of the Irish Land League are recent and conspicuous examples.

Among secular-minded laymen the Coup d'état of Louis Napoleon was, as I have said, differently judged. Few things in French history are more honourable than the determination with which so many men who were the very flower of the French nation refused to take the oath or give their adhesion to the new Government. Great statesmen and a few distinguished soldiers, with a splendid past behind them and with the prospect of an illustrious career before them; men of genius who in their professorial chairs had been the centres of the intellectual life of France; functionaries who had by laborious and persevering industry climbed the steps of their profession and depended for their livelihood on its emoluments, accepted poverty, exile and the long eclipse of the most honourable ambitions rather than take an oath which seemed to justify the usurpation. At the same time, some statesmen of unquestionable honour did not wholly and in all its parts condemn it. Lord Palmerston was conspicuous among them. Without expressing approval of all that had been done, he always maintained that the condition of France was such that a violent subversion of an unworkable Constitution and the establishment of a strong government had become absolutely necessary; that the Coup d'état saved France from the gravest and most imminent danger of anarchy and civil war, and that this fact was its justification. If it had not been for the acts of ferocious tyranny which immediately followed it, his opinion would have been more largely shared.

It is probable that the moral character of Coups d'état may in the future not unfrequently come into discussion in Europe, as it has often done in South America. As the best observers are more and more perceiving, parliamentary government worked upon party lines is by no means an easy thing, and it seldom attains perfection without long experience and without qualities of mind and character which are very unequally distributed among the nations of the world. It requires a spirit of compromise, patience and moderation; the kind of mind which can distinguish the solid, the practical and the well meaning, from the brilliant, the plausible and the ambitious, which cares more for useful results and for the conciliation of many interests and opinions than for any rigid uniformity and consistency of principle; which, while pursuing personal ambitions and party aims, can subordinate them on great occasions to public interests. It needs a combination of independence and discipline which is not common, and where it does not exist parliaments speedily degenerate either into an assemblage of puppets in the hands of party leaders or into disintegrated, demoralised, insubordinate groups. Some of the foremost nations of the world—nations distinguished for noble and brilliant intellect; for splendid heroism; for great achievements in peace and war—have in this form of government conspicuously failed. In England it has grown with our growth and strengthened with our strength. We have practised it in many phases. Its traditions have taken deep root and are in full harmony with the national character. But in the present century this kind of government has been adopted by many nations which are wholly unfit for it, and they have usually adopted it in the most difficult of all forms—that of an uncontrolled democracy resting upon universal suffrage. It is becoming very evident that in many countries such assemblies are wholly incompetent to take the foremost place in government, but they are so fenced round by oaths and other constitutional forms that nothing short of violence can take from them a power which they are never likely voluntarily to relinquish. In such countries democracy tends much less naturally to the parliamentary system than to some form of dictatorship, to some despotism resting on and justified by a plébiscite. It is probable that many transitions in this direction will take place. They will seldom be carried out through purely public motives or without perjury and violence. But public opinion will judge each case on its own merits, and where it can be shown that its results are beneficial and that large sections of the people have desired it, such an act will not be severely condemned.

Cases of conflicting ethical judgments of another kind may be easily cited. One of the best known was that of Governor Eyre at the time of the Jamaica insurrection of 1865. In this case there was no question of personal interest or ambition. The Governor was a man of stainless honour, who in a moment of extreme difficulty and danger had rendered a great service to his country. By his prompt and courageous action a negro insurrection was quickly suppressed, which, if it had been allowed to extend, must have brought untold horrors upon Jamaica. But the martial law which he had proclaimed was certainly continued longer than was necessary, it was exercised with excessive severity, and those who were tried under it were not merely men who had been taken in arms. One conspicuous civilian agitator, who had contributed greatly to stimulate the insurrection, and had been, in the opinion of the Governor, its 'chief cause and origin,' but who, like most men of his kind, had merely incited others without taking any direct part himself, was arrested in a part of the island in which martial law was not proclaimed, and was tried and hanged by orders of a military tribunal in a way which the best legal authorities in England pronounced wholly unwarranted by law. If this act had been considered apart from the general conditions of the island it would have deserved severe punishment. If the services of the Governor had been considered apart from this act they would have deserved high honours from the Crown. In Jamaica the Governor was fully supported by the Legislative Council and the Assembly, but at home public opinion was fiercely divided, and the fact that the chief literary and scientific men in England took sides on the question added greatly to its interest. Carlyle took a leading part in the defence of Governor Eyre. John Stuart Mill was the chairman of a committee who regarded him as a simple criminal, and who for more than two years pursued him with a persistent vindictiveness. As might have been expected the one side dwelt solely on his services and the other side on his misdeeds. Governor Eyre received no reward for the great service he had rendered, and he was involved by his enemies in a ruinous legal expenditure, which, however, was subsequently paid by the Government; but those who desired to bring him to trial for murder were baffled, for the Old Bailey Grand Jury threw out the bill. Public opinion, I think, on the whole, approved of what they had done. Most moderate men had come to the conclusion that Governor Eyre was a brave and honourable man who had rendered great services to the State and had saved countless lives, but who, through no unworthy motive and in a time of extreme danger and panic, had committed a serious mistake which had been very amply expiated.

The more recent events connected with the Jameson raid into the Transvaal may also be cited. Of the raid itself there is little to be said. It was, in truth, one of the most discreditable as well as mischievous events in recent colonial history, and its character was entirely unrelieved by any gleam either of heroism or of skill. Those who took a direct part in it were duly tried and duly punished. A section of English society adopted on this question a disgraceful attitude, but it must at least be said in palliation that they had been grossly deceived, one of the chief and usually most trustworthy organs of opinion having been made use of as an organ of the conspirators.

A more difficult question arose in the case of the statesman who had prepared and organized the expedition against the Transvaal. It is certain that the actual raid had taken place without his knowledge or consent, though when it was brought to his knowledge he abstained from taking any step to stop it. It may be conceded also that there were real grievances to be complained of. By a strange irony of fate some of the largest gold mines of the world had fallen to the possession of perhaps the only people who did not desire them; of a race of hunters and farmers intensely hostile to modern ideas, who had twice abandoned their homes and made long journeys into distant lands in search of solitude and space and of a home where they could live their primitive, pastoral lives, undisturbed by any foreign element. These men now found their country the centre of a vast stream of foreign immigration, and of that most undesirable kind of immigration which gold mines invariably promote. Their laws were very backward, but the part which was most oppressive was that connected with the gold-mining industry which was almost entirely in the hands of the immigrants, and it was this which made it a main object to overthrow their government. The trail of finance runs over the whole story, but it may be acknowledged that, although Mr. Rhodes had made an enormous fortune by mining speculations, and although he was largely interested as a financier in overturning the system of government at Johannesburg, he was not a man likely to be actuated by mere love of money, and that political ambition closely connected with the opening and the civilisation of Africa largely actuated him. Whether the motives of his co-conspirators were of the same kind may be open to question. What, however, he did has been very clearly established. When holding the highly confidential position of Prime Minister of the Cape Colony, and being at the same time a Privy Councillor of the Queen, he engaged in a conspiracy for the overthrow of the government of a neighbouring and friendly State. In order to carry out this design he deceived the High Commissioner whose Prime Minister he was. He deceived his own colleagues in the Ministry. He collected under false pretences a force which was intended to co-operate with an insurrection in Johannesburg. Being a Director of the Chartered Company he made use of that position, without the knowledge of his colleagues, to further the conspiracy. He took an active and secret part in smuggling great quantities of arms into the Transvaal, which were intended to be used in the rebellion; and at a time when his organs in the press were representing Johannesburg as seething with spontaneous indignation against an oppressive government, he, with another millionaire, was secretly expending many thousands of pounds in that town in stimulating and subsidising the rising. He was also directly connected with the shabbiest incident in the whole affair, the concoction of a letter from the Johannesburg conspirators absurdly representing English women and children at Johannesburg as in danger of being shot down by the Boers, and urging the British to come at once to save them. It was a letter drawn up with the sanction of Mr. Rhodes many weeks before the raid, and before any disturbance had arisen, and kept in reserve to be dated and used in the last moment for the purpose of inducing the young soldiers in South Africa to join in the raid, and of subsequently justifying their conduct before the War Office, and also for the purpose of being published in the English press at the same time as the first news of the raid, in order to work upon English public opinion and persuade the English people that the raid, though technically wrong, was morally justifiable.[56]

Mr. Rhodes is a man of great genius and influence, and in the past he has rendered great services to the Empire. At the same time no reasonable judge can question that in these transactions he was more blamable than those who were actually punished by the law for taking part in the raid—far more blamable than those young officers who were, in truth, the most severely punished, and who had been induced to take part in it under a false representation of the wishes of the Government at home, and a grossly false representation of the state of things at Johannesburg. The failure of the raid, and his undoubted complicity with its design, obliged Mr. Rhodes to resign the post of Prime Minister and his directorship of the Chartered Company, and, for a time at least, eclipsed his influence in Africa; but the question confronted the

---

[56] *Report of the Select Committee on British South Africa* (July, 1897).

Ministers whether these resignations alone constituted a sufficient punishment for what he had done.

The question was indeed one of great difficulty. The Government, in my opinion, were right in not attempting a prosecution which, in the face of the fact that the actual raid had certainly been undertaken without the knowledge of Mr. Rhodes, and that the evidence against him was chiefly drawn from his own voluntary admissions before the committee of inquiry, would inevitably have proved abortive. They were, perhaps, right in not taking from him the dignity of Privy Councillor, which had been bestowed on him as a reward for great services in the past, and which had never in the present reign been taken from anyone on whom it had been bestowed. They were right also, I believe, in urging that after a long and elaborate inquiry into the circumstances of the raid, and after a report in which Mr. Rhodes's conduct had been fully examined and severely censured, it was most important for the peace and good government of South Africa that the matter should as soon as possible be allowed to drop, and the raid and the party animosities it had aroused to subside. But what can be thought of the language of a Minister who volunteered to assure the House of Commons that in all the transactions I have described, Mr. Rhodes, though he had made 'a gigantic mistake,' a mistake perhaps as great as a statesman could make, had done nothing affecting his personal honour? [57] The foregoing examples will serve to illustrate the kind of difficulty which every statesman has to encounter in dealing with political misdeeds, and the impossibility of treating them by the clearly defined lines and standards that are applicable to the morals of a private life. Whatever conclusions men may arrive at in the seclusion of their studies, when they take part in active political life they will find it necessary to make large allowances for motives, tendencies, past services, pressing dangers, overwhelming expediencies, opposing interests. Every statesman who is worthy of the name has a strong predisposition to support the public servants who are under him when he knows that they have acted with a sincere desire to benefit the Empire. This is, indeed, a characteristic of all really great statesmen, and it gives a confidence and energy to the public service which in times of difficulty and danger are of supreme importance. In such times a mistaken decision is usually a less evil than timid, vacillating, or procrastinated action, and a wise Minister will go far to defend his subordinates if they have acted promptly and with substantial justice in the way they believed to be best, even though they may have made considerable mistakes, and though the results of their action may have proved unfortunate.

But of all forms of prestige, moral prestige is the most valuable, and no statesman should forget that one of the chief elements of British power is the moral weight that is behind it. It is the conviction that British policy is essentially honourable and straightforward, that the word and honour of its statesmen and diplomatists may be implicitly trusted, and that intrigues and deceptions are wholly alien to their nature.

---

[57] *Parliamentary Debates*, July 26, 1897, 1169, 1170

The statesman must steer his way between rival fanaticisms—the fanaticism of those who pardon everything if it is crowned by success and conduces to the greatness of the Empire, and who act as if weak Powers and savage nations had no moral rights; and the fanaticism of those who always seem to have a leaning against their own country, and who imagine that in times of war, anarchy, or rebellion, and in dealings with savage or half-savage military populations, it is possible to act with the same respect for the technicalities of law, and the same invariably high standard of moral scrupulousness, as in a peaceful age and a highly civilised country. In the affairs of private life the distinction between right and wrong is usually very clear, but it is not so in public affairs. Even the moral aspects of political acts can seldom be rightly estimated without the exercise of a large, judicial, and comprehensive judgment, and the spirit which should actuate a statesman should be rather that of a high-minded and honourable man of the world than that of a theologian, or a lawyer, or an abstract moralist.

In some respects the standard of political morality has undoubtedly risen in modern times; but it is by no means certain that in international politics this is the case. A true history of the wars of the last half of the nineteenth century may well lead us to doubt it, and recent disclosures have shown us that in the most terrible of them—the Franco-German War of 1870—the blame must be much more equally divided than we had been accustomed to believe. Very few massacres in history have been more gigantic or more clearly traced to the action of a government than those perpetrated by Turkish soldiers in our generation, and few signs of the low level of public feeling in Christendom are more impressive than the general indifference with which these massacres were contemplated in most countries. It was made evident that a Power which retains its military strength, and which is therefore sought as an ally and feared as an enemy, may do things with impunity, and even with very little censure, which in the case of a weak nation would produce a swift retribution. Among the minor episodes of nineteenth-century history the historian will not forget how soon after the savage Armenian massacres the sovereign of one of the greatest and most civilised of Christian nations hastened to Constantinople to clasp the hand which was so deeply dyed with Christian blood, and then, having, as he thought, sufficiently strengthened his popularity and influence in that quarter, proceeded to the Mount of Olives, where, amid scenes that are consecrated by the most sacred of all memories, and most fitted to humble the pride of power and dispel the dreams of ambition, he proclaimed himself with melodramatic piety the champion and the patron of the Christian faith! How many instances may be culled from very modern history of the deliberate falsehood of statesmen; of distinct treaty engagements and obligations simply set aside because they were inconvenient to one Power, and could be repudiated with impunity; of weak nations annexed or plundered without a semblance of real provocation! The safety of the weak in the presence of the strong is the best test of international morality. Can it be said that, if measured by this test, the public morality of our time ranks very high? No one can fail to notice with what levity the causes of war with barbarous or semi-civilised nations are scrutinised if only those wars are crowned with success; how strongly the present commercial policy of Europe is stimulating the passion for aggression; how warmly that policy is in all great nations supported by public opinion and by the Press.

The questions of morality arising out of these things are many and complicated, and they cannot be disposed of by short and simple formulæ. How far is a statesman who sees, or thinks he sees, some crushing danger from an aggressive foreign Power impending over his country, justified in anticipating that danger, and at a convenient moment and without any immediate provocation forcing on a war? How far is it his right or his duty to sacrifice the lives of his people through humanitarian motives, for the redress of some flagrant wrong with which he is under no treaty obligation to interfere? How far, if several Powers agree to guarantee the integrity of a small Power, is one Power bound at great risk to interfere in isolation if its co-partners refuse to do so or are even accomplices in a policy of plunder? How far, if the aggression of other Powers places his nation at a commercial or other disadvantage in the competition of nations, may a statesman take measures which, under other circumstances, would be plainly unjustifiable, to guard against such disadvantage? With what degrees of punctiliousness, at what cost of treasure and of life, ought a nation to resent insults directed against its dignity, its subjects and its flag? What is the meaning and what are the limits of national egotism and national unselfishness? There is such a thing as the comity of nations, and even apart from treaty obligations no great nation can pursue a policy of complete isolation, disregarding crimes and aggressions beyond its border. On the other hand, the primary duty of every statesman is to his own country. His task is to secure for many millions of the human race the highest possible amount of peace and prosperity, and a selfishness is at least not a narrow one which, while abstaining from injuring others, restricts itself to promoting the happiness of a vast section of the human race. Sacrifices and dangers which a good man would think it his clear duty to accept if they fell on himself alone wear another aspect if he is acting as trustee for a great nation and for the interests of generations who are yet unborn. Nothing is more calamitous than the divorce of politics from morals, but in practical politics public and private morals will never absolutely correspond. The public opinion of the nation will inevitably inspire and control its statesmen. It creates in all countries an ethical code which with greater or less perfection marks out for them the path of duty, and though a great statesman may do something to raise its level, he can never wholly escape its influence. In different nations it is higher or lower—in truthfulness and sincerity of diplomacy the variations are very great—but it will never be the exact code on which men act in private life. It is certainly widely different from the Sermon on the Mount.

There is one belief, half unconscious, half avowed, which in our generation is passing widely over the world and is practically accepted in a very large measure by the English-speaking nations. It is that to reclaim savage tribes to civilisation, and to place the outlying dominions of civilised countries which are anarchical or grossly misgoverned in the hands of rulers who govern wisely and uprightly, are sufficient justification for aggression and conquest. Many who, as a general rule, would severely censure an unjust and unprovoked war, carried on for the purpose of annexation by a strong Power against a weak one, will excuse or scarcely condemn such a war if it is directed against a country which has shown itself incapable of good government. To place the world in the hands of those who can best govern it is looked upon as a supreme end. Wars are not really undertaken for this end. The philanthropy of nations when it takes the form of war and conquest is seldom or never unmixed with selfishness, though strong gusts of humanitarian enthusiasm often give an impulse, a pretext, or a support to the calculated actions of statesmen. But when wars, however selfish and unprovoked, contribute to enlarge the boundaries of civilisation, to stimulate real progress, to put an end to savage customs, to oppression or to anarchy, they are now very indulgently judged even in the many cases in which the inhabitants of the conquered Power do not desire the change and resist it strenuously in the field.

In domestic as in foreign politics the maintenance of a high moral standard in statesmanship is impossible unless the public opinion of the country is in harmony with it. Moral declension in a nation is very swiftly followed by a corresponding decadence among its public men, and it will indeed be generally found that the standard of public men is apt to be somewhat lower than that of the better section of the public outside. They are exposed to very special temptations, some of which I have already indicated.

The constant habit of regarding questions with a view to party advantage, to proximate issues, to immediate popularity, which is inseparable from parliamentary government, can hardly fail to give some ply to the most honest intellect. Most questions have to be treated more or less in the way of compromise; and alliances and coalitions not very conducive to a severe standard of political morals are frequent. In England the leading men of the opposing parties have happily usually been able to respect one another. The same standard of honour will be found on both sides of the House, but every parliament contains its notorious agitators, intriguers and self-seekers, men who have been connected with acts which may or may not have been brought within the reach of the criminal law, but have at least been sufficient to stamp their character in the eyes of honest men. Such men cannot be neglected in party combinations. Political leaders must co-operate with them in the daily intercourse and business of parliamentary life—must sometimes ask them favours—must treat them with deference and respect. Men who on some subjects and at some times have acted with glaring profligacy, on others act with judgment, moderation and even patriotism, and become useful supporters or formidable opponents. Combinations are in this way formed which are in no degree wrong, but which tend to dull the edge of moral perception and imperceptibly to lower the standard of moral judgment. In the swift changes of the party kaleidoscope the bygone is soon forgotten. The enemy of yesterday is the ally of to-day; the services of the present soon obscure the misdeeds of the past; and men insensibly grow very tolerant not only of diversities of opinion, but also of gross aberrations of conduct. The constant watchfulness of external opinion is very necessary to keep up a high standard of political morality.

Public opinion, it is true, is by no means impeccable. The tendency to believe that crimes cease to be crimes when they have a political object, and that a popular vote can absolve the worst crimes, is only too common; there are few political misdeeds which wealth, rank, genius or success will not induce large sections of English society to pardon, and nations even in their best moments will not judge acts which are greatly for their own advantage with the severity of judgment that they would apply to similar acts of other nations. But when all this is admitted, it still remains true that there is a large body of public opinion in England which carries into all politics a sound moral sense and which places a just and righteous policy higher than any mere party interest. It is on the power and pressure of this opinion that the high character of English government must ultimately depend.

CHAPTER XI

The necessities for moral compromise I have traced in the army, in the law, and in the fields of politics may be found in another form not less conspicuously in the Church. The members, and still more the ministers, of an ancient Church bound to formularies and creeds that were drawn up in long bygone centuries, are continually met by the difficulties of reconciling these forms with the changed conditions of human knowledge, and there are periods when the pressure of these difficulties is felt with more than common force. Such, for example, were the periods of the Renaissance and the Reformation, when changes in the intellectual condition of Europe produced a widespread conviction of the vast amount of imposture and delusion which had received the sanction of a Church that claimed to be infallible, the result being in some countries a silent evanescence of all religious belief among the educated class, even including a large number of the leaders of the Church, and in other countries a great outburst of religious zeal aiming at the restoration of Christianity to its primitive form and a repudiation of the accretions of superstition that had gathered around it. The Copernican theory proving that our world is not, as was long believed, the centre of the universe, but a single planet moving with many others around a central sun, and the discovery, by the instrumentality of the telescope, of the infinitesimally small place which our globe occupies in the universe, altered men's measure of probability and affected widely, though indirectly, their theological beliefs.

A similar change was gradually produced by the Newtonian discovery that the whole system of the universe was pervaded by one great law, and by the steady growth of scientific knowledge, proving that vast numbers of phenomena which were once attributed to isolated and capricious acts of spiritual intervention were regulated by invariable, inexorable, all-pervasive law. Many of the formularies by which we still express our religious beliefs date from periods when comets and eclipses were believed to have been sent to portend calamity; when every great meteorological change was attributed to some isolated spiritual agency; when witchcraft and diabolical possession, supernatural diseases, and supernatural cures were deemed indubitable facts: and when accounts of contemporary miracles, Divine or Satanic, carried with them no sense of strangeness or improbability. It is scarcely surprising that these formularies sometimes seem incongruous with an age when the scientific spirit has introduced very different conceptions of the government of the universe, and when the miraculous, if it is not absolutely discredited, is, at least in the eyes of most educated men, relegated to a distant past.

The present century has seen some powerful reactions towards older religious beliefs, but it has also been to an unusual extent fertile in the kind of changes that most deeply affect them. Not many years have passed since the whole drama of the world's history was believed to have been comprised in the framework of 'Paradise Lost' and 'Paradise Regained.' Man appeared in the universe a faultless being in a faultless world, but he soon fell from his first estate, and his fall entailed world-wide consequences. It introduced into our globe sin, death, suffering, disease, imperfection and decay; all the mischievous and ferocious instincts and tendencies of man and beast; all the multitudinous forms of struggle, terror, anxiety and grief; all that makes life bitter to any living being, and, even as the Fathers were accustomed to say, the briars and weeds and sterility of the earth. Paradise Regained was believed to be indissolubly connected with Paradise Lost. The one was the explanation of the other. The one introduced the disease, the other provided the remedy.

It is idle to deny that the main outlines of this picture have been wholly changed. First came the discovery that the existence of our globe stretches far beyond the period once assigned to the Creation, and that for countless ages before the time when Adam was believed to have lost Paradise, death had been its most familiar fact and its inexorable law; that the animals who inhabited it preyed upon and devoured each other as at present, their claws and teeth being specially adapted for that purpose. Even their half-digested remains have been preserved in fossil.

'Death,' wrote a Pagan philosopher, in sharp contrast to the teaching of the Church, 'is a law and not a punishment,' and geology has fully justified his assertion.

Then came decisive evidence showing that for many thousands of years before his supposed origin man had lived and died upon our globe—a being, as far as can be judged from the remains that have been preserved, not superior but greatly inferior to ourselves, whose almost only art was the manufacture of rude instruments for killing, who appears in structure and in life to have approximated closely to the lowest existing forms of savage life.

Then came the Darwinian theory maintaining that the whole history of the living world is a history of slow and continuous evolution, chiefly by means of incessant strife, from lower to higher forms; that man himself had in this way gradually emerged from the humblest forms of the animal world; that most of the moral deflections which were attributed to the apple in Eden are the remains and traditions of the earlier and lower stages of his existence. The theory of continuous ascent from a lower to a higher stage took the place of the theory of the Fall as the explanation of human history. It is a doctrine which is certainly not without hope for the human race. It gives no explanation of the ultimate origin of things, and it is in no degree inconsistent with the belief either in a Divine and Creative origin or in a settled and Providential plan. But it is as far as possible removed from the conception of human history and human nature which Christendom during eighteen centuries accepted as fundamental truth.

With these things have come influences of another kind. Comparative Mythology has accumulated a vast amount of evidence, showing how myths and miracles are the natural product of certain stages of human history, of certain primitive misconceptions of the course of nature; how legends essentially of the same kind, though with some varieties of detail, have sprung up in many different quarters, and how they have migrated and interacted on each other. Biblical criticism has at the same time decomposed and analysed the Jewish writings, assigning to them dates and degrees of authority very different from those recognised by the Church. It has certainly not impaired their significance as records of successive developments of religious and moral progress, nor has it diminished their value as expressions of the loftiest and most enduring religious sentiments of mankind; but in the eyes of a great section of the educated world it has deprived them of the authoritative and infallible character that was once attributed to them. At the same time historical criticism has brought with it severer standards of proof, more efficient means of distinguishing the historical from the fabulous. It has traced the phases and variations of religions, and the influences that governed them, with a fulness of knowledge and an independence of judgment unknown in the past, and it has led its votaries to regard in these matters a sceptical and hesitating spirit as a virtue, and credulity and easiness of belief as a vice.

This is not a book of theology, and I have no intention of dilating on these things. It must, however, be manifest to all who are acquainted with contemporary thought how largely these influences have displaced theological beliefs among great numbers of educated men; how many things that were once widely believed have become absolutely incredible; how many that were once supposed to rest on the plane of certainty have now sunk to the lower plane of mere probability or perhaps possibility. From the time of Galileo downwards, these changes have been denounced as incompatible with the whole structure of Christian belief. No less an apologist than Bishop Berkeley declared that the belief that the date of the existence of the world was approximately that which could be deduced from the book of Genesis was one of the fundamental beliefs which could not be given up.[58] When the traveller Brydone published his travels in Sicily in 1773, conjecturing, from the deposits of lava, that the world must be much older than the Mosaic cosmogony admitted, his work was denounced as subverting the foundations of the Christian faith. The same charges were brought against the earlier geologists, and in our own day against the early supporters of the Darwinian theory; and many now living can remember the outbursts of indignation against those who first introduced the principles of German criticism into English thought, and who impugned the historical character and the assumed authorship of the Pentateuch.

It is not surprising or unreasonable that it should have been so, for it is impossible to deny that these changes have profoundly altered large portions of the beliefs that were once regarded as essential. One main object of a religion was believed to have been to furnish what may be called a theory of the universe—to explain its origin, its destiny, and the strange contradictions and imperfections it presents. The Jewish theory was a very clear and definite one, but it is certainly not that of modern science.

Yet few things are more remarkable than the facility with which these successive changes have gradually found their places within the Established Church, and how little that Church has been shaken by this fact. Even the Darwinian theory, though it has not yet passed into the circle of fully established truth, is in its main lines constantly mentioned with approbation by the clergy of the Church. The theory of

---

[58] *Alciphron*, 6th Dialogue.

evolution largely pervades their teaching. The doctrine that the Bible was never intended to teach science or scientific facts, and also the main facts and conclusions of modern Biblical criticism, have been largely accepted among the most educated clergy. Very few of them would now deny the antiquity of the world, the antiquity of man, or the antiquity of death, or would maintain that the Mosaic cosmogony was a true and literal account of the origin of the globe and of man, or would very strenuously argue either for the Mosaic authorship or the infallibility of the Pentateuch.

And while changes of this kind have been going on in one direction, another great movement has been taking place in an opposite one. The Church of England was essentially a Protestant Church; though, being constructed more than most other Churches under political influences, by successive stages of progress, and with a view to including large and varying sections of opinion in its fold, it retained, more than other Churches, formularies and tenets derived from the Church it superseded. The earnest Protestant and Puritan party which dominated in Scotland and in the Continental Reformation, and which refused all compromise with Rome, had not become powerful in English public opinion till some time after the framework of the Church was established. The spirit of compromise and conservatism which already characterised the English people; the great part which kings and lawyers played in the formation of the Church; their desire to maintain in England a single body, comprising men who had broken away from the Papacy but who had in other respects no great objection to Roman Catholic forms and doctrines, and also men seriously imbued with the strong Protestant feeling of Germany and Switzerland; the strange ductility of belief and conduct that induced the great majority of the English clergy to retain their preferments and avoid persecution during the successive changes of Henry VIII., Edward VI., Mary, and Elizabeth, all assisted in forming a Church of a very composite character. Two distinct theories found their place within it. According to one school it was simply the pre-Reformation Church purified from certain abuses that had gathered around it, organically united with it through a divinely appointed episcopacy, resting on an authoritative and ecclesiastical basis, and forming one of the three great branches of the Catholic Church. According to the other school it was one of several Protestant Churches, retaining indeed such portions of the old ecclesiastical organisation as might be justified from Scripture, but not regarding them as among the essentials of Christianity; agreeing with other Protestant bodies in what was fundamental, and differing from them mainly on points which were non-essential; accepting cordially the principle that 'the Bible and the Bible alone is the religion of Protestants,' and at the same time separated by the gravest and most vital differences from what they deemed the great apostasy of Rome.

It was argued on the one hand that in its ecclesiastical and legal organisation the Church in England was identical with the Church in the reign of Henry VII.; that there had been no breach of continuity; that bishops, and often the same bishops, sat in the same sees before and after the Reformation; that the great majority of the parochial clergy were unchanged, holding their endowments by the same titles and tenures, subject to the same courts, and meeting in Convocation in the same manner as their predecessors; that the old Catholic services were merely translated and revised, and that although Roman usurpations which had never been completely acquiesced in had been decisively rejected, and although many superstitious novelties had been removed, the Church of England was still the Church of St. Augustine; that it had never, even in the darkest period, lost its distinct existence, and that supernatural graces and sacerdotal powers denied to all schismatics had descended to it through the Episcopacy in an unbroken stream. On the other hand it was argued that the essential of a true Church lay in the accordance of its doctrines with the language of Scripture and not in the methods of Church government, and that whatever might be the case in a legal point of view, the theory of the unity of the Church before and after the Reformation was in a theological sense a delusion. The Church under Henry VII. was emphatically a theocracy or ecclesiastical monarchy, the Pope, as the supposed successor of the supposed prince of the Apostles, being the very keystone of the spiritual arch. Under Henry VIII. and Elizabeth the Church of England had become a kind of aristocracy of bishops, governed very really as well as theoretically by the Crown, totally cut off from what called itself the Chair of Peter, and placed under completely new relations with the Catholic Church of Christendom. In this space of time Anglican Christianity had discarded not only the Papacy but also great part of what for centuries before the change had been deemed vitally and incontestably necessary both in its theology and in its devotions. Though much of the old organisation and many of the old formularies had been retained, its articles, its homilies, the constant teaching of its founders, breathed a spirit of unquestionable Protestantism. The Church which remained attached to Rome, and which held the same doctrines, practised the same devotions, and performed the same ceremonies as the English Church under Henry VII., professed to be infallible, and it utterly repudiated all connection with the new Church of England, and regarded it as nothing more than a Protestant schism; while the Church of England in her authorised formularies branded some of the central beliefs and devotions of the Roman Church as blasphemous, idolatrous, superstitious and deceitful, and was long accustomed to regard that Church as the Church of Antichrist; the Harlot of the Apocalypse, drunk with the blood of the Saints. Each Church during long periods and to the full measure of its powers suppressed or persecuted the other.

In the eyes of the Erastian and also in the eyes of the Puritan the theory of the spiritual unity of these two bodies, and the various sacerdotal consequences that were inferred from it, seemed incredible, nor did the first generation of our reformers shrink from communion, sympathy and co-operation with the non-episcopal Protestants of the Continent. Although they laid great stress on patristic authority, and consented—chiefly through political motives—to leave in the Prayer-book many things derived from the older Church, yet the High Church theory of Anglicanism is much more the product of the seventeenth-century divines than of the reformers, just as Roman Catholicism is much more akin to the later fathers than to primitive Christianity. No one could doubt on what side were the sympathies and what were the opinions of Cranmer, Latimer, Ridley, Jewell and Hooper, and what spirit pervades the articles and the homilies. A Church which does not claim to be infallible; which owes its special form chiefly to the sagacity of statesmen; in which the supreme tribunal, deciding what doctrines may be taught by the clergy, is a secular law court; in which the bands of conformity are so loose that the tendencies and sentiments of the nation give the complexion to the Church, appears in the eyes of men of these schools to have no possible right to claim or share the authority of the Church of Rome. It rests on another basis. It must be justified on other grounds.

These two distinct schools, however, have subsisted in the Church. Each of them can find some support in the Prayer-book, and the old orthodox High Church school which was chiefly elaborated and which chiefly flourished under the Stuarts, has produced a great part of the most learned theology of Christendom, and had in its early days little or no tendency to Rome. It was exclusive and repellent on the side of Nonconformity, and it placed Church authority very high; but the immense majority of its members were intensely loyal to the Anglican Church, and lived and died contentedly within its pale. There were, however, always in that Church men of another kind whose true ideal lay beyond its border. Falkland, in a remarkable speech, delivered in 1640, speaks of them with much bitterness. 'Some,' he says, 'have so industriously laboured to deduce themselves from Rome that they have given great suspicion that in gratitude they desire to return thither, or at least to meet it half way. Some have evidently laboured to bring in an English though not a Roman Popery; I mean not only the outside and dress of it, but equally absolute.... Nay, common fame is more than ordinarily false if none of them have found a way to reconcile the opinions of Rome to the preferments of England, and be so absolutely, directly and cordially Papists that it is all that 1,500*l.* a year can do to keep them from confessing it.'[59]

No wide secession to Rome, however, followed the development of this seventeenth-century school, though it played a large part in the nonjuror schism, and with the decay of that schism and under the latitudinarian tendencies of the eighteenth century it greatly dwindled. Since, however, the Tractarian movement, which carried so many leaders of the English Church to Rome, men of Roman sympathies and Roman ideals have multiplied within the Church to an extraordinary degree. They have not only carried their theological pretensions in the direction of Rome much further than the nonjurors; they have also in many cases so transformed the old and simple Anglican service by vestments and candles, and banners and incense, and genuflexions and whispered prayers, that a stranger might well imagine that he was in a Roman Catholic church. They have put forward sacerdotal pretensions little, if at all, inferior to those of Rome. The whole tendency of their devotional literature and thought flows in the Roman channel, and even in the most insignificant matters of ceremony and dress they are accustomed to pay the greater Church the homage of constant imitation.

---

[59] Nalsons's *Collections*, i. 769, February 9, 1640.

It would be unjust to deny that there are some real differences. The absolute authority and infallibility of the Pope are sincerely repudiated as an usurpation, the ritualist theory only conceding to him a primacy among bishops. The discipline and submission to ecclesiastical authority also, which so eminently distinguish the Roman Church, are wholly wanting in many of its Anglican imitators, and at the same time the English sense of truth has proved sufficient to save the party from the tolerance and propagation of false miracles and of grossly superstitious practices so common in Roman Catholic countries. In this last respect, however, it is probable that English and American Roman Catholics are almost equally distinguished from Catholics in the Southern States of Europe and of America. Still, when all this is admitted, it can hardly be denied that there has grown up in a great section of the English Church a sympathy with Rome and an antipathy to Protestantism and to Protestant types of thought and character utterly alien to the spirit of the Reformers and to the doctrinal formularies of the Church of England.

It is not very easy to form a just estimate of the extent and depth of this movement. There are wide variations in the High Church party; the extreme men are not the most numerous and certainly very far from the ablest, and many influences other than convinced belief have tended to strengthen the party. It has been, indeed, unlike the Tractarian party which preceded it, remarkably destitute of literary or theological ability, and has added singularly little to the large and noble theological literature of the English Church. The mere charm of novelty, which is always especially powerful in the field of religion, draws many to the ritualistic channel, and thousands who care very little for ritualistic doctrines are attracted by the music, the pageantry, the pictorial beauty of the ritualistic services. Æsthetic tastes have of late years greatly increased in England, and the closing of places of amusement on Sunday probably strengthens the craving for more attractive services. The extreme High Church party has chiefly fostered and chiefly benefited by this desire, but it has extended much more widely. It has touched even puritanical and non-episcopal bodies, and it is sometimes combined with extremely latitudinarian opinions. There is, indeed, a type of mind which finds in such services a happy anodyne for half-suppressed doubt. Petitions which in their poignant humiliation and profound emotion no longer correspond to the genuine feelings of the worshipper, seem attenuated and transformed when they are intoned, and creeds which when plainly read shock the understanding and the conscience are readily accepted as parts of a musical performance. Scepticism as well as belief sometimes fills churches. Large classes who have no wish to cut themselves off from religious services have lost all interest in the theological distinctions which once were deemed supremely important and all strong belief in great parts of dogmatic systems, and such men naturally prefer services which by music and ornament gratify their tastes and exercise a soothing or stimulating influence over the imagination.

The extreme High Church party has, however, other elements of attraction. Much of its power is due to the new springs of real spiritual life and the new forms of real usefulness and charity that grew out of its highly developed sacerdotal system and out of the semi-monastic confraternities which at once foster and encourage and organise an active zeal. The power of the party in acting not only on the cultivated classes but also on the poor is very manifest, and it has done much to give the Church of England a democratic character which in past generations it did not possess, and which in the conditions of modern life is supremely important. The multiplication not only of religious services but of communicants, and the great increase in the interest taken in Church life in quarters where the Ritualist party prevail, cannot reasonably be questioned. Its highly ornate services draw many into the churches who never entered them before, and they are often combined with a familiar and at the same time impassioned style of preaching, something like that of a Franciscan friar or a Methodist preacher, which is excellently fitted to act upon the ignorant. If its clergy have been distinguished for their insubordination to their bishops, if they have displayed in no dubious manner a keen desire to aggrandise their own position and authority, it is also but just to add that they have been prominent for the zeal and self-sacrifice with which they have multiplied services, created confraternities, and penetrated into the worst and most obscure haunts of poverty and vice.

The result, however, of all this is that the conflicting tendencies which have always been present in the Church have been greatly deepened. There are to be found within it men whose opinions can hardly be distinguished from simple Deism or Unitarianism, and men who abjure the name of Protestant and are only divided by the thinnest of partitions from the Roman Church. And this diversity exists in a Church which is held together by articles and formularies of the sixteenth century.

It might, perhaps, a priori have been imagined that a Church with so much diversity of opinion and of spirit was an enfeebled and disintegrated Church, but no candid man will attribute such a character to the Church of England. All the signs of corporate vitality are abundantly displayed, and it is impossible to deny that it is playing an active, powerful, and most useful part in English life. Looking at it first of all from the intellectual side, it is plain how large a proportion of the best intellect of the country is contented, not only to live within it, but to take an active part in its ministrations. Compare the amount of higher literature which proceeds from clergymen of the Established Church with the amount which proceeds from the vastly greater body of Catholic priests scattered over the world; compare the place which the English clergy, or laymen deeply imbued with the teaching of the Church, hold in English literature with the place which Catholic priests, or sincere Catholic laymen, hold in the literature of France,—and the contrast will appear sufficiently evident. There is hardly a branch of serious English literature in which Anglican clergy are not conspicuous. There is nothing in a false and superstitious creed incompatible with some forms of literature. It may easily ally itself with the genius of a poet or with great beauty of style either hortatory or narrative. But in the Church of England literary achievement is certainly not restricted to these forms. In the fields of physical science, in the fields of moral philosophy, metaphysics, social and even political philosophy, and perhaps still more in the fields of history, its clergy have won places in the foremost rank. It is notorious that a large proportion of the most serious criticism, of the best periodical writing in England, is the work of Anglican clergymen. No one, in enumerating the leading historians of the present century, would omit such names as Milman, Thirlwall and Merivale, in the generation which has just passed away, or Creighton and Stubbs among contemporaries, and these are only eminent examples of a kind of literature to which the Church has very largely contributed. Their histories are not specially conspicuous for beauty of style, and not only conspicuous for their profound learning; they are marked to an eminent degree by judgment, criticism, impartiality, a desire for truth, a skill in separating the proved from the false or the merely probable. Compare them with the chief histories that have been written by Catholic priests. In past ages some of the greatest works of patient, lifelong industry in all literary history were due to the Catholic priesthood, and especially to members of the monastic orders; even in modern times they have produced some works of great learning, of great dialectic skill, and of great beauty of style; but with scarcely an exception these works bear upon them the stamp of an advocate and are written for the purpose of proving a point, concealing or explaining away the faults on one side, and bringing into disproportioned relief those of the other. No one would look in them for a candid estimate of the merits of an opponent or for a full statement of a hostile case. Döllinger, who would probably once have been cited as the greatest historian the Catholic priesthood had produced in the nineteenth century, died under the anathema of his Church; and how large a proportion of the best writing in modern English Catholicism has come from writers who have been brought up in Protestant universities and who have learnt their skill in the Anglican Church!

It is at least one great test of a living Church that the best intellect of the country can enter into its ministry, that it contains men who in nearly all branches of literature are looked upon by lay scholars with respect or admiration. It is said that the number of young men of ability who take orders is diminishing, and that this is due, not merely to the agricultural depression which has made the Church much less desirable as a profession, and indeed in many cases almost impossible for those who have not some private fortune; not merely to the competitive examination system, which has opened out vast and attractive fields of ambition to the ablest laymen,—but also to the wide divergence of men of the best intellect from the doctrines of the Church, and the conviction that they cannot honestly subscribe its articles and recite its formularies. But although this is, I believe, true, it is also true that there is no other Church which has shown itself so capable of attracting and retaining the services of men of general learning, criticism and ability. One of the most important features of the English ecclesiastical system has been the education of those who are intended for the Church, in common with other students in the great national universities. Other systems of education may produce a clergy of greater professional learning and more intense and exclusive zeal, but no other system of education is so efficacious in maintaining a general harmony of thought and tendency between the Church and the average educated opinion of the nation.

Take another test. Compare the Guardian, which represents better than any other paper the opinions of moderate Churchmen, with the papers which are most read by the French priesthood and have most influence on their opinions. Certainly few English journalists have equalled in ability Louis Veuillot, and few papers have exercised so great an influence over the clergy of the Church as the Univers at the time when he directed it; but no one who read those savagely scurrilous and intolerant pages, burning with an impotent hatred of all the progressive and liberal tendencies of the time, shrinking from no misrepresentation of fact and from no apology for crime if it was in the interest of the Church, could fail to perceive how utterly out of harmony it was with the best lay thought of France. English religious journalism has sometimes, though in a very mitigated degree, exhibited some of these characteristics, but no one who reads the Guardian, which I suppose appeals to a larger clerical public than any other paper, can fail to realise the contrast. It is not merely that it is habitually written in the style and temper of a gentleman, but that it reflects most clearly in its criticism, its impartiality, its tone of thought, the best intellectual influences of the time. Men may agree or differ about its politics or its theology, but no one who reads it can fail to admit that it is thoroughly in touch with cultivated lay opinion, and it is in fact a favourite paper of many who care only for its secular aspects.

The intellectual ability, however, included among the ministers of a Church, though one test, is by no means a decisive and infallible one of its religious life. During the period of the Renaissance, when genuine belief in the Catholic Church had sunk to nearly its lowest point, most men of literary tastes and talents were either members of the priesthood or of the monastic orders. This was not due to any fervour of belief, but simply to the fact that the Church at that time furnished almost the only sphere in which a literary life could be pursued with comfort, without molestation, and with some adequate reward. Much of the literary ability found in the English Church is unquestionably due to the attraction it offers and the facilities it gives to those who simply wish for a studious life. The abolition of many clerical sinecures, and the greatly increased activity of clerical duty imposed by contemporary opinion, have no doubt rendered the profession less desirable from this point of view; but even now there is no other profession outside the universities which lends itself so readily to a literary life, and a great proportion of the most eminent thinkers and writers in the Church of England are eminent in fields that have little or no connection with theology.

Other tests of a flourishing Church are needed, but they can easily be found. Political power is one test, though it is a very coarse and very deceptive one. Perhaps it is not too much to say that the most superstitious creeds are often those which exercise the greatest political influence, for they are those in which the priesthood acquires the most absolute authority. Nor does the decline of superstition among the educated classes always bring with it a corresponding decline in ecclesiastical influence. There have been instances, both in Pagan and Christian times, of a sceptical and highly educated ruling class supporting and allying themselves with a superstitious Church as the best means of governing or moralising the masses. Such Churches, by their skilful organisation, by their ascendency over individual rulers, or by their political alliances, have long exercised an enormous influence, and in a democratic age the preponderance of political power is steadily passing from the most educated classes. At the same time, in a highly civilised and perfectly free country, in which all laws of religious disqualification and coercion have disappeared, and all questions of religion are submitted to perpetual discussion, the political power which the Church of England retains at least proves that she has a vast weight of genuine and earnest opinion behind her. No politician will deny the strength with which the united or greatly preponderating influence of the Church can support or oppose a party. It has been said by a cynical observer that the three things outside their own families that average Englishmen value the most are rank, money, and the Church of England, and certainly no good observer will form a low estimate of the strength or earnestness of the Church feeling in every section of the English people.

Still less can it be denied that the Church retains in a high degree its educational influence. For a long period national education was almost wholly in its hands, and, since all disqualifications and most privileges have been abolished, it still exercises a part in English education which excites the alarm of some and the admiration of others. It has thrown itself heartily into the new political conditions, and the vast number of voluntary schools established under clerical influence, and the immense sums that are annually raised for clerical purposes, show beyond all doubt the amount of support and enthusiasm behind it. In every branch of higher education its clergy are conspicuous, and their influence in training the nation is not confined to the pulpit, the university, or the school. No candid observer of English life will doubt the immense effect of the parochial system in sustaining the moral level both of principle and practice, and the multitude, activity, and value of the philanthropic and moralising agencies which are wholly or largely due to the Anglican Church.

Nor can it be reasonably doubted that the Church has been very efficacious in promoting that spiritual life which, whatever opinion men may form of its origin and meaning, is at least one of the great realities of human nature. The power of a religion is not to be solely or mainly judged by its corporate action; by the institutions it creates; by the part which it plays in the government of the world. It is to be found much more in its action on the individual soul, and especially in those times and circumstances when man is most isolated from society. It is in furnishing the ideals and motives of individual life; in guiding and purifying the emotions; in promoting habits of thought and feeling that rise above the things of earth; in the comfort it can give in age, sorrow, disappointment and bereavement; in the seasons of sickness, weakness, declining faculties, and approaching death, that its power is most felt. No one creed or Church has the monopoly of this power, though each has often tried to identify it with something peculiar to itself. It maybe found in the Catholic and in the Quaker, in the High Anglican who attributes it to his sacramental system, and in the Evangelical in whose eyes that system holds only a very subordinate place. All that need here be said is that no one who studies the devotional literature of the English Church, or who has watched the lives of its more devout members, will doubt that this life can largely exist and flourish within its pale.

The attitude which men who have been born within that Church, but who have come to dissent from large portions of its theology, should bear to this great instrument of good, is certainly not less perplexing than the questions we have been considering in the preceding chapters. The most difficult position is, of course, that of those who are its actual ministers and who have subscribed its formularies. Each man so situated must judge in the light of his own conscience. There is a great difference between the case of men who accept such a position in the Church though they differ fundamentally from its tenets, and the case of men who, having engaged in its service, find their old convictions modified or shaken, perhaps very gradually, by the advance of science or by more matured thought and study. The stringency of the old form of subscription has been much mitigated by an Act of 1865 which substituted a general declaration that the subscriber believed in the doctrine of the Church as a whole, for a declaration that he believed 'all and everything' in the Articles and the Prayer-book. The Church of England does not profess to be an infallible Church; it does profess to be a National Church representing and including great bodies of more or less divergent opinion, and the whole tendency of legal decisions since the Gorham case has been to enlarge the circle of permissible opinion. The possibility of the National Church remaining in touch with the more instructed and intellectual portions of the community depends mainly on the latitude of opinion that is accorded to its clergy, and on their power of welcoming and adopting new knowledge, and it may reasonably be maintained that few greater calamities can befall a nation than the severance of its higher intelligence from religious influences.

It should be remembered, too, that on the latitudinarian side the changes that take place in the teaching of the Church consist much less in the open repudiation of old doctrines than in their silent evanescence. They drop out of the exhortations of the pulpit. The relative importance of different portions of the religious teaching is changed. Dogma sinks into the background. Narratives which are no longer seriously believed become texts for moral disquisitions. The introspective habits and the stress laid on purely ecclesiastical duties which once preponderated disappear. The teaching of the pulpit tends rather to the formation of active, useful and unselfish lives; to a clearer insight into the great masses of remediable suffering and need that still exist in the world; to the duty of carrying into all the walks of secular life a nobler and more unselfish spirit; to a habit of judging men and Churches mainly by their fruits and very little by their beliefs. The disintegration or decadence of old religious beliefs which had long been closely associated with moral teaching always brings with it grave moral dangers, but those dangers are greatly diminished when the change of belief is effected by a gradual transition, without any violent convulsion or disruption severing men from their old religious observances. Such a transition has silently taken place in England among great numbers of educated men, and in some measure under the influence of the clergy. Nor has it, I think, weakened the Church. The standard of duty among such men has not sunk, but has in most departments perceptibly risen: their zeal has not diminished, though it flows rather in philanthropic than in purely ecclesiastical channels. The conviction that the special dogmas which divided other

Protestant bodies from the Establishment rested on no substantial basis and have no real importance tells in favour of the larger and the more liberal Church, and the comprehensiveness which allows highly accentuated sacerdotalism and latitudinarianism in the same Church is in the eyes of many of them rather an element of strength than of weakness.

Few men have watched the religious tendencies of the time with a keener eye than Cardinal Newman, and no man hated with a more intense hatred the latitudinarian tendencies which he witnessed. His judgment of their effect on the Establishment is very remarkable. In a letter to his friend Isaac Williams he says: 'Everything I hear makes me fear that latitudinarian opinions are spreading furiously in the Church of England. I grieve deeply at it. The Anglican Church has been a most useful breakwater against Scepticism. The time might come when you, as well as I, might expect that it would be said above, "Why cumbereth it the ground?" but at present it upholds far more truth in England than any other form of religion would, and than the Catholic Roman Church could. But what I fear is that it is tending to a powerful Establishment teaching direct error, and more powerful than it has ever been; thrice powerful because it does teach error.' [60]

It is, however, of course, evident that the latitude of opinion which may be reasonably claimed by the clergy of a Church encumbered with many articles and doctrinal formularies is not unlimited, and each man must for himself draw the line. The fact, too, that the Church is an Established Church imposes some special obligations on its ministers. It is their first duty to celebrate public worship in such a form that all members of the Church of England may be able to join in it. Whatever interpretations may be placed upon the ceremonies of the Church, those ceremonies, at least, should be substantially the same. A stranger who enters a church which he has never before seen should be able to feel that he is certain of finding public worship intelligibly and decently performed, as in past generations it has been celebrated in all sections of the Established Church. It has, in my opinion, been a gross scandal, following a gross neglect of duty, that this primary obligation has been defied, and that services are held in English churches which would have been almost unrecognisable by the churchmen of a former generation, and which are manifest attempts to turn the English public worship into an imitation of the Romish Mass. Men have a perfect right, within the widest limits, to perform what religious services and to preach what religious doctrines they please, but they have not a right to do so in an Established Church.

The censorship of opinions is another thing, and in the conditions of English life it has never been very effectively maintained. The latitude of opinion granted in an Established Church is, and ought to be, very great, but it is, I think, obvious that on some topics a greater degree of reticence of expression should be observed by a

---

[60] *Autobiography of Isaac Williams*, p. 132. This letter was written in 1863

clergyman addressing a miscellaneous audience from the pulpit of an Established Church than need be required of him in private life or even in his published books.

The attitude of laymen whose opinions have come to diverge widely from the Church formularies is less perplexing, and except in as far as the recent revival of sacerdotal pretensions has produced a reaction, there has, if I mistake not, of late years been a decided tendency in the best and most cultivated lay opinion of this kind to look with increasing favour on the Established Church. The complete abolition of the religious and political disqualifications which once placed its maintenance in antagonism with the interests of large sections of the people; the abolition of the indelibility of orders which excluded clergymen who changed their views from all other means of livelihood; the greater elasticity of opinion permitted within its pale; and the elimination from the statute-book of nearly all penalties and restrictions resting solely upon ecclesiastical grounds,—have all tended to diminish with such men the objections to the Church. It is a Church which does not injure those who are external to it, or interfere with those who are mere nominal adherents. It is more and more looked upon as a machine of well-organised beneficence, discharging efficiently and without corruption functions of supreme utility, and constituting one of the main sources of spiritual and moral life in the community. None of the modern influences of society can be said to have superseded it. Modern experience has furnished much evidence of the insufficiency of mere intellectual education if it is unaccompanied by the education of character, and it is on this side that modern education is most defective. While it undoubtedly makes men far more keenly sensible than in the past to the vast inequalities of human lots, the habit of constantly holding out material prizes as its immediate objects, and the disappearance of those coercive methods of education which once disciplined the will, make it perhaps less efficient as an instrument of moral amelioration.

Some habits of thought also, that have grown rapidly among educated men, have tended powerfully in the same direction. The sharp contrasts between true and false in matters of theology have been considerably attenuated. The point of view has changed. It is believed that in the history of the world gross and material conceptions of religion have been not only natural, but indispensable, and that it is only by a gradual process of intellectual evolution that the masses of men become prepared for higher and purer conceptions. Superstition and illusion play no small part in holding together the great fabric of society. 'Every falsehood,' it has been said, 'is reduced to a certain malleability by an alloy of truth,' and, on the other hand, truths of the utmost moment are, in certain stages of the world's history, only operative when they are clothed with a vesture of superstition. The Divine Spirit filters down to the human heart through a gross and material medium. And what is true of different stages of human history is not less true of different contemporary strata of knowledge and intelligence. In spite of democratic declamation about the equality of man, it is more and more felt that the same kind of teaching is not good for everyone. Truth, when undiluted, is too strong a medicine for many minds. Some things which a highly cultivated intellect would probably discard, and discard without danger, are essential to the moral being of multitudes. There is in all great religious systems something that is transitory and something that is eternal. Theological interpretations of the phenomena of outward nature which surround and influence us, and mythological narratives which have been handed down to us from a remote, uncritical and superstitious past, may be transformed or discredited; but there are elements in religion which have their roots much less in the reason of man than in his sorrows and his affections, and are the expression of wants, moral appetites and aspirations which are an essential, indestructible part of his nature.

No one, I think, can doubt that this way of thinking, whether it be right or wrong, has very widely spread through educated Europe, and it is a habit of thought which commonly strengthens with age. Young men discuss religious questions simply as questions of truth or falsehood. In later life they more frequently accept their creed as a working hypothesis of life; as a consolation in innumerable calamities; as the one supposition under which life is not a melancholy anti-climax; as the indispensable sanction of moral obligation; as the gratification and reflection of needs, instincts and longings which are planted in the deepest recesses of human nature; as one of the chief pillars on which society rests. The proselytising, the aggressive, the critical spirit diminishes. Very often they deliberately turn away their thoughts from questions which appear to them to lead only to endless controversy or to mere negative conclusions, and base their moral life on some strong unselfish interest for the benefit of their kind. In active, useful and unselfish work they find the best refuge from the perplexities of belief and the best field for the cultivation of their moral nature, and work done for the benefit of others seldom fails to react powerfully on their own happiness. Nor is it always those who have most completely abandoned dogmatic systems who are the least sensible to the moral beauty which has grown up around them. The music of the village church, which sounds so harsh and commonplace to the worshipper within, sometimes fills with tears the eyes of the stranger who sits without, listening among the tombs.

It is difficult to say how far the partial truce which has now fallen in England over the great antagonisms of belief is likely to be permanent. No one who knows the world can be insensible to the fact that a large and growing proportion of those who habitually attend our religious services have come to diverge very widely, though in many different degrees, from the beliefs which are expressed or implied in the formularies they use. Custom, fashion, the charm of old associations, the cravings of their own moral or spiritual nature, a desire to support a useful system of moral training, to set a good example to their children, their household, or their neighbours, keep them in their old place when the beliefs which they profess with their lips have in a great measure ebbed away. I do not undertake to blame or to judge them. Individual conscience and character and particular circumstances have, in these matters, a decisive voice. But there are times when the difference between professed belief and real belief is too great for endurance, and when insincerity and half-belief affect seriously the moral character of a nation. 'The deepest, nay, the only theme of the world's history, to which all others are subordinate,' said Goethe, 'is the conflict of faith and unbelief. The epochs in which faith, in whatever form it may be, prevails, are the marked epochs in human history, full of heart-stirring memories and of substantial gains for all after times. The epochs in which unbelief, in whatever form it may be, prevails, even when for the moment they put on the semblance of glory and success, inevitably sink into insignificance in the eyes of posterity, which will not waste its thoughts on things barren and unfruitful.'

Many of my readers have probably felt the force of such considerations and the moral problems which they suggest, and there have been perhaps moments when they have asked themselves the question of the poet—

Tell me, my soul, what is thy creed?

Is it a faith or only a need?

They will reflect, however, that a need, if it be universally felt when human nature is in its highest and purest state, furnishes some basis of belief, and also that no man can venture to assign limits to the transformations which religion may undergo without losing its essence or its power. Even in the field of morals these have been very great, though universal custom makes us insensible to the extent to which we have diverged from a literal observance of Evangelical precepts. We should hardly write over the Savings Bank, 'Take no thought for the morrow, for the morrow will take thought for itself,' or over the Bank of England, 'Lay not up for yourselves treasures upon earth,' 'How hardly shall a rich man enter into the Kingdom of God,' or over the Foreign Office, or the Law Court, or the prison, 'Resist not evil,' 'He that smiteth thee on thy right cheek turn to him the other also,' 'He that taketh away thy coat let him have thy cloak also.' Can it be said that the whole force and meaning of such words are represented by an industrial society in which the formation of habits of constant providence with the object of averting poverty or increasing comfort is deemed one of the first of duties and a main element and measure of social progress; in which the indiscriminate charity which encourages mendicancy and discourages habits of forethought and thrift is far more seriously condemned than an industrial system based on the keenest, the most deadly, and often the most malevolent competition; in which wealth is universally sought, and universally esteemed a good and not an evil, provided only it is honestly obtained and wisely and generously used; in which, although wanton aggression and a violent and quarrelsome temper are no doubt condemned, it is esteemed the duty of every good citizen to protect his rights whenever they are unjustly infringed; in which war and the preparation for war kindle the most passionate enthusiasm and absorb a vast proportion of the energies of Christendom, and in which no Government could remain a week in power if it did not promptly resent the smallest insult to the national flag?

It is a question of a different kind whether the sacerdotal spirit which has of late years so largely spread in the English Church can extend without producing a violent disruption. To cut the tap roots of priestcraft was one of the main aims and objects of the Reformation, and, for reasons I have already stated, I do not believe that the party which would re-establish it has by any means the strength that has been attributed to it. It is true that the Broad Church party, though it reflects faithfully the views of large numbers of educated laymen, has never exercised an influence in active Church life at all proportionate to the eminence of its leading representatives. It is true also that the Evangelical party has in a very remarkable degree lost its old place in the Anglican pulpit and in religious literature, though its tenets still form the staple of the preaching of the Salvation Army and of most other street preachers who exercise a real and widespread influence over the poor. But the middle and lower sections of English society are, I believe, at bottom, profoundly hostile to priestcraft; and although the dread of Popery has diminished, they are very far from being ready to acquiesce in any attempt to restore the dominion which their fathers discarded.

In one respect, indeed, sacerdotalism in the Anglican Church is a worse thing than in the Roman Church, for it is undisciplined and unregulated. The history of the Church abundantly shows the dangers that have sprung from the Confessional, though the Roman Catholic will maintain that its habitually restraining and moralising influence greatly outweighs these occasional abuses. But in the Roman Church the practice of confession is carried on under the most severe ecclesiastical supervision and discipline. Confession can only be made to a celibate priest of mature age, who is bound to secrecy by the most solemn oath; who, except in cases of grave illness, confesses only in an open church; and who has gone through a long course of careful education specially and skilfully designed to fit him for the duty. None of these conditions are observed in Anglican Confession.

In other respects, indeed, the sacerdotal spirit is never likely to be quite the same as in the Roman Church. A married clergy, who have mixed in all the lay influences of an English university, and who still take part in the pursuits, studies, social intercourse and amusements of laymen, are not likely to form a separate caste or to constitute a very formidable priesthood. It is perhaps a little difficult to treat their pretensions with becoming gravity, and the atmosphere of unlimited discussion which envelops Englishmen through their whole lives has effectually destroyed the danger of coercive and restrictive laws directed against opinion. Moral coercion and the tendency to interfere by law on moral grounds with the habits of men, even when those habits in no degree interfere with others, have increased. It is one of the marked tendencies of Anglo-Saxon democracy, and it is very far from being peculiar to, or even specially prominent in, any one Church. But the desire to repress the expression of opinions by force, which for so many centuries marked with blood and fire the power of mediæval sacerdotalism, is wholly alien to modern English nature. Amid all the fanaticisms, exaggerations, and superstitions of belief, this kind of coercion, at least, is never likely to be formidable, nor do I believe that in the most extreme section of the sacerdotal clergy there is any desire for it. There has been one significant contrast between the history of Catholicism and Anglicanism in the present century. In the Catholic Church the Ultramontane element has steadily dominated, restricting liberty of opinion, and important tenets which were once undefined by the Church, and on which sincere Catholics had some latitude of opinion, have been brought under the iron yoke. This is no doubt largely due to the growth of scepticism and indifference, which have made the great body of educated laymen hostile or indifferent to the Church, and have thrown its management mainly into the hands of the priesthood and the more bigoted, ignorant and narrow-minded laymen. But in the Anglican Church educated laymen are much less alienated from Church life, and a tribunal which is mainly lay exercises the supreme authority. As a consequence of these conditions, although the sacerdotal element has greatly increased, the latitude of opinion within the Church has steadily grown.

At the same time, it is difficult to believe that serious dangers do not await the Church if the unprotestantising influences that have spread within it continue to extend. It is not likely that the nation will continue to give its support to the Church if that Church in its main tendencies cuts itself off from the Reformation. The conversions to Catholicism in England, though probably much exaggerated, have been very numerous, and it is certainly not surprising that it should be so. If the Church of Rome permitted Protestantism to be constantly taught in her pulpits, and Protestant types of worship and character to be habitually held up to admiration, there can be little doubt that many of her worshippers would be shaken. If the Church of England becomes in general what it already is in some of its churches, it is not likely that English public opinion will permanently acquiesce in its privileged position in the State. If it ceases to be a Protestant Church, it will not long remain an established one, and its disestablishment would probably be followed by a disruption in which opinions would be more sharply defined, and the latitude of belief and the spirit of compromise that now characterise our English religious life might be seriously impaired.

CHAPTER XII   THE MANAGEMENT OF CHARACTER

Of all the tasks which are set before man in life, the education and management of his character is the most important, and, in order that it should be successfully pursued, it is necessary that he should make a calm and careful survey of his own tendencies, unblinded either by the self-deception which conceals errors and magnifies excellences, or by the indiscriminate pessimism which refuses to recognise his powers for good. He must avoid the fatalism which would persuade him that he has no power over his nature, and he must also clearly recognise that this power is not unlimited. Man is like a card-player who receives from Nature his cards—his disposition, his circumstances, the strength or weakness of his will, of his mind, and of his body. The game of life is one of blended chance and skill. The best player will be defeated if he has hopelessly bad cards, but in the long run the skill of the player will not fail to tell. The power of man over his character bears much resemblance to his power over his body. Men come into the world with bodies very unequal in their health and strength; with hereditary dispositions to disease; with organs varying greatly in their normal condition. At the same time a temperate or intemperate life, skilful or unskilful regimen, physical exercises well adapted to strengthen the weaker parts, physical apathy, vicious indulgence, misdirected or excessive effort, will all in their different ways alter his bodily condition and increase or diminish his chances of disease and premature death. The power of will over character is, however, stronger, or, at least, wider than its power over the body. There are organs which lie wholly beyond its influence; there are diseases over which it can exercise no possible influence, but there is no part of our moral constitution which we cannot in some degree influence or modify.

It has often seemed to me that diversities of taste throw much light on the basis of character. Why is it that the same dish gives one man keen pleasure and to another is loathsome and repulsive? To this simple question no real answer can be given. It is a fact of our nature that one fruit, or meat, or drink will give pleasure to one palate and none whatever to another. At the same time, while the original and natural difference is undoubted, there are many differences which are wholly or largely due to particular and often transitory causes. Dishes have an attraction or the reverse because they are associated with old recollections or habits. Habit will make a Frenchman like his melon with salt, while an Englishman prefers it with sugar. An old association of ideas will make an Englishman shrink from eating a frog or a snail, though he would probably like each if he ate it without knowing it, and he could easily learn to do so. The kind of cookery which one age or one nation generally likes, another age or another nation finds distasteful. The eye often governs the taste, and a dish which, when seen, excites intense repulsion, would have no such repulsion to a blind man. Every one who has moved much about the world, and especially in uncivilised countries, will get rid of many old antipathies, will lose the fastidiousness of his taste, and will acquire new and genuine tastes. The original innate difference is not wholly destroyed, but it is profoundly and variously modified.

These changes of taste are very analogous to what takes place in our moral dispositions. They are for the most part in themselves simply external to morals, though there is at least one conspicuous exception. Many—it is to be hoped most—men might spend their lives with full access to intoxicating liquors without even the temptation of getting drunk. Apart from all considerations of religion, morals, social, physical, or intellectual consequences, they abstain from doing so simply as a matter of taste. With other men the pleasure of excessive drinking is such that it requires an heroic effort of the will to resist it. There are men who not only are so constituted that it is their greatest pleasure, but who are even born with a craving for drink. In no form is the terrible fact of heredity more clearly or more tragically displayed. Many, too, who had originally no such craving gradually acquire it: sometimes by mere social influence, which makes excessive drinking the habit of their circle; more frequently through depression or sorrow, which gives men a longing for some keen pleasure in which they can forget themselves; or through the jaded habit of mind and body which excessive work produces, or through the dreary, colourless, joyless surroundings of sordid poverty. Drink and the sensual pleasures, if viciously indulged, produce (doubtless through physical causes) an intense craving for their gratification. This, however, is not the case with all our pleasures. Many are keenly enjoyed when present, yet not seriously missed when absent. Sometimes, too, the effect of over-indulgence is to vitiate and deaden the palate, so that what was once pleasing ceases altogether to be an object of desire. This, too, has its analogue in other things. We have a familiar example in the excessive novel-reader, who begins with a kind of mental intoxication, and who ends with such a weariness that he finds it a serious effort to read the books which were once his strongest temptation.

Tastes of the palate also naturally change with age and with the accompanying changes of the body. The schoolboy who bitterly repines because the smallness of his allowance restricts his power of buying tarts and sweetmeats will probably grow into a man who, with many shillings in his pocket, daily passes the confectioner's shop without the smallest desire to enter it.

It is evident that there is a close analogy between these things and that collection of likes and dislikes, moral and intellectual, which forms the primal base of character, and which mainly determines the complexion of our lives. As Marcus Aurelius said: 'Who can change the desires of man?' That which gives the strongest habitual pleasure, whether it be innate or acquired, will in the great majority of cases ultimately dominate. Certain things will always be intensely pleasurable, and certain other things indifferent or repellent, and this magnetism is the true basis of character, and with the majority of men it mainly determines conduct. By the associations of youth and by other causes these natural likings and dislikings may be somewhat modified, but even in youth our power is very limited, and in later life it is much less. No real believer in free-will will hold that man is an absolute slave to his desires. No man who knows the world will deny that with average man the strongest passion or desire will prevail—happy when that desire is not a vice.

Passions weaken, but habits strengthen, with age, and it is the great task of youth to set the current of habit and to form the tastes which are most productive of happiness in life. Here, as in most other things, opposite exaggerations are to be avoided. There is such a thing as looking forward too rigidly and too exclusively to the future—to a future that may never arrive. This is the great fault of the over-educationist, who makes early life a burden and a toil, and also of those who try to impose on youth the tastes and pleasures of the man. Youth has its own pleasures, which will always give it most enjoyment, and a happy youth is in itself an end. It is the time when the power of enjoyment is most keen, and it is often accompanied by such extreme sensitiveness that the sufferings of the child for what seem the most trivial causes probably at least equal in acuteness, though not in durability, the sufferings of a man. Many a parent standing by the coffin of his child has felt with bitterness how much of the measure of enjoyment that short life might have known has been cut off by an injudicious education. And even if adult life is attained, the evils of an unhappy childhood are seldom wholly compensated. The pleasures of retrospect are among the most real we possess, and it is around our childish days that our fondest associations naturally cluster. An early over-strain of our powers often leaves behind it lasting distortion or weakness, and a sad childhood introduces into the character elements of morbidness and bitterness that will not disappear.

The first great rule in judging of pleasures is that so well expressed by Seneca: 'Sic præsentibus utaris voluptatibus ut futuris non noceas'—so to use present pleasures as not to impair future ones. Drunkenness, sensuality, gambling, habitual extravagance and self-indulgence, if they become the pleasures of youth, will almost infallibly lead to the ruin of a life. Pleasures that are in themselves innocent lose their power of pleasing if they become the sole or main object of pursuit.

In starting in life we are apt to attach a disproportionate value to tastes, pleasures, and ideals that can only be even approximately satisfied in youth, health, and strength. We have, I think, an example of this in the immense place which athletic games and out-of-door sports have taken in modern English life. They are certainly not things to be condemned. They have the direct effect of giving a large amount of intense and innocent pleasure, and they have indirect effects which are still more important. In so far as they raise the level of physical strength and health, and dispel the morbidness of temperament which is so apt to accompany a sedentary life and a diseased or inert frame, they contribute powerfully to lasting happiness. They play a considerable part in the formation of friendships which is one of the best fruits of the period between boyhood and mature manhood. Some of them give lessons of courage, perseverance, energy, self-restraint, and cheerful acquiescence in disappointment and defeat that are of no small value in the formation of character, and when they are not associated with gambling they have often the inestimable advantage of turning young men away from vicious pleasures. At the same time it can hardly be doubted that they hold an exaggerated prominence in the lives of young Englishmen of the present generation. It is not too much to say that among large sections of the students at our Universities, and at a time when intellectual ambition ought to be most strong and when the acquisition of knowledge is most important, proficiency in cricket or boating or football is more prized than any intellectual achievement. I have heard a good judge, who had long been associated with English University life, express his opinion that during the last forty or fifty years the relative intellectual position of the upper and middle classes in England has been materially changed, owing to the disproportioned place which outdoor amusements have assumed in the lives of the former. It is the impression of very competent judges that a genuine love, reverence and enthusiasm for intellectual things is less common among the young men of the present day than it was in the days of their fathers. The predominance of the critical spirit which chills enthusiasm, and still more the cram system which teaches young men to look on the prizes that are to be won by competitive examinations as the supreme end of knowledge, no doubt largely account for this, but much is also due to the extravagant glorification of athletic games.

If we compare the class of pleasures I have described with the taste for reading and kindred intellectual pleasures, the superiority of the latter is very manifest. To most young men, it is true, a game will probably give at least as much pleasure as a book. Nor must we measure the pleasure of reading altogether by the language of the genuine scholar. It is not every one who could say, like Gibbon, that he would not exchange his love of reading for all the wealth of the Indies. Very many would agree with him; but Gibbon was a man with an intense natural love of knowledge, and the weak health of his early life intensified this predominant passion. But while the tastes which require physical strength decline or pass with age, that for reading steadily grows. It is illimitable in the vistas of pleasure it opens; it is one of the most easily satisfied, one of the cheapest, one of the least dependent on age, seasons, and the varying conditions of life. It cheers the invalid through years of weakness and confinement; illuminates the dreary hours of the sleepless night; stores the mind with pleasant thoughts, banishes ennui, fills up the unoccupied interstices and enforced leisures of an active life; makes men for a time at least forget their anxieties and sorrows, and if it is judiciously managed it is one of the most powerful means of training character and disciplining and elevating thought. It is eminently a pleasure which is not only good in itself but enhances many others. By extending the range of our knowledge, by enlarging our powers of sympathy and appreciation, it adds incalculably to the pleasures of society, to the pleasures of travel, to the pleasures of art, to the interest we take in the vast variety of events which form the great world-drama around us.

To acquire this taste in early youth is one of the best fruits of education, and it is especially useful when the taste for reading becomes a taste for knowledge, and when it is accompanied by some specialisation and concentration and by some exercise of the powers of observation. 'Many tastes and one hobby' is no bad ideal to be aimed at. The boy who learns to collect and classify fossils, or flowers, or insects, who has acquired a love for chemical experiments, who has begun to form a taste for some particular kind or department of knowledge, has laid the foundation of much happiness in life.

In the selection of pleasures and the cultivation of tastes much wisdom is shown in choosing in such a way that each should form a complement to the others; that different pleasures should not clash, but rather cover different areas and seasons of life; that each should tend to correct faults or deficiencies of character which the others may possibly produce. The young man who starts in life with keen literary tastes and also with a keen love of out-of-door sports, and who possesses the means of gratifying each, has perhaps provided himself with as many elements of happiness as mere amusements can ever furnish. One set of pleasures, however, often kills the capacity for enjoying others, and some which in themselves are absolutely innocent, by blunting the enjoyment of better things, exercise an injurious influence on character. Habitual novel-reading, for example, often destroys the taste for serious literature, and few things tend so much to impair a sound literary perception and to vulgarise the character as the habit of constantly saturating the mind with inferior literature, even when that literature is in no degree immoral. Sometimes an opposite evil may be produced. Excessive fastidiousness greatly limits our enjoyments, and the inestimable gift of extreme concentration is often dearly bought. The well-known confession of Darwin that his intense addiction to science had destroyed his power of enjoying even the noblest imaginative literature represents a danger to which many men who have achieved much in the higher and severer forms of scientific thought are subject. Such men are usually by their original temperament, and become still more by acquired habit, men of strong, narrow, concentrated natures, whose thoughts, like a deep and rapid stream confined in a restricted channel, flow with resistless energy in one direction. It is by the sacrifice of versatility that they do so much, and the result is amply sufficient to justify it. But it is a real sacrifice, depriving them of many forms both of capacity and of enjoyment.

The same pleasures act differently on different characters, especially on the differences of character that accompany difference of sex. I have myself no doubt that the movement which in modern times has so widely opened to women amusements that were once almost wholly reserved for men has been on the whole a good one. It has produced a higher level of health, stronger nerves, and less morbid characters, and it has given keen and innocent enjoyment to many who from their circumstances and surroundings once found their lives very dreary and insipid. Yet most good observers will agree that amusements which have no kind of evil effect on men often in some degree impair the graces or characters of women, and that it is not quite with impunity that one sex tries to live the life of the other. Some pleasures, too, exercise a much larger influence than others on the general habits of life. It is not too much to say that the invention of the bicycle, bringing with it an immense increase of outdoor life, of active exercise, and of independent habits, has revolutionised the course of many lives. Some amusements which may in themselves be but little valued are wisely cultivated as helping men to move more easily in different spheres of society, or as providing a resource for old age. Talleyrand was not wholly wrong in his reproach to a man who had never learned to play whist: 'What an unhappy old age you are preparing for yourself!'

I have already mentioned the differences that may be found in different countries and ages, in the relative importance attached to external circumstances and to dispositions of mind as means of happiness, and the tendency in the more progressive nations to seek their happiness mainly in improved circumstances. Another great line of distinction is between education that acts specially upon the desires, and that which acts specially upon the will. The great perfection of modern systems of education is chiefly of the former kind. Its object is to make knowledge and virtue attractive, and therefore an object of desire. It does so partly by presenting them in the most alluring forms, partly by connecting them as closely as possible with rewards. The great principle of modern moral education is to multiply innocent and beneficent interests, tastes, and ambitions. It is to make the path of virtue the natural, the easy, the pleasing one; to form a social atmosphere favourable to its development, making duty and interest as far as possible coincident. Vicious pleasures are combated by the multiplication of healthy ones, and by a clearer insight into the consequences of each. An idle or inert character is stimulated by holding up worthy objects of interest and ambition, and it is the aim alike of the teacher and the legislator to make the grooves and channels of life such as tend naturally and easily towards good. But the education of the will—the power of breasting the current of the desires and doing for long periods what is distasteful and painful—is much less cultivated than in some periods of the past.

Many things contribute to this. The rush and hurry of modern existence and the incalculable multitude and variety of fleeting impressions that in the great centres of civilisation pass over the mind are very unfavourable to concentration, and perhaps still more to the direct cultivation of mental states. Amusements, and the appetite for amusements, have greatly extended. Life has become more full. The long leisures, the introspective habits, the vita contemplativa so conspicuous in the old Catholic discipline, grow very rare. Thoughts and interests are more thrown on the external; and the comfort, the luxury, the softness, the humanity of modern life, and especially of modern education, make men less inclined to face the disagreeable and endure the painful.

The starting-point of education is thus silently changing. Perhaps the extent of the change is best shown by the old Catholic ascetic training. Its supreme object was to discipline and strengthen the will: to accustom men habitually to repudiate the pleasurable and accept the painful; to mortify the most natural tastes and affections; to narrow and weaken the empire of the desires; to make men wholly independent of outward circumstances; to preach self-renunciation as itself an end.

Men will always differ about the merits of this system. In my own opinion it is difficult to believe that in the period of Catholic ascendency the moral standard was, on the whole and in its broad lines, higher than our own. The repression of the sensual instincts was the central fact in ascetic morals; but, even tested by this test, it is at least very doubtful whether it did not fail. The withdrawal from secular society of the best men did much to restrict the influences for good, and the habit of aiming at an unnatural ideal was not favourable to common, everyday, domestic virtue. The history of sacerdotal and monastic celibacy abundantly shows how much vice that might easily have been avoided grew out of the adoption of an unnatural standard, and how often it led in those who had attained it to grave distortions of character. Affections and impulses which were denied their healthy and natural vent either became wholly atrophied or took other and morbid forms, and the hard, cruel, self-righteous fanatic, equally ready to endure or to inflict suffering, was a not unnatural result. But whatever may have been its failures and its exaggerations, Catholic asceticism was at least a great school for disciplining and strengthening the will, and the strength and discipline of the will form one of the first elements of virtue and of happiness.

In the grave and noble type of character which prevailed in English and American life during the seventeenth century, the strength of will was conspicuously apparent. Life was harder, simpler, more serious, and less desultory than at present, and strong convictions shaped and fortified the character. 'It was an age,' says a great American writer, 'when what we call talent had far less consideration than now, but the massive materials which produce stability and dignity of character a great deal more. The people possessed by hereditary right the quality of reverence, which, in their descendants, if it survive at all, exists in smaller proportion and with a vastly diminished force in the selection and estimate of public men. The change may be for good or ill, and is partly, perhaps, for both. In that old day the English settler on these rude shores, having left king, nobles, and all degrees of awful rank behind, while still the faculty and necessity of reverence were strong in him, bestowed it on the white hair and venerable brow of age; on long-tried integrity; on solid wisdom and sad-coloured experience; on endowments of that grave and weighty order which give the idea of permanence and come under the general definition of respectability. These primitive statesmen, therefore,—Bradstreet, Endicott, Dudley, Bellingham, and their compeers,—who were elevated to power by the early choice of the people, seem to have been not often brilliant, but distinguished by a ponderous sobriety rather than activity of intellect. They had fortitude and self-reliance, and in time of difficulty or peril stood up for the welfare of the State like a line of cliffs against a tempestuous tide.'[61]

The power of the will, however, even when it exists in great strength, is often curiously capricious. History is full of examples of men who in great trials and emergencies have acted with admirable and persevering heroism, yet who readily succumbed to private vices or passions. The will is not the same as the desires, but the connection between them is very close. A love for a distant end; a dominating ambition or passion, will call forth long perseverance in wholly distasteful work in men whose will in other fields of life is lamentably feeble. Every one who has embarked with real earnestness in some extended literary enterprise which as a whole represents the genuine bent of his talent and character will be struck with his

---

[61] Hawthorne's *Scarlet Letter*, ch. xxii.

exceptional power of traversing perseveringly long sections of this enterprise for which he has no natural aptitude and in which he takes no pleasure. Military courage is with most men chiefly a matter of temperament and impulse, but there have been conspicuous instances of great soldiers and sailors who have frankly acknowledged that they never lost in battle an intense constitutional shrinking from danger, though by the force of a strong will they never suffered this timidity to govern or to weaken them. With men of very vivid imagination there is a natural tendency to timidity as they realise more than ordinary men danger and suffering. On the other hand it has often been noticed how calmly the callous, semi-torpid temperament that characterises many of the worst criminals enables them to meet death upon the gallows.

In courage itself, too, there are many varieties. The courage of the soldier and the courage of the martyr are not the same, and it by no means follows that either would possess that of the other. Not a few men who are capable of leading a forlorn hope, and who never shrink from the bayonet and the cannon, have shown themselves incapable of bearing the burden of responsibility, enduring long-continued suspense, taking decisions which might expose them to censure or unpopularity. The active courage that encounters and delights in danger is often found in men who show no courage in bearing suffering, misfortune, or disease. In passive courage the woman often excels the man as much as in active courage the man exceeds the woman. Even in active courage familiarity does much; sympathy and enthusiasm play great and often very various parts, and curious anomalies may be found. The Teutonic and the Latin races are probably equally distinguished for their military courage, but there is a clear difference between them in the nature of that courage and in the circumstances or conditions under which it is usually most splendidly displayed. The danger incurred by the gladiator was far greater than that which was encountered by the soldier, but Tacitus [62] mentions that when some of the bravest gladiators were employed in the Roman army they were found wholly inefficient, as they were much less capable than the ordinary soldiers of military courage.

The circumstances of life are the great school for forming and strengthening the will, and in the excessive competition and struggle of modern industrialism this school is not wanting. But in ethical and educational systems the value of its cultivation is often insufficiently felt. Yet nothing which is learned in youth is so really valuable as the power and the habit of self-restraint, of self-sacrifice, of energetic, continuous and concentrated effort. In the best of us evil tendencies are always strong and the path of duty is often distasteful. With the most favourable wind and tide the bark will never arrive at the harbour if it has ceased to obey the rudder. A weak nature which is naturally kindly, affectionate and pure, which floats through life under the impulse of the feelings, with no real power of self-restraint, is indeed not without its charm, and in a well-organised society, with good surroundings and few temptations, it may attain a high degree of beauty; but its besetting failings will steadily grow; without fortitude,

---

[62] *Hist.* ii. 35.

perseverance and principle, it has no recuperative energy, and it will often end in a moral catastrophe which natures in other respects much less happily compounded would easily avoid. Nothing can permanently secure our moral being in the absence of a restraining will basing itself upon a strong sense of the difference between right and wrong, upon the firm groundwork of principle and honour.

Experience abundantly shows how powerfully the steady action of such a will can operate upon innate defects, converting the constitutional idler into the indefatigably industrious, checking, limiting and sometimes almost destroying constitutional irritability and vicious passions. The natural power of the will in different men differs greatly, but there is no part of our nature which is more strengthened by exercise or more weakened by disuse. The minor faults of character it can usually correct; but when a character is once formed, and when its tendencies are essentially vicious, radical cure or even considerable amelioration is very rare. Sometimes the strong influence of religion effects it. Sometimes it is effected by an illness, a great misfortune, or the total change of associations that follows emigration. Marriage perhaps more frequently than any other ordinary agency in early life transforms or deeply modifies the character, for it puts an end to powerful temptations and brings with it a profound change of habits and motives, associations and desires. But we have all of us encountered in life depraved natures in which vicious self-indulgence had attained such a strength, and the recuperating and moralising elements were so fatally weak, that we clearly perceive the disease to be incurable, and that it is hardly possible that any change of circumstances could even seriously mitigate it. In what proportion this is the fault or the calamity of the patient no human judgment can accurately tell.

Few things are sadder than to observe how frequently the inheritance of great wealth or even of easy competence proves the utter and speedy ruin of a young man, except when the administration of a large property, or the necessity of carrying on a great business, or some other propitious circumstance provides him with a clearly defined sphere of work. The majority of men will gladly discard distasteful work which their circumstances do not require; and in the absence of steady work, and in the possession of all the means of gratification, temptations assume an overwhelming strength, and the springs of moral life are fatally impaired. It can hardly be doubted that the average longevity in this small class is far less than in that of common men, and that even when natural capacity is considerable it is more rarely displayed. To a man with a real desire for work such circumstances are indeed of inestimable value, giving him the leisure and the opportunities of applying himself without distraction and from early manhood to the kind of work that is most suited to him. Sometimes this takes place, but much more frequently vicious tastes or a simply idle or purposeless life are the result. Sometimes, indeed, a large amount of desultory and unregulated energy remains, but the serious labour of concentration is shunned and no real result is attained. The stream is there, but it turns no mill.

Most men escape this danger through the circumstances of life which make serious and steady work necessary to their livelihood, and in the majority of cases the kind of work is so clearly marked out that they have little choice. When some choice exists, the rule which I have already laid down should not be forgotten. Men should choose their work not only according to their talents and their opportunities, but also, as far as possible, according to their characters. They should select the kinds which are most fitted to bring their best qualities into exercise, or should at least avoid those which have a special tendency to develop or encourage their dominant defects. On the whole it will be found that men's characters are much more deeply influenced by their pursuits than by their opinions.

The choice of work is one of the great agencies for the management of character in youth. The choice of friends is another. In the words of Burke, 'The law of opinion ... is the strongest principle in the composition of the frame of the human mind, and more of the happiness and unhappiness of man reside in that inward principle than in all external circumstances put together.'[63] This is true of the great public opinion of an age or country which envelops us like an atmosphere, and by its silent pressure steadily and almost insensibly shapes or influences the whole texture of our lives. It is still more true of the smaller circle of our intimacies which will do more than almost any other thing to make the path of virtue easy or difficult. How large a proportion of the incentives to a noble ambition, or of the first temptations to evil, may be traced to an early friendship, and it is often in the little circle that gathers round a college table that the measure of life is first taken, and ideals and enthusiasms are formed which give a colour to all succeeding years. To admire strongly and to admire wisely is, indeed, one of the best means of moral improvement.

Very much, however, of the management of character can only be accomplished by the individual himself acting in complete isolation upon his own nature and in the chamber of his own mind. The discipline of thought; the establishment of an ascendency of the will over our courses of thinking; the power of casting away morbid trains of reflection and turning resolutely to other subjects or aspects of life; the power of concentrating the mind vigorously on a serious subject and pursuing continuous trains of thought,—form perhaps the best fruits of judicious self-education. Its importance, indeed, is manifold. In the higher walks of intellect this power of mental concentration is of supreme value. Newton is said to have ascribed mainly to an unusual amount of it his achievements in philosophy, and it is probable that the same might be said by most other great thinkers. In the pursuit of happiness hardly anything in external circumstances is so really valuable as the power of casting off worry, turning in times of sorrow to healthy work, taking habitually the brighter view of things. It is in such exercises of will that we chiefly realise the truth of the lines of Tennyson:

Oh, well for him whose will is strong,

He suffers, but he will not suffer long.

In moral culture it is not less important to acquire the power of discarding the demoralising thoughts and imaginations that haunt so many, and meeting temptation

---

[63] Speech on the Impeachment of Warren Hastings

by calling up purer, higher and restraining thoughts. The faculty we possess of alternating and intensifying our own motives by bringing certain thoughts, or images, or subjects into the foreground and throwing others into the background, is one of our chief means of moral progress. The cultivation of this power is a far wiser thing than the cultivation of that introspective habit of mind which is perpetually occupied with self-analysis or self-examination, and which is constantly and remorsefully dwelling upon past faults or upon the morbid elements in our nature. In the morals which are called minor, though they affect deeply the happiness of mankind, the importance of the government of thought is not less apparent. The secret of good or bad temper is our habitual tendency to dwell upon or to fly from the irritating and the inevitable. Content or discontent, amiability or the reverse, depend mainly upon the disposition of our minds to turn specially to the good or to the evil sides of our own lot, to the merits or to the defects of those about us. A power of turning our thoughts from a given subject, though not the sole element in self-control, is at least one of its most important ingredients.

This power of the will over the thoughts is one in which men differ enormously. Thus—to take the most familiar instance—the capacity for worry, with all the exaggerations and distortions of sentiment it implies, is very evidently a constitutional thing, and where it exists to a high degree neither reason nor will can effectually cure it. Such a man may have the clearest possible intellectual perception of its uselessness and its folly. Yet it will often banish sleep from his pillow, follow him with an habitual depression in all the walks of life, and make his measure of happiness much less than that of others who with far less propitious circumstances are endued by nature with the gift of lightly throwing off the past and looking forward with a sanguine and cheerful spirit to the future. It is hardly possible to exaggerate the different degrees of suffering the same trouble will produce in different men, and it is probable that the happiness of a life depends much less on the amount of pleasurable or painful things that are encountered, than upon the turn of thought which dwells chiefly on one or on the other. It is very evident that buoyancy of temperament is not a thing that increases with civilisation or education. It is mainly physical. It is greatly influenced by climate and by health, and where no very clear explanation of this kind can be given it is a thing in which different nations differ greatly. Few good observers will deny that persistent and concentrated will is more common in Great Britain than in Ireland, but that the gift of a buoyant temperament is more common among Irishmen than among Englishmen. Yet it co-exists in the national character with a strong vein of very genuine melancholy, and it is often accompanied by keen sensitiveness to suffering. This combination is a very common one. Every one who has often stood by a deathbed knows how frequently it will be found that the mourner who is utterly prostrated by grief, and whose tears flow in torrents, casts off her grief much more completely and much sooner than one whose tears refuse to flow and who never for a moment loses her self-command.

But though natural temperament enables one man to do without effort what another man with the utmost effort fails to accomplish, there are some available remedies that can palliate the disease. Society, travel and other amusements can do something, and such words as 'diversion' and 'distraction' embalm the truth that the chief virtue of many pleasures is to divert or distract our minds from painful thoughts. Pascal considered this a sign of the misery and the baseness of our nature, and he describes as a deplorable spectacle a man who rose from his bed weighed down with anxiety and grave sorrow, and who could for a time forget it all in the passionate excitement of the chase. But, in truth, the possession of such a power—weak and transient though it be—is one of the great alleviations of the lot of man. Religion, with its powerful motives and its wide range of consolatory and soothing thoughts and images, has much power in this sphere when it does not take a morbid form and intensify instead of alleviating sorrow; and the steady exercise of the will gives us some real and increasing, though imperfect, control over the current of our feelings as well as of our ideas.

Often the power of dreaming comes to our aid. When we cannot turn from some painfully pressing thought to serious thinking of another kind, we can give the reins to our imaginations and soon lose ourselves in ideal scenes. There are men who live so habitually in a world of imagination that it becomes to them a second life, and their strongest temptations and their keenest pleasures belong to it. To them 'common life seems tapestried with dreams.' Not unfrequently they derive a pleasure from imagined or remembered enjoyments which the realities themselves would fail to give. They select in imagination certain aspects or portions, throw others into the shade, intensify or attenuate impressions, transform and beautify the reality of things. The power of filling their existence with happy day-dreams is their most precious luxury. They feel the full force of the pathetic lines of an Irish poet:[64]

> Sweet thoughts, bright dreams my comfort be,
> I have no joy beside;
> Oh, throng around and be to me
> Power, country, fame and bride.

To train this side of our nature is no small part of the management of character. There is a great sphere of happiness and misery which is almost or altogether unconnected with surrounding circumstances, and depends upon the thoughts, images, hopes and fears on which our minds are chiefly concentrated. The exercise of this form of imagination has often a great influence, both intellectually and morally. In childhood, as every teacher knows, it is often a distracting influence, and with men also it is sometimes an obstacle to concentrated reasoning and observation, turning the mind away from sober and difficult thought; but there is a kind of dreaming which is eminently conducive to productive thought. It enables a man to place himself so

---

[64] Davis.

completely in other conditions of thought and life that the ideas connected with those conditions rise spontaneously in the mind. A true and vivid realisation of characters and circumstances unlike his own is acquired. The mere fact of placing himself in other circumstances and investing himself with imaginary powers and functions sometimes suggests possible remedies for great human ills, and gives clearer views of the proportions, difficulties and conditions of governments and societies. Much discovery in science has been due to this power of the imagination to realise conditions that are unseen, and the habit or faculty of living other lives than our own is scarcely less valuable to the historian, and even to the statesman, than to the poet or the novelist or the dramatist. It gives the magic touch which changes mere lifeless knowledge into realisation.

Its effect upon character also is great and various. No one can fail to recognise the depraving influence of a corrupt imagination; and the corruption may spring, not only from suggestions from without, but from those which rise spontaneously in our minds. Nor is even the imagination which is wholly pure absolutely without its dangers. It is a well-known law of our nature that an excessive indulgence in emotion that does not end in action tends rather to deaden than to stimulate the moral nerve. It has been often noticed that the exaggerated sentimentality which sheds passionate tears over the fictitious sorrows of a novel or a play is no certain sign of a benevolent and unselfish nature, and is quite compatible with much indifference to real sorrows and much indisposition to make efforts for their alleviation. It is, however, no less true, as Dugald Stewart says, that the apparent coldness and selfishness of men are often simply due to a want of that kind of imagination which enables us to realise sufferings with which we have never been brought into direct contact, and that once this power of realisation is acquired, the coldness is speedily dispelled. Nor can it be doubted that in the management of thought, the dream power often plays a most important part in alleviating human suffering; illuminating cheerless and gloomy lives, and breaking the chain of evil or distressing thoughts.

The immense place which the literature of fiction holds in the world shows how widely some measure of it is diffused, and how large an amount of time and talent is devoted to its cultivation. It is probable, however, that it is really stronger in the earlier and uncultivated than in the later stages of humanity, as it is more vivid in childhood and in youth than in mature life. 'A child,' as an American writer [65] has well said, 'can afford to sleep without dreaming; he has plenty of dreams without sleep.' The childhood of the world is also eminently an age of dreams. There are stages of civilisation in which the dream world blends so closely with the world of realities, in which the imagination so habitually and so spontaneously transfigures or distorts, that men become almost incapable of distinguishing between the real and the fictitious. This is the true age of myths and legends; and there are strata in contemporary society in which something of the same conditions is reproduced. 'To those who do not read

---

[65] Cable.

or write much,' says an acute observer, 'even in our days, dreams are much more real than to those who are continually exercising the imagination.... Since I have been occupied with literature my dreams have lost all vividness and are less real than the shadows of the trees; they do not deceive me even in my sleep. At every hour of the day I am accustomed to call up figures at will before my eyes, which stand out well defined and coloured to the very hue of their faces.... The less literary a people the more they believe in dreams; the disappearance of superstition is not due to the cultivation of reason or the spread of knowledge, but purely to the mechanical effect of reading, which so perpetually puts figures and aërial shapes before the mental gaze that in time those that occur naturally are thought no more of than those conjured into existence by a book. It is in far-away country places, where people read very little, that they see phantoms and consult the oracles of fate. Their dreams are real.'[66]

The last point I would notice in the management of character is the importance of what may be called moral safety-valves. One of the most fatal mistakes in education is the attempt which is so often made by the educator to impose his own habits and tastes on natures that are essentially different. It is common for men of lymphatic temperaments, of studious, saintly, and retiring tastes, to endeavor to force a high-spirited young man starting in life into their own mould—to prescribe for him the cast of tastes and pursuits they find most suited for themselves, forgetting that such an ideal can never satisfy a wholly different nature, and that in aiming at it a kind of excellence which might easily have been attained is missed. This is one of the evils that very frequently arise when the education of boys after an early age is left in the hands of women. It is the true explanation of the fact, which has so often been noticed, that children of clergymen, or at least children educated on a rigidly austere, puritanical system, so often go conspicuously to the bad. Such an education, imposed on a nature that is unfit for it, generally begins by producing hypocrisy, and not unfrequently ends by a violent reaction into vice. There is no greater mistake in education than to associate virtue in early youth with gloomy colours and constant restrictions, and few people do more mischief in the world than those who are perpetually inventing crimes. In circles where smoking, or field sports, or going to the play, or reading novels, or indulging in any boisterous games or in the most harmless Sunday amusements, are treated as if they were grave moral offences, young men constantly grow up who end by looking on grave moral offences as not worse than these things. They lose all sense of proportion and perspective in morals, and those who are always straining at gnats are often peculiarly apt to swallow camels. It is quite right that men who have formed for themselves an ideal of life of the kind that I have described should steadily pursue it, but it is another thing to impose it upon others, and to prescribe it as of general application. By teaching as absolutely wrong things that are in reality only culpable in their abuse or their excess, they destroy the habit of

---

[66] Jefferies, *Field and Hedgerow*, p. 242

moderate and restrained enjoyment, and a period of absolute prohibition is often followed by a period of unrestrained license.

The truth is there are elements in human nature which many moralists might wish to be absent, as they are very easily turned in the direction of vice, but which at the same time are inherent in our being, and, if rightly understood, are essential elements of human progress. The love of excitement and adventure; the fierce combative instinct that delights in danger, in struggle, and even in destruction; the restless ambition that seeks with an insatiable longing to better its position and to climb heights that are yet unscaled; the craving for some enjoyment which not merely gives pleasure but carries with it a thrill of passion,—all this lies deep in human nature and plays a great part in that struggle for existence, in that harsh and painful process of evolution by which civilisation is formed, faculty stimulated to its full development, and human progress secured. In the education of the individual, as in the education of the race, the true policy in dealing with these things is to find for them a healthy, useful, or at least harmless sphere of action. In the chemistry of character they may ally themselves with the most heroic as well as with the worst parts of our nature, and the same passion for excitement which in one man will take the form of ruinous vice, in another may lead to brilliant enterprise, while in a third it may be turned with no great difficulty into channels which are very innocent.

Take, for example, the case to which I have already referred, of a perfectly commonplace boy who, on coming of age, finds himself with a competence that saves him from the necessity of work; and who has no ambition, literary or artistic taste, love of work, interest in politics, religious or philanthropic earnestness, or special talent. What will become of him? In probably the majority of cases ruin, disease, and an early death lie before him. He seeks only for amusement and excitement, and three fatal temptations await him—drink, gambling, and women. If he falls under the dominion of these, or even of one of them, he almost infallibly wrecks either his fortune or his constitution, or both. It is perfectly useless to set before him high motives or ideals, or to incite him to lines of life for which he has no aptitude and which can give him no pleasure. What, then, can save him? Most frequently a happy marriage; but even if he is fortunate enough to attain this, it will probably only be after several years, and in those years a fatal bias is likely to be given to his life which can never be recovered. Yet experience shows that in cases of this kind a keen love of sport can often do much. With his gun and with his hunter he finds an interest, an excitement, an employment which may not be particularly noble, but which is at least sufficiently absorbing, and is not injurious either to his morals, his health, or his fortune. It is no small gain if, in the competition of pleasures, country pleasures take the place of those town pleasures which, in such cases as I have described, usually mean pleasures of vice.

Nor is it by any means only in such cases that field sports prove a great moral safety-valve, scattering morbid tastes and giving harmless and healthy vent to turns of character or feeling which might very easily be converted into vice. Among the influences that form the character of the upper classes of Englishmen they have a great part, and in spite of the exaggerations and extravagances that often accompany them, few good observers will doubt that they have an influence for good. However much of the Philistine element there may be in the upper classes in England, however manifest may be their limitations and their defects, there can be little doubt that on the whole the conditions of English life have in this sphere proved successful. There are few better working types within the reach of commonplace men than that of an English gentleman with his conventional tastes, standard of honour, religion, sympathies, ideals, opinions and instincts. He is not likely to be either a saint or a philosopher, but he is tolerably sure to be both an honourable and a useful man, with a fair measure of good sense and moderation, and with some disposition towards public duties. A crowd of out-of-door amusements and interests do much to dispel his peccant humours and to save him from the stagnation and the sensuality that have beset many foreign aristocracies. County business stimulates his activity, mitigates his class prejudices, and forms his judgment: and his standard of honour will keep him substantially right amid much fluctuation of opinions.

The reader, from his own experience of individual characters, will supply other illustrations of the lines of thought I am enforcing. Some temptations that beset us must be steadily faced and subdued. Others are best met by flight—by avoiding the thoughts or scenes that call them into activity; while other elements of character which we might wish to be away are often better treated in the way of marriage—that is by a judicious regulation and harmless application—than in the way of asceticism or attempted suppression. It is possible for men—if not in educating themselves, at least in educating others—to pitch their standard and their ideal too high. What they have to do is to recognise their own qualities and the qualities of those whom they influence as they are, and endeavour to use these usually very imperfect materials to the best advantage for the formation of useful, honourable and happy lives. According to the doctrine of this book, man comes into the world with a free will. But his free will, though a real thing, acts in a narrower circle and with more numerous limitations than he usually imagines. He can, however, do much so to dispose, regulate and modify the circumstances of his life as to diminish both his sufferings and his temptations, and to secure for himself the external conditions of a happy and upright life, and he can do something by judicious and persevering self-culture to improve those conditions of character on which, more than on any external circumstances, both happiness and virtue depend.

CHAPTER XIII   MONEY

I do not think that I can better introduce the few pages which I propose to write on the relations of money to happiness and to character than by a pregnant passage from one of the essays [67] of Sir Henry Taylor. 'So manifold are the bearings of money upon the lives and characters of mankind, that an insight which should search out the life of a man in his pecuniary relations would penetrate into almost every cranny of his nature. He who knows like St. Paul both how to spare and how to abound has a great knowledge; for if we take account of all the virtues with which money is mixed up— honesty, justice, generosity, charity, frugality, forethought, self-sacrifice, and of their correlative vices, it is a knowledge which goes near to cover the length and breadth of humanity, and a right measure in getting, saving, spending, giving, taking, lending, borrowing and bequeathing would almost argue a perfect man.'

There are few subjects on which the contrast between the professed and the real beliefs of men is greater than in the estimate of money. More than any other single thing it is the object and usually the lifelong object of human effort, and any accession of wealth is hailed by the immense majority of mankind as an unquestionable blessing. Yet if we were to take literally much of the teaching we have all heard we should conclude that money, beyond what is required for the necessaries of life, is far more a danger than a good; that it is the pre-eminent source of evil and temptation; that one of the first duties of man is to emancipate himself from the love of it, which can only mean from any strong desire for its increase.

In this, as in so many other things, the question is largely one of degree. No one who knows what is meant by the abject poverty to which a great proportion of the human race is condemned will doubt that at least such an amount of money as raises them from this condition is one of the greatest of human blessings. Extreme poverty means a lifelong struggle for the bare means of living; it means a life spent in wretched hovels, with insufficient food, clothes and firing, in enforced and absolute ignorance; an existence almost purely animal, with nearly all the higher faculties of man undeveloped. There is a far greater real difference in the material elements of happiness between the condition of such men and that of a moderately prosperous artizan in a civilised country than there is between the latter and the millionaire.

Money, again, at least to such an amount as enables men to be in some considerable degree masters of their own course in life, is also on the whole a great good. In this second degree it has less influence on happiness than health, and probably than character and domestic relations, but its influence is at least very great. Money is a good thing because it can be transformed into many other things. It gives the power of education which in itself does much to regulate the character and opens out countless tastes and spheres of enjoyment. It saves its possessor from the fear of a destitute old age and of the destitution of those he may leave behind, which is the

---

[67] *Notes on Life*

harrowing care of multitudes who cannot be reckoned among the very poor. It enables him to intermit labour in times of sickness and sorrow and old age, and in those extremes of heat and cold during which active labour is little less than physical pain. It gives him and it gives those he loves increased chances of life and increased hope of recovery in sickness. Few of the pains of penury are more acute than those of a poor man who sees his wife or children withering away through disease, and who knows or believes that better food or medical attendance, or a surgical operation, or a change of climate, might have saved them. Money, too, even when it does not dispense with work, at least gives a choice of work and longer intervals of leisure. For the very poor this choice hardly exists, or exists only within very narrow limits, and from want of culture or want of leisure some of their most marked natural aptitudes are never called into exercise. With the comparatively rich this is not the case. Money enables them to select the course of life which is congenial to their tastes and most suited to their natural talents, or, if their strongest taste cannot become their work, money at least gives them some leisure to cultivate it. The command of leisure, when it is fruitful leisure spent in congenial work, is to many, perhaps, the greatest boon it can bestow. 'Riches,' said Charles Lamb, 'are chiefly good because they give us Time.' 'All one's time to oneself! for which alone I rankle with envy at the rich. Books are good and pictures are good, and money to buy them is therefore good—but to buy time—in other words, life!'

To some men money is chiefly valuable because it makes it possible for them not to think of money. Except in the daily regulation of ordinary life, it enables them to put aside cares which are to them both harassing and distasteful, and to concentrate their thoughts and energies on other objects. An assured competence also, however moderate, gives men the priceless blessing of independence. There are walks of life, there are fields of ambition, there are classes of employments in which between inadequate remuneration and the pressure of want on the one side, and the facilities and temptations to illicit gain on the other, it is extremely difficult for a poor man to walk straight. Illicit gain does not merely mean gain that brings a man within the range of the criminal law. Many of its forms escape legal and perhaps social censure, and may be even sanctioned by custom. A competence, whether small or large, is no sure preservative against that appetite for gain which becomes one of the most powerful and insatiable of passions. But it at least diminishes temptation. It takes away the pressure of want under which so many natures that were once substantially honest have broken down.

In the expenditure of money there is usually a great deal of the conventional, the factitious, the purely ostentatious, but we are here dealing with the most serious realities of life. There are few or no elements of happiness and character more important than those I have indicated, and a small competence conduces powerfully to them. Let no man therefore despise it, for if wisely used it is one of the most real blessings of life. It is of course only within the reach of a small minority, but the number might easily be much larger than it is. Often when it is inherited in early youth it is scattered in one or two years of gambling and dissipation, followed by a lifetime of regret. In other cases it crumbles away in a generation, for it is made an excuse for a life of idleness, and when children multiply or misfortunes arrive, what was once a competence becomes nothing more than bare necessity. In a still larger number of cases many of its advantages are lost because men at once adopt a scale of living fully equal to their income. A man who with one house would be a wealthy man, finds life with two houses a constant struggle. A set of habits is acquired, a scale or standard of luxury is adopted, which at once sweeps away the margin of superfluity. Riches or poverty depend not merely on the amount of our possessions, but quite as much on the regulation of our desires, and the full advantages of competence are only felt when men begin by settling their scheme of life on a scale materially within their income. When the great lines of expenditure are thus wisely and frugally established, they can command a wide latitude and much ease in dealing with the smaller ones.

It is of course true that the power of a man thus to regulate his expenditure is by no means absolute. The position in society in which a man is born brings with it certain conventionalities and obligations that cannot be discarded. A great nobleman who has inherited a vast estate and a conspicuous social position will, through no fault of his own, find himself involved in constant difficulties and struggles on an income a tenth part of which would suffice to give a simple private gentleman every reasonable enjoyment in life. A poor clergyman who is obliged to keep up the position of a gentleman is in reality a much poorer man than a prosperous artizan, even though his actual income may be somewhat larger. But within the bounds which the conventionalities of society imperatively prescribe many scales of expenditure are possible, and the wise regulation of these is one of the chief forms of practical wisdom.

It may be observed, however, that not only men but nations differ widely in this respect, and the difference is not merely that between prudence and folly, between forethought and passion, but is also in a large degree a difference of tastes and ideals. In general it will be found that in Continental nations a man of independent fortune will place his expenditure more below his means than in England, and a man who has pursued some lucrative employment will sooner be satisfied with the competence he has acquired and will gladly exchange his work for a life of leisure. The English character prefers a higher rate of expenditure and work continued to the end.

It is probable that, so far as happiness depends on money, the happiest lot—though it is certainly not that which is most envied—is that of a man who possesses a realised fortune sufficient to save him from serious money cares about the present and the future, but who at the same time can only keep up the position in society he has chosen for himself, and provide as he desires for his children, by adding to it a professional income. Work is necessary both to happiness and to character, and experience shows that it most frequently attains its full concentration and continuity when it is professional, or, in other words, money-making. Men work in traces as they will seldom work at liberty. The compulsory character, the steady habits, the constant emulation of professional life mould and strengthen the will, and probably the happiest lot is when this kind of work exists, but without the anxiety of those who depend solely on it.

It is also a good thing when wealth tends to increase with age. 'Old age,' it has been said, 'is a very expensive thing.' If the taste for pleasure diminishes, the necessity for comfort increases. Men become more dependent and more fastidious, and hardships that are indifferent to youth become acutely painful. Beside this, money cares are apt to weigh with an especial heaviness upon the old. Avarice, as has been often observed, is eminently an old-age vice, and in natures that are in no degree avaricious it will be found that real money anxieties are more felt and have a greater haunting power in age than in youth. There is then the sense of impotence which makes men feel that their earning power has gone. On the other hand youth, and especially early married life spent under the pressure of narrow circumstances, will often be looked back upon as both the happiest and the most fruitful period of life. It is the best discipline of character. It is under such circumstances that men acquire habits of hard and steady work, frugality, order, forethought, punctuality, and simplicity of tastes. They acquire sympathies and realisations they would never have known in more prosperous circumstances. They learn to take keen pleasure in little things, and to value rightly both money and time. If wealth and luxury afterwards come in overflowing measure, these lessons will not be wholly lost.

The value of money as an element of happiness diminishes rapidly in proportion to its amount. In the case of the humbler fortunes, each accession brings with it a large increase of pleasure and comfort, and probably a very considerable addition to real happiness. In the case of rich men this is not the case, and of colossal fortunes only a very small fraction can be truly said to minister to the personal enjoyment of the owner. The disproportion in the world between pleasure and cost is indeed almost ludicrous. The two or three shillings that gave us our first Shakespeare would go but a small way towards providing one of the perhaps untasted dishes on the dessert table. The choicest masterpieces of the human mind—the works of human genius that through the long course of centuries have done most to ennoble, console, brighten, and direct the lives of men, might all be purchased—I do not say by the cost of a lady's necklace, but by that of one or two of the little stones of which it is composed. Compare the relish with which the tired pedestrian eats his bread and cheese with the appetites with which men sit down to some stately banquet; compare the level of spirits at the village dance with that of the great city ball whose lavish splendour fills the society papers with admiration; compare the charm of conversation in the college common room with the weary faces that may be often seen around the millionaire's dinner table,—and we may gain a good lesson of the vanity of riches. The transition from want to comfort brings with it keen enjoyment and much lasting happiness. The transition from mere comfort to luxury brings incomparably less and costs incomparably more. Let a man of enormous wealth analyse his life from day to day and try to estimate what are the things or hours that have afforded him real and vivid pleasure. In many cases he will probably say that he has found it in his work—in others in the hour spent with his cigar, his newspaper, or his book, or in his game of cricket, or in the excitement of the hunting-field, or in his conversation with an old friend, or in hearing his daughters sing, or in welcoming his son on his return from school. Let him look round the splendid adornments of his home and ask how many of these things have ever given him a pleasure at all proportionate to their cost. Probably in many cases, if he deals honestly with himself, he would confess that his armchair and his bookshelves are almost the only exceptions.

Steam, the printing press, the spread of education, and the great multiplication of public libraries, museums, picture galleries and exhibitions have brought the chief pleasures of life in a much larger degree than in any previous age within the reach of what are called the working classes, while in the conditions of modern life nearly all the great sources of real enjoyment that money can give are open to a man who possesses a competent but not extraordinary fortune and some leisure. Intellectual tastes he may gratify to the full. Books, at all events in the great centres of civilisation, are accessible far in excess of his powers of reading. The pleasures of the theatre, the pleasures of society, the pleasures of music in most of its forms, the pleasures of travel with all its variety of interests, and many of the pleasures of sport, are abundantly at his disposal. The possession of the highest works of art has no doubt become more and more a monopoly of the very rich, but picture galleries and exhibitions and the facilities of travel have diffused the knowledge and enjoyment of art over a vastly wider area than in the past. The power of reproducing works of art has been immensely increased and cheapened, and in one form at least the highest art has been brought within the reach of a man of very moderate means. Photography can reproduce a drawing with such absolute perfection that he may cover his walls with works of Michael Angelo and Leonardo da Vinci that are indistinguishable from the originals. The standard of comfort in mere material things is now so high in well-to-do households that to a healthy nature the millionaire can add little to it. Perhaps among the pleasures of wealth that which has the strongest influence is a country place, especially when it brings with it old remembrances, and associations that appeal powerfully to the affections and the imagination. More than any other inanimate thing it throws its tendrils round the human heart and becomes the object of a deep and lasting affection. But even here it will be probably found that this pleasure is more felt by the owner of one country place than by the great proprietor whose life is spent alternately in several—by the owner of a place of moderate dimensions than by the owner of those vast parks which can only be managed at great expense and trouble and by much delegated supervision, and which are usually thrown open with such liberality to the public that they probably give more real pleasure to others than to their owners.

Among the special pleasures of the enormously rich the collecting passion is conspicuous, and of course a very rich man can carry it into departments which men of moderate fortune can hardly touch. In the rare case when the collector is a man of strong and genuine artistic taste the possession of works of beauty is a thing of enduring pleasure, but in general the mere love of collecting, though it often becomes a passion almost amounting to a mania, bears very little proportion to pecuniary value. The intelligent collector of fossils has as much pleasure as the collector of gems— probably indeed more, as the former pursuit brings with it a much greater variety of interest, and usually depends much more on the personal exertions of the collector. It is pleasant, in looking over a geological collection, to think that every stone we see has given a pleasure. A collector of Caxtons, a collector of large printed or illustrated editions, a collector of first editions of famous books, a collector of those editions that are so much prized because an author has made in them some blunder which he afterwards corrected; a collector of those unique books which have survived as rarities because no one thought it worth while to reprint them or because they are distinguished by some obsolete absurdity, will probably not derive more pleasure, though he will spend vastly more money, than the mere literary man who, being interested in some particular period or topic, loves to hunt up in old bookshops the obscure and forgotten literature relating to it. Much the same thing may be said of other tastes. The gratification of a strong taste or hobby will always give pleasure, and it makes little difference whether it is an expensive or an inexpensive one.

The pleasures of acquisition, the pleasures of possession, and the pleasures of ostentation, are no doubt real things, though they act in very different degrees on different natures, and some of them much more on one sex than on the other. In general, however, they tend to grow passive and inert. A state of luxury and splendour is little appreciated by those who are born to it, though much if it follows a period of struggle and penury. Yet even then the circumstances and surroundings of life soon become a second nature. Men become so habituated to them that they are accepted almost mechanically and cease to give positive pleasure, though a deprivation of them gives positive pain. The love of power, the love of society, and—what is not quite the same thing—the love of social influence, are, however, much stronger and more enduring, and great wealth is largely valued because it helps to give them, though it does not give them invariably, and though there are other things that give them in an equal or greater degree. To many very rich men some form of field sports is probably the greatest pleasure that money affords. It at least gives a genuine thrill of unmistakable enjoyment.

Few of the special pleasures of the millionaire can be said to be purely selfish, for few are concentrated altogether on himself. His great park is usually open to the public. His pictures are lent for exhibition or exhibited in his house. If he keeps a pack of hounds others hunt with it. If he preserves game to an enormous extent he invites many to shoot it, and at his great entertainments it will often be found that no one derives less pleasure than the weary host.

At the same time no thinking man can fail to be struck with the great waste of the means of enjoyment in a society in which such gigantic sums are spent in mere conventional ostentation which gives little or no pleasure; in which the best London houses are those which are the longest untenanted; in which some of the most enchanting gardens and parks are only seen by their owners for a few weeks in the year.

Hamerton, in his Essay on Bohemianism, has very truly shown that the rationale of a great deal of this is simply the attempt of men to obtain from social intercourse the largest amount of positive pleasure or amusement it can give by discarding the forms, the costly conventionalities, the social restrictions that encumber and limit it. One of the worst tendencies of a very wealthy society is that by the mere competition of ostentation the standard of conventional expense is raised, and the intercourse of men limited by the introduction of a number of new and costly luxuries which either give no pleasure or give pleasure that bears no kind of proportion to their cost. Examples may sometimes be seen of a very rich man who imagines that he can obtain from life real enjoyment in proportion to his wealth and who uses it for purely selfish purposes. We may find this in the almost insane extravagance of vulgar ostentation by which the parvenu millionaire tries to gratify his vanity and dazzle his neighbours; in the wild round of prodigal dissipation and vice by which so many young men who have inherited enormous fortunes have wrecked their constitutions and found a speedy path to an unhonoured grave. They sought from money what money cannot give, and learned too late that in pursuing shadows they missed the substance that was within their reach.

To the intelligent millionaire, however, and especially to those who are brought up to great possessions, wealth is looked on in a wholly different light. It is a possession and a trust carrying with it many duties as well as many interests and accompanied by a great burden of responsibility. Mere pleasure-hunting plays but a small and wholly subsidiary part in such lives, and they are usually filled with much useful work. This man, for example, is a banker on a colossal scale. Follow his life, and you will find that for four days in the week he is engaged in his office as steadily, as unremittingly as any clerk in his establishment. He has made himself master not only of the details of his own gigantic business but of the whole great subject of finance in all its international relations. He is a power in many lands. He is consulted in every crisis of finance. He is an important influence in a crowd of enterprises, most of them useful as well as lucrative, some of them distinctively philanthropic. Saturday and Sunday he spends at his country place, usually entertaining a number of guests. One other day during the hunting season he regularly devotes to his favourite sport. His holiday is the usual holiday of a professional man, with rather a tendency to abridge than to lengthen it, as the natural bent of his thoughts is so strongly to his work that time soon begins to hang heavily when he is away from it.

Another man is an ardent philanthropist, and his philanthropy probably blends with much religious fervour, and he becomes in consequence a leader in the religious world. Such a life cannot fail to be abundantly filled. Religious meetings, committees, the various interests of the many institutions with which he is connected, the conflicting and competing claims of different religious societies, fully occupy his time and thoughts, sometimes to the great neglect of his private affairs.

Another man is of a different type. Shy, retiring, hating publicity, and not much interested in politics, he is a gigantic landowner, and the work of his life is concentrated on the development of his own estate. He knows the circumstances of every village, almost of every farm. It is his pride that no labourer on his estate is badly housed, that no part of it is slovenly or mismanaged or poverty-stricken. He endows churches and hospitals, he erects public buildings, encourages every local industry, makes in times of distress much larger remissions of rent than would be possible for a poorer man, superintends personally the many interests on his property, knows accurately the balance of receipts and expenditure, takes a great interest in sanitation, in new improvements and experiments in agriculture, in all the multifarious matters that affect the prosperity of his numerous tenantry. He subscribes liberally to great national undertakings, as he considers it one of the duties of his position, but his heart is not in such things, and the well-being of his own vast estate and of those who live upon it is the aim and the work of his life. For a few weeks of the year he exercises the splendid and lavish hospitality which is expected from a man in his position, and he is always very glad when those weeks are over. He has, however, his own expensive hobby, which gives him real pleasure—his yacht, his picture gallery, his museum, his collection of wild animals, his hothouses or his racing establishment. One or more of these form the real amusement of his active and useful life.

A more common type in England is that of the active politician. Great wealth and especially great landed property bring men easily into Parliament, and, if united with industry and some measure of ability, into official life, and public life thus becomes a profession and in many cases a very laborious one. There are few better examples of a well-filled life and of the skilful management and economy of time than are to be found in the lives of some great noblemen who take a leading part in politics and preside over important Government departments without suffering their gigantic estates to fall into mismanagement, or neglecting the many social duties and local interests connected with them. Most of their success is indeed due to the wise use of money in economising time by trustworthy and efficient delegation. Yet the superintending brain, the skilful choice, the personal control cannot be dispensed with. In a life so fully occupied the few weeks of pleasure which may be spent on a Scotch moor or in a Continental watering-place will surely not be condemned.

The economy of time and the elasticity of brain and character such lives develop are, however, probably exceeded by another class. Nothing is more remarkable in the social life of the present generation than the high pressure under which a large number of ladies in great positions habitually live. It strikes every Continental observer, for there is nothing approaching it in any other European country, and it certainly far exceeds anything that existed in England in former generations. Pleasure-seeking, combined, however, on a large scale with pleasure-giving, holds a much more prominent place in these lives than in those I have just described. With not a few women, indeed, of wealth and position, it is the all-in-all of life, and in general it is probable that women obtain more pleasure from most forms of society than men, though it is also true that they bear a much larger share of its burdens. There are, however, in this class, many who combine with society a truly surprising number and variety of serious interests. Not only the management of a great house, not only the superintendence of schools and charities and local enterprises connected with a great estate, but also a crowd of philanthropic, artistic, political, and sometimes literary interests fill their lives. Few lives, indeed, in any station are more full, more intense, more constantly and variously occupied. Public life, which in most foreign countries is wholly outside the sphere of women, is eagerly followed. Public speaking, which in the memory of many now living was almost unknown among women of any station in English society, has become the most ordinary accomplishment. Their object is to put into life from youth to old age as much as life can give, and they go far to attain their end. A wonderful nimbleness and flexibility of intellect capable of turning swiftly from subject to subject has been developed, and keeps them in touch with a very wide range both of interests and pleasures.

There are no doubt grave drawbacks to all this. Many will say that this external activity must be at the sacrifice of the duties of domestic life, but on this subject there is, I think, at least much exaggeration. Education has now assumed such forms and attained such a standard that usually for many hours in the day the education of the young in a wealthy family is in the hands of accomplished specialists, and I do not think that the most occupied lives are those in which the cares of a home are most neglected. How far, however, this intense and constant strain is compatible with physical well-being is a graver question, and many have feared that it must bequeath weakened constitutions to the coming generation. Nor is a life of incessant excitement in other respects beneficial. In both intellectual and moral hygiene the best life is that which follows nature and alternates periods of great activity with periods of rest. Retirement, quiet, steady reading, and the silent thought which matures character and deepens impressions are things that seem almost disappearing from many English lives. But lives such as I have described are certainly not useless, undeveloped, or wholly selfish, and they in a large degree fulfil that great law of happiness, that it should be sought for rather in interests than in pleasures.

I have already referred to the class who value money chiefly because it enables them to dismiss money thoughts and cares from their minds. On the whole, this end is probably more frequently attained by men of moderate but competent fortunes than by the very rich. This is at least the case when they are sufficiently rich to invest their money in securities which are liable to no serious risk or fluctuation. A gigantic fortune is seldom of such a nature that it does not bring with it great cares of administration and require much thought and many decisions. There is, however, one important exception. When there are many children the task of providing for their future falls much more lightly on the very rich than on those of medium fortune.

There is a class, however, who are the exact opposite of these and who make the simple acquisition of money the chief interest and pleasure of their lives. Money-making in some form is the main occupation of the great majority of men, but it is usually as a means to an end. It is to acquire the means of livelihood, or the means of maintaining or improving a social position, or the means of providing as they think fit for the children who are to succeed them. Sometimes, however, with the very rich and without any ulterior object, money-making for its own sake becomes the absorbing interest. They can pursue it with great advantage; for, as has been often said, nothing makes money like money, and the possession of an immense capital gives innumerable facilities for increasing it. The collecting passion takes this form. They come to care more for money than for anything money can purchase, though less for money than for the interest and the excitement of getting it. Speculative enterprise, with its fluctuations, uncertainties and surprises, becomes their strongest interest and their greatest amusement.

When it is honestly conducted there is no real reason why it should be condemned. On these conditions a life so spent is, I think, usually useful to the world, for it generally encourages works that are of real value. All that can be truly said is that it brings with it grave temptations and is very apt to lower a man's moral being. Speculation easily becomes a form of gambling so fierce in its excitement that, when carried on incessantly and on a great scale, it kills all capacity for higher and tranquil pleasures, strengthens incalculably the temptations to unscrupulous gain, disturbs the whole balance of character, and often even shortens life. With others the love of accumulation has a strange power of materialising, narrowing and hardening. Habits of meanness—sometimes taking curious and inconsistent forms, and applying only to particular things or departments of life—steal insensibly over them, and the love of money assumes something of the character of mania. Temptations connected with money are indeed among the most insidious and among the most powerful to which we are exposed. They have probably a wider empire than drink, and, unlike the temptations that spring from animal passion, they strengthen rather than diminish with age. In no respect is it more necessary for a man to keep watch over his own character, taking care that the unselfish element does not diminish, and correcting the love of acquisition by generosity of expenditure.

It is probable that the highest form of charity, involving real and serious self-denial, is much more common among the poor, and even the very poor, than among the rich. I think most persons who have had much practical acquaintance with the dealings of the poor with one another will confirm this. It is certainly far less common among those who are at the opposite pole of fortune. They have not had the same discipline, or indeed the same possibility of self-sacrifice, or the same means of realising the pains of poverty, and there is another reason which tends not unnaturally to check their benevolence. A man with the reputation of great wealth soon finds himself beleaguered by countless forms of mendicancy and imposture. He comes to feel that there is a general conspiracy to plunder him, and he is naturally thrown into an attitude of suspicion and self-defence. Often, though he may give largely and generously, he will do so under the veil of strict anonymity, in order to avoid a reputation for generosity which will bring down upon him perpetual solicitations. If he is an intellectual man he will probably generalise from his own experience. He will be deeply impressed with the enormous evils that have sprung from ill-judged charity, and with the superiority even from a philanthropic point of view of a productive expenditure of money.

And in truth it is difficult to overrate the evil effects of injudicious charities in discouraging thrift, industry, foresight and self-respect. They take many forms; some of them extremely obvious, while others can only be rightly judged by a careful consideration of remote consequences. There are the idle tourists who break down, in a once unsophisticated district, that sense of self-respect which is one of the most valuable lessons that early education can give, by flinging pence to be scrambled for among the children, or who teach the poor the fatal lesson that mendicancy or something hardly distinguishable from mendicancy will bring greater gain than honest and continuous work. There is the impulsive, uninquiring charity that makes the trade of the skilful begging-letter writer a lucrative profession, and makes men and women who are rich, benevolent and weak, the habitual prey of greedy impostors. There is the old-established charity for ministering to simple poverty which draws to its centre all the pauperism of the neighbouring districts, depresses wages, and impoverishes the very district or class it was intended to benefit. There are charities which not only largely diminish the sufferings that are the natural consequence and punishment of vice; but even make the lot of the criminal and the vicious a better one than that of the hard-working poor. There are overlapping charities dealing with the same department, but kept up with lavish waste through the rivalry of different religious denominations, or in the interests of the officials connected with them; belated or superannuated charities formed to deal with circumstances or sufferings that have in a large degree passed away—useless, or almost useless, charities established to carry out some silly fad or to gratify some silly vanity; sectarian charities intended to further ends which, in the eyes of all but the members of one sect, are not only useless but mischievous; charities that encourage thriftless marriages, or make it easy for men to neglect obvious duties, or keep a semi-pauper population stationary in employments and on a soil where they can never prosper, or in other ways handicap, impede or divert the natural and healthy course of industry. Illustrations of all these evils will occur to every careful student of the subject. Unintelligent, thoughtless, purely impulsive charity, and charity which is inspired by some other motive than a real desire to relieve suffering, will constantly go wrong, but every intelligent man can find without difficulty vast fields on which the largest generosity may be expended with abundant fruit.

Hospitals and kindred institutions for alleviating great unavoidable calamities, and giving the sick poor something of the same chances of recovery as the rich, for the most part fall under this head. Money will seldom be wasted which is spent in promoting kinds of knowledge, enterprise or research that bring no certain remuneration proportioned to their value; in assisting poor young men of ability and industry to develop their special talents; in encouraging in their many different forms thrift, self-help and co-operation; in alleviating the inevitable suffering that follows some great catastrophe on land or sea, or great transitions of industry, or great fluctuations and depressions in class prosperity; in giving the means of healthy recreation or ennobling pleasures to the denizens of a crowded town. The vast sphere of education opens endless fields for generous expenditure, and every religious man will find objects which, in the opinion not only of men of his own persuasion, but also of many others, are transcendently important. Nor is it a right principle that charity should be denied to all calamities which are in some degree due to the fault of the sufferer, or which might have been averted by exceptional forethought or self-denial. Some economists write as if a far higher standard of will and morals should be expected among the poor and the uneducated than can be found among the rich. Good sense and right feeling will here easily draw the line, abstaining from charities that have a real influence in encouraging improvidence or vice, yet making due allowance for the normal weaknesses of our nature.

In all these ways the very rich can find ample opportunities for useful benevolence. It is the prerogative of great wealth that it can often cure what others can only palliate, and can establish permanent sources of good which will continue long after the donors have passed away. In dealing with individual cases of distress, rich men who have neither the time nor the inclination to investigate the special circumstances will do well to rely largely on the recommendation of others. If they choose trustworthy, competent and sensible advisers with as much judgment as they commonly show in the management of their private affairs, they are not likely to go astray. There never was a period when a larger amount of intelligent and disinterested labour was employed in careful and detailed examination of the circumstances and needs of the poor. The parish clergyman, the district visitor, the agents of the Charity Organization Society which annually selects its special cases of well-ascertained need, will abundantly furnish them with the knowledge they require.

The advantage or disadvantage of the presence in a country of a large class of men possessing fortunes far exceeding anything that can really administer to their enjoyment is a question which has greatly divided both political economists and moralists. The former were long accustomed to maintain somewhat exclusively that laws and institutions should be established with the object of furthering the greatest possible accumulation of wealth, and that a system of unrestricted competition, coupled with equal laws, giving each man the most complete security in the possession and disposal of his property, was the best means of attaining this end. They urged with great truth that, although under such a system the inequalities of fortune will be enormous, most of the wealth of the very rich will inevitably be distributed in the form of wages, purchases, and industrial enterprises through the community at large, and that, other things being equal, the richest country will on the whole be the happiest. They clearly saw the complete delusion of the common assertions that the more millionaires there are in a country the more paupers will multiply, and that society is dividing between the enormously rich and the abjectly poor. The great industrial communities, in which there are the largest number of very wealthy men, are also the centres in which we find the most prosperous middle class, and the highest and most progressive rates of wages and standards of comfort among the poor. Great corruption in many forms no doubt exists in them, but it can scarcely be maintained with confidence that the standard of integrity is on the whole lower in these than in other countries, and they at least escape what in many poor countries is one of the most fruitful causes of corruption in all branches of administration—the inadequate pay of the servants of the Crown. The path of liberty in the eyes of economists of this school is the path of wisdom, and they were profoundly distrustful of all legislative attempts to restrict or interfere with the course of industrial progress.

In our own generation a somewhat different tendency has manifestly strengthened. It has been said that past political economists paid too much attention to the accumulation and too little to the distribution of wealth. Men have become more sensible to the high level of happiness and moral well-being that has been attained in some of the smaller and somewhat stagnant countries of Europe, where wealth is more generally attained by thrift and steady industry than by great industrial or commercial enterprise, in which there are few large fortunes but little acute poverty, a low standard of luxury, but a high standard of real comfort. The enormous evils that have grown up in wealthy countries, in the form of company-mongering, excessive competition, extravagant and often vicious luxury, and dishonest administration of public funds, are more and more felt, and it is only too true that in these countries there are large and influential circles of society in which all considerations of character, intellect, or manners seem lost in an intense thirst for wealth and for the things that it can give. Sometimes we find vast fortunes in countries where there is but little enterprise and a very low standard of comfort among the people, and where this is the case it is usually due to unequal laws or corrupt administration. In the free, democratic, and industrial communities great fluctuations and disparities of wealth are inevitable, and some of the most colossal fortunes have, no doubt, been made by the evil methods I have described. They are, however, only a minority, and not a very large one. Like all the great successes of life, abnormal accumulation of wealth is usually due to the combination in different proportions of ability, character, and chance, and is not tainted with dishonesty. On the whole, the question that should be asked is not what a man has, but how he obtained it and how he uses it. When wealth is honestly acquired and wisely and generously used, the more rich men there are in a country the better.

There has probably never been a period in the history of the world when the conditions of industry, assisted by the great gold discoveries in several parts of the globe, were so favourable to the formation of enormous fortunes as at present, and when the race of millionaires was so large. The majority belong to the English-speaking race; probably most of their gigantic fortunes have been rapidly accumulated, and bring with them none of the necessary, hereditary, and clearly defined obligations of a great landowner, while a considerable proportion of them have fallen to the lot of men who, through their education or early habits, have not many cultivated or naturally expensive tastes. In England many of the new millionaires become great landowners and set up great establishments. In America, where country tastes are less marked and where the difficulties of domestic service are very great, this is less common. In both countries the number of men with immense fortunes, absolutely at their own disposal, has enormously increased, and the character of their expenditure has become a matter of real national importance.

Much of it, no doubt, goes in simple luxury and ostentation, or in mere speculation, or in restoring old and dilapidated fortunes through the marriages of rank with money which are so characteristic of our time; but much also is devoted to charitable or philanthropic purposes. In this, as in most things, motives are often very blended. To men of such fortunes, such expenditure, even on a large scale, means no real self-sacrifice, and the inducements to it are not always of the highest kind. To some men it is a matter of ambition—a legitimate and useful ambition—to obtain the enduring and honourable fame which attaches to the founder of a great philanthropic or educational establishment. Others find that, in England at least, large philanthropic expenditure is one of the easiest and shortest paths to social success, bringing men and women of low extraction and bad manners into close and frequent connection with the recognised leaders of society; while others again have discovered that it is the quickest way of effacing the stigma which still in some degree attaches to wealth which has been acquired by dishonourable or dubious means. Fashion, social ambition, and social rivalries are by no means unknown in the fields of charity. There are many, however, in whose philanthropy the element of self has no place, and whose sole desire is to expend their money in forms that can be of most real and permanent benefit to others.

Such men have great power, and, if their philanthropic expenditure is wisely guided, it may be of incalculable benefit. I have already indicated many of the channels in which it may safely flow, but one or two additional hints on the subject may not be useless. Perhaps as a general rule these men will find that they can act most wisely by strengthening and enlarging old charities which are really good, rather than by founding new ones. Competition is the soul of industry, but certainly not of charity, and there is in England a deplorable waste of money and machinery through the excessive multiplication of institutions intended for the same objects. The kind of ambition to which I have just referred tends to make men prefer new charities which can be identified with their names; the paid officials connected with charities have become a large and powerful profession, and their influence is naturally used in the same direction; the many different religious bodies in the country often refuse to combine, and each desires to have its own institutions; and there are fashions in charity which, while they greatly stimulate generosity, have too often the effect of diverting it from the older and more unobtrusive forms. On the other hand, one of the most important facts in our present economical condition is that an extraordinary and almost unparalleled development of industrial prosperity has been accompanied by extreme and long-continued agricultural depression and by a great fall in the rate of interest. Wealth in many forms is accumulating with wonderful rapidity, and the increased rate of wages is diffusing prosperity among the working classes; but those who depend directly or indirectly on agricultural rents or on interest of money invested in trust securities have been suffering severely, and they comprise some of the most useful, blameless, and meritorious classes in the community. The same causes that have injured them have fallen with crushing severity on old-established institutions which usually derive their income largely or entirely from the rent of land or from money invested in the public funds. The bitter cry of distress that is rising from the hospitals and many other ancient charities, from the universities, from the clergy of the Established Church, abundantly proves it.

The preference, however, to be given to old charities rather than to new ones is subject to very many exceptions. It does not apply to new countries or to the many cases in which changes and developments of industry have planted vast agglomerations of population in districts which were once but thinly populated, and therefore but little provided with charitable or educational institutions. Nor does it apply to the many cases in which the circumstances of modern life have called into existence new forms of charity, new wants, new dangers and evils to be combated, new departments of knowledge to be cultivated. One of the greatest difficulties of the older universities is that of providing, out of their shrinking endowments, for the teaching of branches of science and knowledge which have only come into existence, or at least into prominence, long after these universities were established, and some of which require not only trained teachers but costly apparatus and laboratories. Increasing international competition and enlarged scientific knowledge have rendered necessary an amount of technical and agricultural education never dreamed of by our ancestors; and the rise of the great provincial towns and the greater intensity of provincial life and provincial patriotism, as well as the changes that have passed over the position both of the working and middle classes, have created a genuine demand for educational establishments of a different type from the older universities. The higher education of women is essentially a nineteenth-century work, and it has been carried on without the assistance of old endowments and with very little help from modern Parliaments. In the distribution of public funds a class which is wholly unrepresented in Parliament seldom gets its fair share; and higher education, like most forms of science, like most of the higher forms of literature, and like many valuable forms of research, never can be self-supporting. There are great branches of knowledge which without established endowments must remain uncultivated, or be cultivated only by men of considerable private means. Some invaluable curative agencies, such as convalescent homes in different countries and climates and for different diseases, have grown up in our own generation, as well as some of the most fruitful forms of medical research and some of the most efficacious methods of giving healthy change and brightness to the lives that are most monotonous and overstrained. Every great revolution in industry, in population, and even in knowledge, brings with it new and special wants, and there are cases in which assisted emigration is one of the best forms of charity.

These are but a few illustrations of the directions in which the large surplus funds which many of the very rich are prepared to expend on philanthropic purposes may profitably go. There is a marked and increasing tendency in our age to meet all the various exigencies of Society, as they arise, by State aid resting on compulsory taxation. In countries where the levels of fortune are such that few men have incomes greatly in excess of their real or factitious wants, this method will probably be necessary; but many of the wants I have described can be better met by the old English method of intelligent private generosity, and in a country in which the number of the very rich is so great and so increasing, this generosity should not be wanting.

CHAPTER XIV MARRIAGE

The beautiful saying of Newton, that he felt like a child who had been picking up a few pebbles on the shore of the great ocean of undiscovered truth, may well occur to any writer who attempts to say something on the vast subject of marriage. The infinite variety of circumstances and characters affects it in infinitely various ways, and all that can here be done is to collect a few somewhat isolated and miscellaneous remarks upon it. Yet it is a subject which cannot be omitted in a book like this. In numerous cases it is the great turning-point of a life, and in all cases when it takes place it is one of the most important of its events. Whatever else marriage may do or fail to do, it never leaves a man unchanged. His intellect, his character, his happiness, his way of looking on the world, will all be influenced by it. If it does not raise or strengthen him it will lower or weaken. If it does not deepen happiness it will impair it. It brings with it duties, interests, habits, hopes, cares, sorrows, and joys that will penetrate into every fissure of his nature and modify the whole course of his life.

It is strange to think with how much levity and how little knowledge a contract which is so indissoluble and at the same time so momentous is constantly assumed; sometimes under the influence of a blinding passion and at an age when life is still looked upon as a romance or an idyll; sometimes as a matter of mere ambition and calculation, through a desire for wealth or title or position. Men and women rely on the force of habit and necessity to accommodate themselves to conditions they have never really understood or realised.

In most cases different motives combine, though in different degrees. Sometimes an overpowering affection for the person is the strongest motive and eclipses all others. Sometimes the main motive to marriage is a desire to be married. It is to obtain a settled household and position; to be relieved from the 'unchartered freedom' and the 'vague desires' of a lonely life; to find some object of affection; to acquire the steady habits and the exemption from household cares which are essential to a career; to perpetuate a race; perhaps to escape from family discomforts, or to introduce a new and happy influence into a family. With these motives a real affection for a particular person is united, but it is not of such a character as to preclude choice, judgment, comparison, and a consideration of worldly advantages.

It is a wise saying of Swift that there would be fewer unhappy marriages in the world if women thought less of making nets and more of making cages. The qualities that attract, fascinate, and dazzle are often widely different from those which are essential to a happy marriage. Sometimes they are distinctly hostile to it. More frequently they conduce to it, but only in an inferior or subsidiary degree. The turn of mind and character that makes the accomplished flirt is certainly not that which promises best for the happiness of a married life; and distinguished beauty, brilliant talents, and the heroic qualities that play a great part in the affairs of life, and shine conspicuously in the social sphere, sink into a minor place among the elements of married happiness. In marriage the identification of two lives is so complete that it brings every faculty and gift into play, but in degrees and proportions very different from public life or casual intercourse and relations. The most essential are often wanting in a brilliant life, and are largely developed in lives and characters that rise little, if at all, above the commonplace. In the words of a very shrewd man of the world: 'Before marriage the shape, the figure, the complexion carry all before them; after marriage the mind and character unexpectedly claim their share, and that the largest, of importance.'[68]

The relation is one of the closest intimacy and confidence, and if the identity of interest between the two partners is not complete, each has an almost immeasurable power of injuring the other. A moral basis of sterling qualities is of capital importance. A true, honest, and trustworthy nature, capable of self-sacrifice and self-restraint, should rank in the first line, and after that a kindly, equable, and contented temper, a power of sympathy, a habit of looking at the better and brighter side of men and things. Of intellectual qualities, judgment, tact, and order are perhaps the most valuable. Above almost all things, men should seek in marriage perfect sanity, and dread everything like hysteria. Beauty will continue to be a delight, though with much diminished power, but grace and the charm of manner will retain their full attraction to the last. They brighten in innumerable ways the little things of life, and life is mainly made up of little things, exposed to petty frictions, and requiring small decisions and small sacrifices. Wide interests and large appreciations are, in the marriage relation, more important than any great constructive or creative talent, and the power to soothe, to sympathise, to counsel, and to endure, than the highest qualities of the hero or the saint. It is by these alone that the married life attains its full measure of perfection.

'Tu mihi curarum requies, tu nocte vel atrâ
Lumen, et in solis tu mihi turba locis.'[69]

But while this is true of all marriages, it is obvious that different professions and circumstances of life will demand different qualities. A hard-working labouring man, or a man who, though not labouring with his hands, is living a life of poverty and struggle, will not seek in marriage a type of character exactly the same as a man who is born to a great position, and who has large social and administrative duties to discharge. The wife of a clergyman immersed in the many interests of a parish; the wife of a soldier or a merchant, who may have to live in many lands, with long periods of separation from her husband, and perhaps amid many hardships; the wife of an active and ambitious politician; the wife of a busy professional man incessantly occupied outside his home; the wife of a man whose health or business or habits keep him constantly in his house, will each need some special qualities. There are few things in which both men and women naturally differ more than in the elasticity and adaptiveness of their natures, in their power of bearing monotony, in the place which habit, routine, and variety hold in their happiness; and in different kinds of life these

---

[68] *Melbourne Papers*, p. 72.

[69] Tibullus.

things have very different degrees of importance. Special family circumstances, such as children by a former marriage, or difficult and delicate relations with members of the family of one partner, will require the exercise of special qualities. Such relations, indeed, are often one of the most searching and severe tests of the sterling qualities of female character.

Probably, on the whole, the best presumption of a successful choice in marriage will be found where the wife has not been educated in circumstances or ideas absolutely dissimilar from those of her married life. Marriages of different races or colours are rarely happy, and the same thing is true of marriages between persons of social levels that are so different as to entail great differences of manners and habits. Other and minor disparities of circumstances between girl life and married life will have their effect, but they are less strong and less invariable. Some of the happiest marriages have been marriages of emancipation, which removed a girl from uncongenial family surroundings, and placed her for the first time in an intellectual and moral atmosphere in which she could freely breathe. At the same time, in the choice of a wife, the character, circumstances, habits, and tone of the family in which she has been brought up will always be an important element. There are qualities of race, there are pedigrees of character, which it is never prudent to neglect. Franklin quotes with approval the advice of a wise man to choose a wife 'out of a bunch,' as girls brought up together improve each other by emulation, learn mutual self-sacrifice and forbearance, rub off their angularities, and are not suffered to develop overweening self-conceit. A family where the ruling taste is vulgar, where the standard of honour is low, where extravagance and self-indulgence and want of order habitually prevail, creates an atmosphere which it needs a strong character altogether to escape. There is also the great question of physical health. A man should seek in marriage rather to raise than to depress the physical level of his family, and above all not to introduce into it grave, well-ascertained hereditary disease. Of all forms of self-sacrifice hardly any is at once so plainly right and so plainly useful as the celibacy of those who are tainted with such disease.

There is no subject on which religious teachers have dwelt more than upon marriage and the relation of the sexes, and it has been continually urged that the propagation of children is its first end. It is strange, however, to observe how almost absolutely in the popular ethics of Christendom such considerations as that which I have last mentioned have been neglected. If one of the most responsible things that a man can do is to bring a human being into the world, one of his first and most obvious duties is to do what he can to secure that it shall come into the world with a sound body and a sane mind. This is the best inheritance that parents can leave their children, and it is in a large degree within their reach. Immature marriage, excessive child-bearing, marriages of near relations, and, above all, marriages with some grave hereditary physical or mental disease or some great natural defect, may bring happiness to the parents, but can scarcely fail to entail a terrible penalty upon their children. It is clearly recognised that one of the first duties of parents to their children is to secure them in early life not only good education, but also, as far as is within their power, the conditions of a healthy being. But the duty goes back to an earlier stage, and in marriage the prospects of the unborn should never be forgotten. This is one of the considerations which in the ethics of the future is likely to have a wholly different place from any that it has occupied in the past.

A kindred consideration, little less important and almost equally neglected in popular teaching, is that it is a moral offence to bring children into the world with no prospect of being able to provide for them. It is difficult to exaggerate the extent to which the neglect of these two duties has tended to the degradation and unhappiness of the world.

The greatly increased importance which the Darwinian theory has given to heredity should tend to make men more sensible of the first of these duties. In marriage there are not only reciprocal duties between the two partners; there are also, more than in any other act of life, plain duties to the race. The hereditary nature of insanity and of some forms of disease is an indisputable truth. The hereditary transmission of character has not, it is true, as yet acquired this position; and there is a grave schism on the subject in the Darwinian school. But that it exists to some extent few close observers will doubt, and it is in a high degree probable that it is one of the most powerful moulding influences of life. No more probable explanation has yet been given of the manner in which human nature has been built up, and of the various instincts and tastes with which we are born, than the doctrine that habits and modes of thought and feeling indulged in and produced by circumstances in former generations have gradually become innate in the race, and exhibit themselves spontaneously and instinctively and quite independently of the circumstances that originally produced them. According to this theory the same process is continually going on. Man has slowly emerged from a degraded and bestial condition. The pressure of long-continued circumstances has moulded him into his special type; but new feelings and habits, or modifications of old feelings and habits, are constantly passing not only into his life but into his nature, taking root there, and in some degree at least reproducing themselves by the force of heredity in the innate disposition of his offspring. If this be true, it gives a new and terrible importance both to the duty of self-culture and to the duty of wise selection in marriage. It means that children are likely to be influenced not only by what we do and by what we say, but also by what we are, and that the characters of the parents in different degrees and combinations will descend even to a remote posterity.

It throws a not less terrible light upon the miscalculations of the past. On this hypothesis, as Mr. Galton has truly shown, it is scarcely possible to exaggerate the evil which has been brought upon the world by the religious glorification of celibacy and by the enormous development and encouragement of the monastic life. Generation after generation, century after century, and over the whole wide surface of Christendom, this conception of religion drew into a sterile celibacy nearly all who were most gentle, most unselfish, most earnest, studious, and religious, most susceptible to moral and intellectual enthusiasm, and thus prevented them from transmitting to posterity the very qualities that are most needed for the happiness and the moral progress of the race. Whenever the good and evil resulting from different religious systems come to be impartially judged, this consideration is likely to weigh heavily in the scale.[70]

Returning, however, to the narrower sphere of particular marriages, it may be observed that although full confidence, and, in one sense, complete identification of interests, are the characteristics of a perfect marriage, this does not by any means imply that one partner should be a kind of duplicate of the other. Woman is not a mere weaker man; and the happiest marriages are often those in which, in tastes, character, and intellectual qualities, the wife is rather the complement than the reflection of her husband. In intellectual things this is constantly shown. The purely practical and prosaic intellect is united with an intellect strongly tinged with poetry and romance; the man whose strength is in facts, with the woman whose strength is in ideas; the man who is wholly absorbed in science or politics or economical or industrial problems and pursuits, with a woman who possesses the talent or at least the temperament of an artist or musician. In such cases one partner brings sympathies or qualities, tastes or appreciations or kinds of knowledge in which the other is most defective; and by the close and constant contact of two dissimilar types each is, often insensibly, but usually very effectually, improved. Men differ greatly in their requirements of intellectual sympathy. A perfectly commonplace intellectual surrounding will usually do something to stunt or lower a fine intelligence, but it by no means follows that each man finds the best intellectual atmosphere to be that which is most in harmony with his own special talent.

To many, hard intellectual labour is an eminently isolated thing, and what they desire most in the family circle is to cast off all thought of it. I have known two men who were in the first rank of science, intimate friends, and both of them of very domestic characters. One of them was accustomed to do nearly all his work in the presence of his wife, and in the closest possible co-operation with her. The other used to congratulate himself that none of his family had his own scientific tastes, and that when he left his work and came into his family circle he had the rest of finding himself in an atmosphere that was entirely different. Some men of letters need in their work constant stimulus, interest, and sympathy. Others desire only to develop their talent uncontrolled, uninfluenced, and undisturbed, and with an atmosphere of cheerful quiet around them.

What is true of intellect is also in a large degree true of character. Two persons living constantly together should have many tastes and sympathies in common, and their characters will in most cases tend to assimilate. Yet great disparities of character may subsist in marriage, not only without evil but often with great advantage. This is especially the case where each supplies what is most needed in the other. Some natures

---

[70] Galton's *Hereditary Genius*, pp. 357-8. It may be argued, on the other side, that the monasteries consigned to celibacy a great proportion of the weaker physical natures, who would otherwise have left sickly children behind them. This, and the much greater mortality of weak infant life, must have strengthened the race in an age when sanitary science was unknown and when external conditions were very unfavourable.

require sedatives and others tonics; and it will often be found in a happy marriage that the union of two dissimilar natures stimulates the idle and inert, moderates the impetuous, gives generosity to the parsimonious and order to the extravagant, imparts the spirit of caution or the spirit of enterprise which is most needed, and corrects, by contact with a healthy and cheerful nature, the morbid and the desponding.

Marriage may also very easily have opposite effects. It is not unfrequently founded on the sympathy of a common weakness, and when this is the case it can hardly fail to deepen the defect. On the whole, women, in some of the most valuable forms of strength—in the power of endurance and in the power of perseverance—are at least the equals of men. But weak and tremulous nerves, excessive sensibility, and an exaggerated share of impulse and emotion, are indissolubly associated with certain charms, both of manner and character, which are intensely feminine, and to many men intensely attractive. When a nature of this kind is wedded to a weak or a desponding man, the result will seldom be happiness to either party, but with a strong man such marriages are often very happy. Strength may wed with weakness or with strength, but weakness should beware of mating itself with weakness. It needs the oak to support the ivy with impunity, and there are many who find the constant contact of a happy and cheerful nature the first essential of their happiness.

As it is not wise or right that either partner in marriage should lose his or her individuality, so it is right that each should have an independent sphere of authority. It is assumed, of course, that there is the perfect trust which should be the first condition of marriage and also a reasonable judgment. Many marriages have been permanently marred because the woman has been given no independence in money matters and is obliged to come for each small thing to her husband. In general the less the husband meddles in household matters, or the wife in professional ones, the better. The education of very young children of both sexes, and of girls of a mature age, will fall almost exclusively to the wife. The education of the boys when they have emerged from childhood will be rather governed by the judgment of the man. Many things will be regulated in common; but the larger interests of the family will usually fall chiefly to one partner, the smaller and more numerous ones to the other.

On such matters, however, generalisations have little value, as exceptions are very numerous. Differences of character, age, experience, and judgment, and countless special circumstances, will modify the family type, and it is in discovering these differences that wisdom in marriage mainly consists. The directions in which married life may influence character are also very many; but in the large number of cases in which it brings with it a great weight of household cares and family interests it will usually be found with both partners, but especially with the woman, at once to strengthen and to narrow unselfishness. She will live very little for herself, but very exclusively for her family. On the intellectual side such marriages usually give a sounder judgment and a wider knowledge of the world rather than purely intellectual tastes. It is a good thing when the education which precedes marriage not only prepares for the duties of the married life, but also furnishes a fair share of the interests and tastes which that state will probably tend to weaken. The hard battle of life, and the anxieties and sorrows that a family seldom fails to bring, will naturally give an increased depth and seriousness to character. There are, however, natures which, though they may be tainted by no grave vice, are so incurably frivolous that even this education will fail to influence them. As Emerson says, 'A fly is as untameable as a hyæna.'

The age that is most suited for marriage is also a matter which will depend largely on individual circumstances. The ancients, as is well known, placed it, in the case of the man, far back, and they desired a great difference of age between the man and the woman. Plato assigned between thirty and thirty-five, and Aristotle thirty-seven, as the best age for a man to marry, while they would have the girls married at eighteen or twenty.[71] In their view, however, marriage was looked upon very exclusively from the side of the man and of the State. They looked on it mainly as the means of producing healthy citizens, and it was in their eyes almost wholly dissociated from the passion of love. Montaigne, in one of his essays, has expounded this view with the frankest cynicism.[72] Yet few things are so important in marriage as that the man should bring into it the freshness and the purity of an untried nature, and that the early poetry and enthusiasm of life should at least in some degree blend with the married state. Nor is it desirable that a relation in which the formation of habits plays so large a part should be deferred until character has lost its flexibility, and until habits have been irretrievably hardened.

On the other hand there are invincible arguments against marriages entered into at an age when neither partner has any real knowledge of the world and of men. Only too often they involve many illusions and leave many regrets. Some kinds of knowledge, such as that given by extended travel, are far more easily acquired before than after marriage. Usually very early marriages are improvident marriages, made with no sufficient provision for the children, and often they are immature marriages, bringing with them grave physical evils. In those cases in which a great place or position is to be inherited, it is seldom a good thing that the interval of age between the owner and his heir should be so small that inheritance will probably be postponed till the confines of old age.

Marriages entered into in the decline of life stand somewhat apart from others, and are governed by other motives. What men chiefly seek in them is a guiding hand to lead them gently down the last descent of life.

On this, as on most subjects connected with marriage, no general or inflexible rule can be laid down. Moralists have chiefly dilated on the dangers of deferred marriages; economists on the evils of improvident marriages. Each man's circumstances and disposition must determine his course. On the whole, however, in most civilised countries the prevailing tendencies are in the direction of an increased postponement of marriage. Among the rich, the higher standard of luxury and requirements, the

---

[71] *Republic*, Book V. *Politics*, Book VII

[72] *Livre* III. Ch. 5.

comforts of club life, and also, I think, the diminished place which emotion is taking in life, all lead to this, while the spread of providence and industrial habits among the poor has the same tendency.

A female pen is so much more competent than a masculine one for dealing with marriage from the woman's point of view that I do not attempt to enter on that field. It is impossible, however, to overlook the marked tendency of nineteenth-century civilisation to give women, both married and unmarried, a degree of independence and self-reliance far exceeding that of the past. The legislation of most civilised countries has granted them full protection for their property and their earnings, increased rights of guardianship over their children, a wider access to professional life, and even a very considerable voice in the management of public affairs; and these influences have been strengthened by great improvement in female education, and by a change in the social tone which has greatly extended their latitude of independent action. For my own part, I have no doubt that this movement is, on the whole, beneficial, not only to those who have to fight a lonely battle in life, but also to those who are in the marriage state. Larger interests, wider sympathies, a more disciplined judgment, and a greater power of independence and self-control naturally accompany it; and these things can never be wholly wasted. They will often be called into active exercise by the many vicissitudes of the married life. They will, perhaps, be still more needed when the closest of human ties is severed by the great Divorce of Death.

CHAPTER XV SUCCESS

One of the most important lessons that experience teaches is that on the whole, and in the great majority of cases, success in life depends more on character than on either intellect or fortune. Many brilliant exceptions, no doubt, tend to obscure the rule, and some of the qualities of character that succeed the best may be united with grave vices or defects; but on the whole the law is one that cannot be questioned, and it becomes more and more apparent as civilisation advances. Temperance, industry, integrity, frugality, self-reliance, and self-restraint are the means by which the great masses of men rise from penury to comfort, and it is the nations in which these qualities are most diffused that in the long run are the most prosperous. Chance and circumstance may do much. A happy climate, a fortunate annexation, a favourable vicissitude in the course of commerce, may vastly influence the prosperity of nations; anarchy, agitation, unjust laws, and fraudulent enterprise may offer many opportunities of individual or even of class gains; but ultimately it will be found that the nations in which the solid industrial virtues are most diffused and most respected pass all others in the race. The moral basis of character was the true foundation of the greatness of ancient Rome, and when that foundation was sapped the period of her decadence began. The solid, parsimonious, and industrious qualities of the French peasantry have given their country the recuperative force which has enabled its greatness to survive the countless follies and extravagances of its rulers.

Character, it may be added, is especially pre-eminent in those kinds and degrees of success that affect the greatest numbers of men and influence most largely their real happiness—in the success which secures a high level of material comfort; which makes domestic life stable and happy; which wins for a man the respect and confidence of his neighbours. If we have melancholy examples that very different qualities often gain splendid prizes, it is still true that there are few walks in life in which a character that inspires complete confidence is not a leading element of success.

In the paths of ambition that can only be pursued by the few, intellectual qualities bear a larger part, and there are, of course, many works of genius that are in their own nature essentially intellectual. Yet even the most splendid successes of life will often be found to be due much less to extraordinary intellectual gifts than to an extraordinary strength and tenacity of will, to the abnormal courage, perseverance, and work-power that spring from it, or to the tact and judgment which make men skilful in seizing opportunities, and which, of all intellectual qualities, are most closely allied with character.

Strength of will and tact are not necessarily, perhaps not generally, conjoined, and often the first seems somewhat to impair the second. The strong passion, the intense conviction, the commanding and imperious nature overriding obstacles and defying opposition, that often goes with a will of abnormal strength, does not naturally harmonise with the reticence of expression, the delicacy of touch and management that characterise a man who possesses in a high degree the gift of tact. There are circumstances and times when each of these two things is more important than the other, and the success of each man will mainly depend upon the suitability of his peculiar gift to the work he has to do. 'The daring pilot in extremity' is often by no means the best navigator in a quiet sea; and men who have shown themselves supremely great in moments of crisis and appalling danger, who have built up mighty nations, subdued savage tribes, guided the bark of the State with skill and courage amid the storms of revolution or civil war, and written their names in indelible letters on the page of history, have sometimes proved far less successful than men of inferior powers in the art of managing assemblies, satisfying rival interests or assuaging by judicious compromise old hatreds and prejudices. We have had at least one conspicuous example of the difference of these two types in our own day in the life of the great founder of German Unity.

Sometimes, however, men of great strength of will and purpose possess also in a high degree the gift of tact; and when this is combined with soundness of judgment it usually leads to a success in life out of all proportion to their purely intellectual qualities. In nearly all administrative posts, in all the many fields of labour where the task of man is to govern, manage, or influence others, to adjust or harmonise antagonisms of race or interests or prejudices, to carry through difficult business without friction and by skilful co-operation, this combination of gifts is supremely valuable. It is much more valuable than brilliancy, eloquence, or originality. I remember the comment of a good judge of men on the administration of a great governor who was pre-eminently remarkable for this combination. 'He always seemed to gain his point, yet he never appeared to be in antagonism with anyone.' The steady pressure of a firm and consistent will was scarcely felt when it was accompanied by the ready recognition of everything that was good in the argument of another, and by a charm of manner and of temper which seldom failed to disarm opposition and win personal affection.

The combination of qualities which, though not absolutely incompatible, are very usually disconnected, is the secret of many successful lives. Thus, to take one of the most homely, but one of the most useful and most pleasing of all qualities—good-nature—it will too often be found that when it is the marked and leading feature of a character it is accompanied by some want of firmness, energy, and judgment. Sometimes, however, this is not the case, and there are then few greater elements of success. It is curious to observe the subtle, magnetic sympathy by which men feel whether their neighbour is a harsh or a kind judge of others, and how generally those who judge harshly are themselves harshly judged, while those who judge others rather by their merits than by their defects, and perhaps a little above their merits, win popularity.

No one, indeed, can fail to notice the effect of good-nature in conciliating opposition, securing attachment, smoothing the various paths of life, and, it must be added, concealing grave faults. Laxities of conduct that might well blast the reputation of a man or a woman are constantly forgotten, or at least forgiven, in those who lead a life of tactful good-nature, and in the eyes of the world this quality is more valued than others of far higher and more solid worth. It is not unusual, for example, to see a lady in society, who is living wholly or almost wholly for her pleasures, who has no high purpose in life, no real sense of duty, no capacity for genuine and serious self-sacrifice, but who at the same time never says an unkind thing of her neighbours, sets up no severe standard of conduct either for herself or for others, and by an innate amiability of temperament tries, successfully and without effort, to make all around her cheerful and happy. She will probably be more admired, she will almost certainly be more popular, than her neighbour whose whole life is one of self-denial for the good of others, who sacrifices to her duties her dearest pleasures, her time, her money, and her talents, but who through some unhappy turn of temper, strengthened perhaps by a narrow and austere education, is a harsh and censorious judge of the frailties of her fellows.

It is also a curious thing to observe how often, when the saving gift of tact is wanting, the brilliant, the witty, the ambitious, and the energetic are passed in the race of life by men who in intellectual qualities are greatly their inferiors. They dazzle, agitate, and in a measure influence, and they easily win places in the second rank; but something in the very exercise of their talents continually trammels them, while judgment, tact, and good-nature, with comparatively little brilliancy, quietly and unobtrusively take the helm. There is the excellent talker who, by his talents and his acquirements, is eminently fitted to delight and to instruct, yet he is so unable to repress some unseemly jest or some pointed sarcasm or some humorous paradox that he continually leaves a sting behind him, creates enemies, destroys his reputation for sobriety of thought, and makes himself impossible in posts of administration and trust. There is the parliamentary speaker who, amid shouts of applause, pursues his adversary with scathing invective or merciless ridicule, and who all the time is accumulating animosities against himself, shutting the door against combinations that would be all important to his career, and destroying his chances of party leadership. There is the advocate who can state his case with consummate power, but who, by an aggressive manner or a too evident contempt for his adversary, or by the over-statement of a good cause, habitually throws the minds of his hearers into an attitude of opposition. There are the many men who, by ill-timed or too frequent levity, lose all credit for their serious qualities, or who by pretentiousness or self-assertion or restless efforts to distinguish themselves, make themselves universally disliked, or who by their egotism or their repetitions or their persistence, or their incapacity of distinguishing essentials from details, or understanding the dispositions of others, or appreciating times and seasons, make their wearied and exasperated hearers blind to the most substantial merits. By faults of tact men of really moderate opinions get the reputation of extremists; men of substantially kindly natures sow animosities wherever they go; men of real patriotism are regarded as mere jesters or party gamblers; men who possess great talents and have rendered great services to the world sink into inveterate bores and never obtain from their contemporaries a tithe of the success which is their due. Tact is not merely shown in saying the right thing at the right time and to the right people; it is shown quite as much in the many things that are left unsaid and apparently unnoticed, or are only lightly and evasively touched.

It is certainly not the highest of human endowments, but it is as certainly one of the most valuable, for it is that which chiefly enables a man to use his other gifts to advantage, and which most effectually supplies the place of those that are wanting. It lies on the borderland of character and intellect. It implies self-restraint, good temper, quick and kindly sympathy with the feelings of others. It implies also a perception of the finer shadings of character and expression, the intellectual gift which enables a man to place himself in touch with great varieties of disposition, and to catch those more delicate notes of feeling to which a coarser nature is insensible.

It is perhaps in most cases more developed among women than among men, and it does not necessarily imply any other remarkable gift. It is sometimes found among both men and women of very small general intellectual powers; and in numerous cases it serves only to add to the charm of private life and to secure social success. Where it is united with real talents it not only enables its possessor to use these talents to the greatest advantage; it also often leads those about him greatly to magnify their amount. The presence or absence of this gift is one of the chief causes why the relative value of different men is often so differently judged by contemporaries and by posterity; by those who have come in direct personal contact with them, and by those who judge them from without, and by the broad results of their lives. Real tact, like good manners, is or becomes a spontaneous and natural thing. The man of perfectly refined manners does not consciously and deliberately on each occasion observe the courtesies and amenities of good society. They have become to him a second nature, and he observes them as by a kind of instinct, without thought or effort. In the same way true tact is something wholly different from the elaborate and artificial attempts to conciliate and attract which may often be seen, and which usually bring with them the impression of manoeuvre and insincerity.

Though it may be found in men of very different characters and grades of intellect, tact has its natural affinities. Seeking beyond all things to avoid unnecessary friction, and therefore with a strong leaning towards compromise, it does not generally or naturally go with intense convictions, with strong enthusiasms, with an ardently impulsive or emotional temperament. Nor is it commonly found among men of deep and concentrated genius, intensely absorbed in some special subject. Such men are often among the most unobservant of the social sides of life, and very bad judges of character, though there will frequently be found among them an almost childlike unworldliness and simplicity of nature, and an essential moderation of temperament which, combined with their superiority of intellect, gives them a charm peculiarly their own. Tact, however, has a natural affinity to a calm, equable, and good-natured temper. It allies itself with a quick sense of opportunity, proportion, and degree; with the power of distinguishing readily and truly between the essential and the unimportant; with that soundness of judgment which not only guides men among the varied events of life, and in their estimate of those about them, but also enables them to take a true measure of their own capacities, of the tasks that are most fitted for them, of the objects of ambition that are and are not within their reach.

Though in its higher degrees it is essentially a natural gift, and is sometimes conspicuous in perfectly uneducated men, it may be largely cultivated and improved; and in this respect the education of good society is especially valuable. Such an education, whatever else it may do, at least removes many jarring notes from the rhythm of life. It tends to correct faults of manner, demeanour, or pronunciation which tell against men to a degree altogether disproportioned to their real importance, and on which, it is hardly too much to say, the casual judgments of the world are mainly formed; and it also fosters moral qualities which are essentially of the nature of tact.

We can hardly have a better picture of a really tactful man than in some sentences taken from the admirable pages in which Cardinal Newman has painted the character of the perfect gentleman.

'It is almost a definition of a gentleman to say he is one who never inflicts pain.... He carefully avoids whatever may cause a jar or a jolt in the minds of those with whom he is cast—all clashing of opinion or collision of feeling, all restraint or suspicion or gloom or resentment; his great concern being to make everyone at ease and at home. He has his eyes on all his company; he is tender towards the bashful, gentle towards the distant, and merciful towards the absurd; he can recollect to whom he is speaking; he guards against unreasonable allusions or topics that may irritate; he is seldom prominent in conversation, and never wearisome. He makes light of favours while he does them, and seems to be receiving when he is conferring. He never speaks of himself except when compelled, never defends himself by a mere retort; he has no ears for slander or gossip, is scrupulous in imputing motives to those who interfere with him, and interprets everything for the best. He is never mean or little in his disputes, never takes an unfair advantage, never mistakes personalities or sharp sayings for arguments, or insinuates evil which he dare not say out.... He has too much good sense to be affronted at insult; he is too busy to remember injuries, and too indolent to bear malice.... If he engages in controversy of any kind his disciplined intellect preserves him from the blundering discourtesy of better though less educated minds, who, like blunt weapons, tear and hack instead of cutting clean.... He may be right or wrong in his opinion, but he is too clear-headed to be unjust; he is as simple as he is forcible, and as brief as he is decisive. Nowhere shall we find greater candour, consideration, indulgence. He throws himself into the minds of his opponents, he accounts for their mistakes. He knows the weakness of human nature as well as its strength, its province, and its limits.'[73]

I have said at the beginning of this chapter that character bears, on the whole, a larger part in promoting success than any other things, and that a steady perseverance in the industrial virtues seldom fails to bring some reward in the directions that are most conducive to human happiness. At the same time it is only too evident that success in life is by no means measured by merit, either moral or intellectual. Life is a

---

[73] Newman's *Scope and Nature of University Education*, Discourse IX

great lottery, in which chance and opportunity play an enormous part. The higher qualities are often less successful than the medium and the lower ones. They are often most successful when they are blended with other and inferior elements, and a large share of the great prizes fall to the unscrupulous, the selfish, and the cunning. Probably, however, the disparity between merit and success diminishes if we take the larger averages, and the fortunes of nations correspond with their real worth much more nearly than the fortunes of individuals. Success, too, is far from being a synonym for happiness, and while the desire for happiness is inherent in all human nature, the desire for success—at least beyond what is needed for obtaining a fair share of the comforts of life—is much less universal. The force of habit, the desire for a tranquil domestic life, the love of country and of home, are often, among really able men, stronger than the impulse of ambition; and a distaste for the competitions and contentions of life, for the increasing responsibilities of greatness, and for the envy and jealousies that seldom fail to follow in its trail, may be found among men who, if they chose to enter the arena, seem to have every requisite for success. The strongest man is not always the most ardent climber, and the tranquil valleys have to many a greater charm than the lofty pinnacles of life.

CHAPTER XVI   TIME

Considering the countless ages that man has lived upon this globe, it seems a strange thing that he has so little learned to acquiesce in the normal conditions of humanity. How large a proportion of the melancholy which is reflected in the poetry of all ages, and which is felt in different degrees in every human soul, is due not to any special or peculiar misfortune, but to things that are common to the whole human race! The inexorable flight of time; the approach of old age and its infirmities; the shadow of death; the mystery that surrounds our being; the contrast between the depth of affection and the transitoriness and uncertainty of life; the spectacle of the broken lives and baffled aspirations and useless labours and misdirected talents and pernicious energies and long-continued delusions that fill the path of human history; the deep sense of vanity and aimlessness that must sometimes come over us as we contemplate a world in which chance is so often stronger than wisdom; in which desert and reward are so widely separated; in which living beings succeed each other in such a vast and bewildering redundance—eating, killing, suffering, and dying for no useful discoverable purpose,—all these things belong to the normal lot or to the inevitable setting of human life. Nor can it be said that science, which has so largely extended our knowledge of the Universe, or civilisation, which has so greatly multiplied our comforts and alleviated our pains, has in any degree diminished the sadness they bring. It seems, indeed, as if the more man is raised above a purely animal existence, and his mental and moral powers are developed, the more this kind of feeling increases.

In few if any periods of the world's history has it been more perceptible in literature than at present. Physical constitution and temperament have a vast and a humiliating power of deepening or lightening it, and the strength or weakness of religious belief largely affects it, yet the best, the strongest, the most believing, and the most prosperous cannot wholly escape it. Sometimes it finds its true expression in the lines of Raleigh:

> Even such is time; which takes in trust
> Our youth, our joys, and all we have!
> And pays us nought but age and dust,
> Which in the dark and silent grave,
> When we have wandered all our ways,
> Shuts up the story of our days;
> And from which grave and earth and dust,
> The Lord shall raise me up, I trust.

Sometimes it takes the tone of a lighter melancholy touched with cynicism:

La vie est vaine:
  Un peu d'amour,
  Un peu de haine,
  Et puis—bon jour.

La vie est brève,
  Un peu d'espoir,
  Un peu de rêve,
  Et puis—bon soir. [74]

There are few sayings which deserve better to be brought continually before our minds than that of Franklin: 'You value life; then do not squander time, for time is the stuff of life.' Of all the things that are bestowed on men, none is more valuable, but none is more unequally used, and the true measurement of life should be found less in its duration than in the amount that is put into it. The waste of time is one of the oldest of commonplaces, but it is one of those which are never really stale. How much of the precious 'stuff of life' is wasted by want of punctuality; by want of method involving superfluous and repeated effort; by want of measure prolonging things that are pleasurable or profitable in moderation to the point of weariness, satiety, and extravagance; by want of selection dwelling too much on the useless or the unimportant; by want of intensity, growing out of a nature that is listless and apathetic both in work and pleasure. Time is, in one sense, the most elastic of things. It is one of the commonest experiences that the busiest men find most of it for exceptional work, and often a man who, under the strong stimulus of an active professional life, repines bitterly that he finds so little time for pursuing some favourite work or study, discovers, to his own surprise, that when circumstances have placed all his time at his disposal he does less in this field than in the hard-earned intervals of a crowded life. The art of wisely using the spare five minutes, the casual vacancies or intervals of life, is one of the most valuable we can acquire. There are lives in which the main preoccupation is to get through time. There are others in which it is to find time for all that has to be got through, and most men, in different periods of their lives, are acquainted with both extremes. With some, time is mere duration, a blank, featureless thing, gliding swiftly and insensibly by. With others every day, and almost every hour, seems to have its distinctive stamp and character, for good or ill, in work or pleasure. There are vast differences in this respect between different ages of history, and between different generations in the same country, between town and country life, and between different countries. 'Better fifty years of Europe than a cycle of Cathay' is profoundly true, and no traveller can fail to be insensible to the difference in the value of time in a Northern and in a Southern country. The leisure of some nations seems

---

[74] Monte-Naken

busier than the work of others, and few things are more resting to an overwrought and jaded Anglo-Saxon nature than to pass for a short season into one of those countries where time seems almost without value.

On the whole there can be little doubt that life in the more civilised nations has, in our own generation, largely increased. It is not simply that its average duration is extended. This, in a large degree, is due to the diminished amount of infant mortality. The improvement is shown more conclusively in the increased commonness of vigorous and active old age, in the multitude of new contrivances for economising and therefore increasing time, in the far greater intensity of life both in the forms of work and in the forms of pleasure. 'Life at high pressure' is not without its drawbacks and its evils, but it at least means life which is largely and fully used.

All intermissions of work, however, even when they do not take the form of positive pleasure, are not waste of time. Overwork, in all departments of life, is commonly bad economy, not so much because it often breaks down health—most of what is attributed to this cause is probably rather due to anxiety than to work—as because it seldom fails to impair the quality of work. A great portion of our lives passes in the unconsciousness of sleep, and perhaps no part is more usefully spent. It not only brings with it the restoration of our physical energies, but it also gives a true and healthy tone to our moral nature. Of all earthly things sleep does the most to place things in their true proportions, calming excited nerves and dispelling exaggerated cares. How many suicides have been averted, how many rash enterprises and decisions have been prevented, how many dangerous quarrels have been allayed, by the soothing influence of a few hours of steady sleep! 'Sleep that knits up the ravell'd sleeve of care' is, indeed, in a careworn world, one of the chief of blessings. Its healing and restorative power is as much felt in the sicknesses of the mind as in those of the body, and, in spite of the authority of Solomon, it is probably a wise thing for men to take the full measure of it, which undoctored nature demands. The true waste of time of the sluggard is not in the amount of natural sleep he enjoys, but in the time idly spent in bed when sleep has ceased, and in misplaced and mistimed sleep, which is not due to any genuine craving of the body for rest, but simply to mental sluggishness, to lack of interest and attention.

Some men have claimed for sleep even more than this. 'The night-time of the body,' an ancient writer has said, 'is the day-time of the soul,' and some, who do not absolutely hold the old belief that it is in the dreams of the night that the Divine Spirit most communicates with man, have, nevertheless, believed that the complete withdrawal of our minds from those worldly cares which haunt our waking hours and do so much to materialise and harden our natures is one of the first conditions of a higher life. 'In proportion,' said Swedenborg, 'as the mind is capable of being withdrawn from things sensual and corporeal, in the same proportion it is elevated into things celestial and spiritual.' It has been noticed that often thoughts and judgments, scattered and entangled in our evening hours, seem sifted, clarified, and arranged in sleep; that problems which seemed hopelessly confused when we lay down are at once and easily solved when we awake, 'as though a reason more perfect than reason had been at work when we were in our beds.' Something analogous to this, it has been contended, takes place in our moral natures. 'A process is going on in us during those hours which is not, and cannot be, brought so effectually, if at all, at any other time, and we are spiritually growing, developing, ripening more continuously while thus shielded from the distracting influences of the phenomenal world than during the hours in which we are absorbed in them.... Is it not precisely the function of sleep to give us for a portion of every day in our lives a respite from worldly influences which, uninterrupted, would deprive us of the instruction, of the spiritual reinforcements, necessary to qualify us to turn our waking experiences of the world to the best account without being overcome by them? It is in these hours that the plans and ambitions of our external worldly life cease to interfere with or obstruct the flow of the Divine life into the will.' [75]

Without, however, following this train of thought, it is at least sufficiently clear that no small portion of the happiness of life depends upon our sleeping hours. Plato has exhorted men to observe carefully their dreams as indicating their natural dispositions, tendencies, and temptations, and—perhaps with more reason—Burton and Franklin have proposed 'the art of procuring pleasant dreams' as one of the great, though little recognised, branches of the science of life. This is, no doubt, mainly a question of diet, exercise, efficient ventilation, and a wise distribution of hours, but it is also largely influenced by moral causes.

> Somnia quæ mentes ludunt volitantibus umbris,
> Nec delubra deum, nec ab æthere numina mittunt,
> Sed sibi quisque facit.

To appease the perturbations of the mind, to live a tranquil, upright, unremorseful life, to cultivate the power of governing by the will the current of our thoughts, repressing unruly passions, exaggerated anxieties, and unhealthy desires, is at least one great recipe for banishing from our pillows those painful dreams that contribute not a little to the unhappiness of many lives.

An analogous branch of self-culture is that which seeks to provide some healthy aliment for the waking hours of the night, when time seems so unnaturally prolonged, and when gloomy thoughts and exaggerated and distempered views of the trials of life peculiarly prevail. Among the ways in which education may conduce to the real happiness of man, its power of supplying pleasant or soothing thoughts for those dreary hours is not the least, though it is seldom or never noticed in books or speeches. It is, perhaps, in this respect that the early habit of committing poetry—and especially religious poetry—to memory is most important.

---

[75] See *The Mystery of Sleep*, by John Bigelow.

In estimating the value of those intermissions of labour which are not spent in active enjoyment one other consideration may be noted. There are times when the mind should lie fallow, and all who have lived the intellectual life with profit have perceived that it is often in those times that it most regains the elasticity it may have lost and becomes most prolific in spontaneous thought. Many periods of life which might at first sight appear to be merely unused time are, in truth, among the most really valuable.

We have all noticed the curious fact of the extreme apparent inequalities of time, though it is, in its essence, of all things the most uniform. Periods of pain or acute discomfort seem unnaturally long, but this lengthening of time is fortunately not true of all the melancholy scenes of life, nor is it peculiar to things that are painful. An invalid life with its almost unbroken monotony, and with the large measure of torpor that often accompanies it, usually flies very quickly, and most persons must have observed how the first week of travel, or of some other great change of habits and pursuits, though often attended with keen enjoyment, appears disproportionately long. Routine shortens and variety lengthens time, and it is therefore in the power of men to do something to regulate its pace. A life with many landmarks, a life which is much subdivided when those subdivisions are not of the same kind, and when new and diverse interests, impressions, and labours follow each other in swift and distinct succession, seems the most long, and youth, with its keen susceptibility to impressions, appears to move much more slowly than apathetic old age. How almost immeasurably long to a young child seems the period from birthday to birthday! How long to the schoolboy seems the interval between vacation and vacation! How rapid as we go on in life becomes the awful beat of each recurring year! When the feeling of novelty has grown rare, and when interests have lost their edge, time glides by with an ever-increasing celerity. Campbell has justly noticed as a beneficent provision of nature that it is in the period of life when enjoyments are fewest, and infirmities most numerous, that the march of time seems most rapid.

The more we live, more brief appear
Our life's succeeding stages,
A day to childhood seems a year,
And years like passing ages.

When Joys have lost their bloom and breath,
And life itself is vapid,
Why as we reach the Falls of death
Feel we its tide more rapid?

Heaven gives our years of fading strength
  Indemnifying fleetness;
And those of youth a seeming length
  Proportioned to their sweetness.

The shortness of life is one of the commonplaces of literature. Yet though we may easily conceive beings with faculties both of mind and body adapted to a far longer life than ours, it will usually be found, with our existing powers, that life, if not prematurely shortened, is long enough. In the case of men who have played a great part in public affairs, the best work is nearly always done before old age. It is a remarkable fact that although a Senate, by its very derivation, means an assembly of old men, and although in the Senate of Rome, which was the greatest of all, the members sat for life, there was a special law providing that no Senator, after sixty, should be summoned to attend his duty.[76] In the past centuries active septuagenarian statesmen were very rare, and in parliamentary life almost unknown. In our own century there have been brilliant exceptions, but in most cases it will be found that the true glory of these statesmen rests on what they had done before old age, and sometimes the undue prolongation of their active lives has been a grave misfortune, not only to their own reputations, but also to the nations they influenced. Often, indeed, while faculties diminish, self-confidence, even in good men, increases. Moral and intellectual failings that had been formerly repressed take root and spread, and it is no small blessing that they have but a short time to run their course. In the case of men of great capacities the follies of age are perhaps even more to be feared than the follies of youth. When men have made a great reputation and acquired a great authority, when they become the objects of the flattery of nations, and when they can, with little trouble or thought or study, attract universal attention, a new set of temptations begins. Their heads are apt to be turned. The feeling of responsibility grows weaker; the old judgment, caution, deliberation, self-restraint, and timidity disappear. Obstinacy and prejudice strengthen, while at the same time the force of the reasoning will diminishes. Sometimes, through a failing that is partly intellectual, but partly also moral, they almost wholly lose the power of realising or recognising new conditions, discoveries and necessities. They view with jealousy the rise of new reputations and of younger men, and the well-earned authority of an old man becomes the most formidable obstacle to improvement. In the field of politics, in the field of science, and in the field of military organisation, these truths might be abundantly illustrated. In the case of great but maleficent genius the shortness of life is a priceless blessing. Few greater curses could be imagined for the human race than the prolongation for centuries of the life of Napoleon.

---

[76] Seneca, *de Brevitate Vitæ*, cap. XX

In literature also the same law may be detected. A writer's best thoughts are usually expressed long before extreme old age, though the habit and desire of production continue. The time of repetition, of diluted force, and of weakened judgment—the age when the mind has lost its flexibility and can no longer assimilate new ideas or keep pace with the changing modes and tendencies of another generation—often sets in while physical life is but little enfeebled. In this case, it is true, the evil is not very great, for Time may be trusted to sift the chaff from the wheat, and though it may not preserve the one it will infallibly discard the other. 'While I live,' Victor Hugo said with some grandiloquence, but also with some justice, 'it is my duty to produce. It is the duty of the world to select, from what I produce, that which is worth keeping. The world will discharge its duty. I shall discharge mine.' At the same time, no one can have failed to observe how much in our own generation the long silence of Newman in his old age added to his dignity and his reputation, and the same thing might have been said of Carlyle if a beneficent fire had destroyed the unrevised manuscripts which he wrote or dictated when a very old man.

We are here, however, dealing with great labours, and with men who are filling a great place in the world's strife. The decay of faculty and will, that impairs power in these cases, is often perceptible long before there is any real decay in the powers that are needed for ordinary business or for the full enjoyment of life. But the time comes when children have grown into maturity, and when it becomes desirable that a younger generation should take the government of the world, should inherit its wealth, its power, its dignities, its many means of influence and enjoyment; and this cannot be fully done till the older generation is laid to rest. Often, indeed, old age, when it is free from grave infirmities and from great trials and privations, is the most honoured, the most tranquil, and perhaps on the whole the happiest period of life. The struggles, passions, and ambitions of other days have passed. The mellowing touch of time has allayed animosities, subdued old asperities of character, given a larger and more tolerant judgment, cured the morbid sensitiveness that most embitters life. The old man's mind is stored with the memories of a well-filled and honourable life. In the long leisures that now fall to his lot he is often enabled to resume projects which in a crowded professional life he had been obliged to adjourn; he finds (as Adam Smith has said) that one of the greatest pleasures in life is reverting in old age to the studies of youth, and he himself often feels something of the thrill of a second youth in his sympathy with the children who are around him. It is the St. Martin's summer, lighting with a pale but beautiful gleam the brief November day. But the time must come when all the alternatives of life are sad, and the least sad is a speedy and painless end. When the eye has ceased to see and the ear to hear, when the mind has failed and all the friends of youth are gone, and the old man's life becomes a burden not only to himself but to those about him, it is far better that he should quit the scene. If a natural clinging to life, or a natural shrinking from death, prevents him from clearly realising this, it is at least fully seen by all others.

Nor, indeed, does this love of life in most cases of extreme old age greatly persist. Few things are sadder than to see the young, or those in mature life, seeking, according to the current phrase, to find means of "killing time." But in extreme old age, when the power of work, the power of reading, the pleasures of society, have gone, this phrase acquires a new significance. As Madame de Staël has beautifully said, 'On dépose fleur à fleur la couronne de la vie.' An apathy steals over every faculty, and rest—unbroken rest—becomes the chief desire. I remember a touching epitaph in a German churchyard: 'I will arise, O Christ, when Thou callest me; but oh! let me rest awhile, for I am very weary.'

After all that can be said, most men are reluctant to look Time in the face. The close of the year or a birthday is to them merely a time of revelry, into which they enter in order to turn away from depressing thought. They shrink from what seems to them the dreary truth, that they are drifting to a dark abyss. To many the milestones along the path of life are tombstones, every epoch being mainly associated in their memories with a death. To some, past time is nothing—a closed chapter never to be reopened.

The past is nothing, and at last,

The future can but be the past.

To others, the thought of the work achieved in the vanished years is the most real and abiding of their possessions. They can feel the force of the noble lines of Dryden:

Not Heaven itself upon the past has power,

But what has been has been, and I have had my hour.

He who would look Time in the face without illusion and without fear should associate each year as it passes with new developments of his nature; with duties accomplished, with work performed. To fill the time allotted to us to the brim with action and with thought is the only way in which we can learn to watch its passage with equanimity.

CHAPTER XVII 'THE END'

It is easy to conceive circumstances not widely different from those of actual life that would, if not altogether, at least very largely, take from death the gloom that commonly surrounds it. If all the members of the human race died either before two or after seventy; if death was in all cases the swift and painless thing that it is with many; and if the old man always left behind him children to perpetuate his name, his memory, and his thoughts, Death, though it might still seem a sad thing, would certainly not excite the feelings it now so often produces. Of all the events that befall us, it is that which owes most of its horror not to itself, but to its accessories, its associations, and to the imaginations that cluster around it. 'Death,' indeed, as a great stoical moralist said, 'is the only evil that can never touch us. When we are, death is not. When death comes, we are not.'

The composition of treatises of consolation intended to accustom men to contemplate death without terror was one of the favourite exercises of the philosophers in the Augustan and in the subsequent periods of Pagan Rome. The chapter which Cicero has devoted to this subject in his treatise on old age is a beautiful example of how it appeared to a virtuous pagan, who believed in a future life which would bring him into communion with those whom he had loved and lost on earth, but who at the same time recognised this only as a probability, not a certainty. "Death," he said, 'is an event either utterly to be disregarded if it extinguish the soul's existence, or much to be wished if it convey her to some region where she shall continue to exist for ever. One of these two consequences must necessarily follow the disunion of soul and body; there is no other possible alternative. What then have I to fear if after death I shall either not be miserable or shall certainly be happy?'

Vague notions, however, of a dim, twilight, shadowy world where the ghosts of the dead lived a faint and joyless existence, and whence they sometimes returned to haunt the living in their dreams, were widely spread through the popular imaginations, and it was as the extinction of all superstitious fears that the school of Lucretius and Pliny welcomed the belief that all things ended with death—'Post mortem nihil est, ipsaque mors nihil.' Nor is it by any means certain that even in the school of Plato the thought of another life had a great and operative influence on minds and characters. Death was chiefly represented as rest; as the close of a banquet; as the universal law of nature which befalls all living beings, though the immense majority encounter it at an earlier period than man. It was thought of simply as sleep—dreamless, undisturbed sleep—the final release from all the sorrows, sufferings, anxieties, labours, and longings of life.

We are such stuff
As dreams are made on, and our little life
Is rounded with a sleep.[77]

The best of rest is sleep,
And that thou oft provok'st; yet grossly fear'st
Thy death, which is no more.[78]

To die is landing on some silent shore
Where billows never break, nor tempests roar.[79]

It is a strange thing to observe to what a height not only of moral excellence, but also of devotional fervour, men have arisen without any assistance from the doctrine of a future life. Only the faintest and most dubious glimmer of such a belief can be traced in the Psalms, in which countless generations of Christians have found the fullest expression of their devotional feelings, or in the Meditations of Marcus Aurelius, which are perhaps the purest product of pagan piety.

As I have already said, I am endeavouring in this book to steer clear of questions of contested theologies; but it is impossible to avoid noticing the great changes that have been introduced into the conception of death by some of the teaching which in different forms has grown up under the name of Christianity, though much of it may be traced in germ to earlier periods of human development. Death in itself was made incomparably more terrible by the notion that it was not a law but a punishment; that sufferings inconceivably greater than those of Earth awaited the great masses of the human race beyond the grave; that an event which was believed to have taken place ages before we were born, or small frailties such as the best of us cannot escape, were sufficient to bring men under this condemnation; that the only paths to safety were to be found in ecclesiastical ceremonies; in the assistance of priests; in an accurate choice among competing theological doctrines. At the same time the largest and most powerful of the Churches of Christendom has, during many centuries, done its utmost to intensify the natural fear of death by associating it in the imaginations of men with loathsome images and appalling surroundings. There can be no greater contrast than that between the Greek tomb with its garlands of flowers, its bright, youthful and restful imagery, and the mortuary chapels that may often be found in Catholic countries, with their ghastly pictures of the saved souls writhing in purgatorial flames,

---

[77] The Tempest.

[78] Measure for Measure.

[79] Garth.

while the inscription above and the moneybox below point out the one means of alleviating their lot.

Fermati, O Passagiero, mira tormenti.

Siamo abbandonati dai nostri parenti.

Di noi abbiate pietà, o voi amici cari.

This is one side of the picture. On the other hand it cannot be questioned that the strong convictions and impressive ceremonies, even of the most superstitious faith, have consoled and strengthened multitudes in their last moments, and in the purer and more enlightened forms of Christianity death now wears a very different aspect from what it did in the teaching of mediæval Catholicism, or of some of the sects that grew out of the Reformation. Human life ending in the weakness of old age and in the corruption of the tomb will always seem a humiliating anti-climax, and often a hideous injustice. The belief in the rightful supremacy of conscience, and in an eternal moral law redressing the many wrongs and injustices of life, and securing the ultimate triumph of good over evil; the incapacity of earth and earthly things to satisfy our cravings and ideals; the instinctive revolt of human nature against the idea of annihilation, and its capacity for affections and attachments, which seem by their intensity to transcend the limits of earth and carry with them in moments of bereavement a persuasion or conviction of something that endures beyond the grave,—all these things have found in Christian beliefs a sanction and a satisfaction that men had failed to find in Socrates or Cicero, or in the vague Pantheism to which unassisted reason naturally inclines.

Looking, however, on death in its purely human aspects, the mourner should consider how often in a long illness he wished the dying man could sleep; how consoling to his mind was the thought of every hour of peaceful rest; of every hour in which the patient was withdrawn from consciousness, insensible to suffering, removed for a time from the miseries of a dying life. He should ask himself whether these intervals of insensibility were not on the whole the happiest in the illness—those which he would most have wished to multiply or to prolong. He should accustom himself, then, to think of death as sleep—undisturbed sleep—the only sleep from which man never wakes to pain.

You find yourself in the presence of what is a far deeper and more poignant trial than an old man's death—a young life cut off in its prime; the eclipse of a sun before the evening has arrived. Accustom yourself to consider the life that has passed as a whole. A human being has been called into the world—has lived in it ten, twenty, thirty years. It seems to you an intolerable instance of the injustice of fate that he is so early cut off. Estimate, then, that life as a whole, and ask yourself whether, so judged, it has been a blessing or the reverse. Count up the years of happiness. Count up the days, or perhaps weeks, of illness and of pain. Measure the happiness that this short life has given to some who have passed away; who never lived to see its early close.

Balance the happiness which during its existence it gave to those who survived, with the poignancy and the duration of pain caused by the loss. Here, for example, is one who lived perhaps twenty-five years in health and vigour; whose life during that period was chequered by no serious misfortune; whose nature, though from time to time clouded by petty anxieties and cares, was on the whole bright, buoyant, and happy; who had the capacity of vivid enjoyment and many opportunities of attaining it; who felt all the thrill of health and friendship and ecstatic pleasure. Then came a change,— a year or two with a crippled wing—life, though not abjectly wretched, on the whole a burden, and then the end. You can easily conceive—you can ardently desire—a better lot, but judge fairly the lights and shades of what has been. Does not the happiness on the whole exceed the evil? Can you honestly say that this life has been a curse and not a blessing?—that it would have been better if it had never been called out of nothingness?—that it would have been better if the drama had never been played? It is over now. As you lay in his last home the object of so much love, ask yourself whether, even in a mere human point of view, this parenthesis between two darknesses has not been on the whole productive of more happiness than pain to him and to those around him.

It was an ancient saying that 'he whom the gods love dies young,' and more than one legend representing speedy and painless death as the greatest of blessings has descended to us from pagan antiquity; while other legends, like that of Tithonus, anticipated the picture which Swift has so powerfully but so repulsively drawn of the misery of old age and its infirmities, if death did not come as a release. I have elsewhere related an old Irish legend embodying this truth. 'In a certain lake in Munster, it is said, there were two islands; into the first death could never enter, but age and sickness, and the weariness of life and the paroxysms of fearful suffering were all known there, and they did their work till the inhabitants, tired of their immortality, learned to look upon the opposite island as upon a haven of repose. They launched their barks upon its gloomy waters; they touched its shore, and they were at rest.'[80]

No one, however, can confidently say whether an early death is a misfortune, for no one can really know what calamities would have befallen the dead man if his life had been prolonged. How often does it happen that the children of a dead parent do things or suffer things that would have broken his heart if he had lived to see them! How often do painful diseases lurk in germ in the body which would have produced unspeakable misery if an early and perhaps a painless death had not anticipated their development! How often do mistakes and misfortunes cloud the evening and mar the beauty of a noble life, or moral infirmities, unperceived in youth or early manhood, break out before the day is over! Who is there who has not often said to himself as he looked back on a completed life, how much happier it would have been had it ended sooner? 'Give us timely death' is in truth one of the best prayers that man can pray. Pain, not Death, is the real enemy to be combated, and in this combat, at least, man

---

[80] *History of European Morals*, i. p. 203. The legend is related by Camden.

can do much. Few men can have lived long without realising how many things are worse than death, and how many knots there are in life that Death alone can untie.

Remember, above all, that whatever may lie beyond the tomb, the tomb itself is nothing to you. The narrow prison-house, the gloomy pomp, the hideousness of decay, are known to the living and the living alone. By a too common illusion of the imagination, men picture themselves as consciously dead,—going through the process of corruption, and aware of it; imprisoned with the knowledge of the fact in the most hideous of dungeons. Endeavour earnestly to erase this illusion from your mind, for it lies at the root of the fear of death, and it is one of the worst sides of mediæval and of much modern teaching and art that it tends to strengthen it. Nothing, if we truly realise it, is less real than the grave. We should be no more concerned with the after fate of our discarded bodies than with that of the hair which the hair-cutter has cut off. The sooner they are resolved into their primitive elements the better. The imagination should never be suffered to dwell upon their decay.

Bacon has justly noticed that while death is often regarded as the supreme evil, there is no human passion that does not become so powerful as to lead men to despise it. It is not in the waning days of life, but in the full strength of youth, that men, through ambition or the mere love of excitement, fearlessly and joyously encounter its risk. Encountered in hot blood it is seldom feared, and innumerable accounts of shipwrecks and other accidents, and many episodes in every war, show conclusively how calmly honour, duty, and discipline can enable men of no extraordinary characters, virtues, or attainments, to meet it even when it comes before them suddenly, as an inevitable fact, and without any of that excitement which might blind their eyes. If we analyse our own feelings on the death of those we love, we shall probably find that, except in cases where life is prematurely shortened and much promise cut off, pity for the dead person is rarely a marked element. The feelings which had long been exclusively concentrated on the sufferings of the dying man take a new course when the moment of death arrives. It is the sudden blank; the separation from him who is dear to us; the cessation of the long reciprocity of love and pleasure,—in a word our own loss,—that affects us then. 'A happy release' is perhaps the phrase most frequently heard around a death-bed. And as we look back through the vista of a few years, and have learned to separate death more clearly from the illness that preceded it, the sense of its essential peacefulness and naturalness grows upon us. A vanished life comes to be looked upon as a day that has past, but leaving many memories behind it.

It is, I think, a healthy tendency that is leading men in our own generation to turn away as much as possible from the signs and the contemplation of death. The pomp and elaboration of funerals; protracted mournings surrounding us with the gloom of an ostentatious and artificial sorrow; above all, the long suspension of those active habits which nature intended to be the chief medicine of grief, are things which at least in the English-speaking world are manifestly declining. We should try to think of those who have passed away as they were at their best, and not in sickness or in decay. True sorrow needs no ostentation, and the gloom of death no artificial enhancement. Every good man, knowing the certainty of death and the uncertainty of its hour, will make it one of his first duties to provide for those he loves when he has himself passed away, and to do all in his power to make the period of bereavement as easy as possible. This is the last service he can render before the ranks are closed, and his place is taken, and the days of forgetfulness set in. In careers of riot and of vice the thought of death may have a salutary restraining influence; but in a useful, busy, well-ordered life it should have little place. It was not the Stoics alone who 'bestowed too much cost on death, and by their preparations made it more fearful.'[81] As Spinoza has taught, 'the proper study of a wise man is not how to die but how to live,' and as long as he is discharging this task aright he may leave the end to take care of itself. The great guiding landmarks of a wise life are indeed few and simple; to do our duty—to avoid useless sorrow—to acquiesce patiently in the inevitable.

---

[81] Bacon

formation can be obtained
CGtesting.com
the USA
0640140720
V00002B/190

9 781406 851939

CPSIA i
at www.I
Printed i
BVHW0
583600

CPSIA information can be obtained
at www.ICGtesting.com
Printed in the USA
BVHW070640140720
583600BV00002B/190

9 781406 851939